ANSWERING TO US

Answering to Us

WHY DEMOCRACY DEMANDS ACCOUNTABILITY

MINH LY

PRINCETON UNIVERSITY PRESS

PRINCETON & OXFORD

Published by Princeton University Press
41 William Street, Princeton, New Jersey 08540
99 Banbury Road, Oxford OX2 6JX
press.princeton.edu

GPSR Authorized Representative: Easy Access System Europe - Mustamäe tee 50, 10621 Tallinn, Estonia, gpsr.requests@easproject.com

ISBN 978-0-691-19861-3
ISBN (e-book) 978-0-691-22971-3

Library of Congress Control Number 2025937250

British Library Cataloging-in-Publication Data is available

Editorial: Matt Rohal and Alena Chekanov
Production Editorial: Jill Harris
Jacket Design: Katie Osborne
Production: Erin Suydam
Publicity: William Pagdatoon

Cover images copyright © Leonard Freed / Magnum Photos; Ben Stevens / Adobe Stock

This book has been composed in Arno

10 9 8 7 6 5 4 3 2 1

To my family, especially
Cam, Chung, and Theodora

CONTENTS

Acknowledgments   ix

1 The Need for Democratic Accountability:
   The Crisis in Democracy   1

2 The Rights of Democratic Accountability   39

3 The Duties of Democratic Accountability   87

4 Defending the Duties of Democratic Accountability   127

5 Justice as the Standard of Democratic Accountability:
   The Equal Accountability Principle, Equal Human Rights
   Principle, and Inclusion Principle   170

6 The Human Right to Democratic Accountability:
   Democratic Self-Determination   212

   Conclusion. The Equal Accountability
   Theory of Democracy   263

Index   273

ACKNOWLEDGMENTS

A book is a voyage of discovery made possible by the help of friends. The poet Alfred Lord Tennyson once hailed the sailors who aided Ulysses:

> There lies the port; the vessel puffs her sail:
> There gloom the dark, broad seas. My mariners,
> Souls that have toil'd, and wrought, and thought with me—
> That ever with a frolic welcome took
> The thunder and the sunshine.[1]

I have been exceptionally fortunate in the family and friends who have lit a bright beacon of hope to bring this book home.

I can think of no one who better epitomizes the ideal of an editor than Matt Rohal. He has championed the book from the beginning and charted it adroitly through the review process. He elevated the quality of my manuscript with his astute suggestions and eye for clarity. I thank his colleagues at Princeton University Press, who are consummate professionals, from the publisher in political theory Rob Tempio to the production editor Jill Harris, copyeditor Irina du Quenoy, and director Christie Henry. Katie Osborne designed the cover, elegantly conveying the duty of democratic solidarity among citizens with the linked arms of the protestors and the duty of oversight with the eyes looking toward the reader.

I thank my marvelous dissertation committee at Brown University. Corey Brettschneider has been the most extraordinary mentor

1. Alfred Lord Tennyson, "Ulysses," Poetry Foundation, accessed July 16, 2025, https://www.poetryfoundation.org/poems/45392/ulysses.

imaginable, devoting countless hours to intellectual conversations, the job search, and my work. I am incredibly grateful for how he has supported me in this project, not only as an adviser, but as a friend. I thank John Tomasi for his discussion of Rawls and Hayek and his leadership of the Political Theory Project. I am in debt to Sharon Krause, whose attentive reading improved my arguments, and led me to engage more closely with Aristotle and Habermas. I am grateful to Dave Estlund and Jim Morone for their conversations on democracy. Jim, Kevin McGravey, and Jeremy Johnson organized a talk and gave incisive comments. I am indebted to Mark Blyth, both for his teaching me everything I know about international political economy and his Herculean labors in my placement.

After graduate school, Chuck Beitz and Helen Milner invited me to join the University Center for Human Values and the Niehaus Center for Globalization and Governance in the Princeton School of Public and International Affairs. I benefited from the unmatched critical acumen of Annie Stilz in her comments on my work. Her research, in its clarity, precision, and depth, has set an exemplar for my own writing. I am thankful that Annie invited me to continue my postdoctoral research position under the auspices of the Program in Values and Public Life. Steve Macedo's wide-ranging erudition enlightened me about the policy implications of political theory, both in the seminar room and in conversations. Philip Pettit served on the selection committee for my postdoc and enriched my perspective with his thoughts on freedom. Peter Singer was a guiding force on global justice and introduced me to the Press. I thought more deeply about office and the Ancient Athenians because of Melissa Lane and Ian Walling; human rights because of Chuck Beitz, Bob Keohane, and Lucia Rafanelli; democracy and populism because of Jan-Werner Müller, Kim Lane Scheppele, Steve Macedo, and Ted Lechterman; the ethics of resistance because of Desmond Jagmohan and Shuk Ying Chan; and equal recognition because of Alan Patten. The faculty, LSR fellows, and graduate students made research a joy with their company.

My remarkable friends at Stanford sponsored my lectureship, with special thanks to the generosity of Emilee Chapman, Dan Edelstein, Pam

Karlan, Alison McQueen, Josh Ober, Rob Reich, Debra Satz, and Leif Wenar. I am especially grateful to Rob, who directed the Center for Ethics in Society that hosted my lectureship, Josh who founded the Civics Initiative where I was affiliated, and Debra and Dan who helped to fund my lectureship through Citizenship in the 21st Century. I appreciate the opportunity to teach with them, alongside Larry Diamond, Jim Fishkin, Scott Sagan, and Allen Weiner. Lauren Hirshberg, Dongxian Jiang, and Katie Lennard shared thoughts on the book and lessons on effective pedagogy as fellow Lecturers. These scholars at Stanford, including also Eamonn Callan, Brian Coyne, Hakeem Jefferson, Philip Petrov, Jack Rakove, Barry Weingast, and the graduate students in political science have created a vibrant intellectual community. Rob, Josh, and Emilee gave me the unforgettable opportunity to teach the PhD students in political theory in the Department of Political Science. Brian invited me to present in the faculty seminar in political theory, with instructive comments from Natasha Patel and the participants. Emilee became the first professor to teach *Answering to Us* in her graduate democratic theory course. I presented an initial draft of a chapter at the Nature of Rights Revisited Workshop at Stanford Law School, convened by Geoff Sigalet and Francisco Urbina, where Paul Yowell commented on the relation between my view and Ronald Dworkin's on democracy. Father Xavier Lavagetto and Father Dominic DeLay were sources of spiritual sustenance in the Stanford Catholic Community. I am thankful to Ellen Woods, Parna Sengupta, Lindsay Garratt, and Dayo Mitchell in Thinking Matters. My co-instructor Pam Karlan provided me an ongoing lesson in leadership with her advocacy on behalf of the marginalized and work at the head of the US Department of Justice Civil Rights Division.

I warmly thank the kindness of my friends at my home in the University of Vermont. I consider myself very lucky to count as colleagues my Chair, Peter VonDoepp, and my Dean, Bill Falls. My fellow theorists Jan Feldman, Bob Pepperman Taylor, and Alex Zakaras have set a high standard for me to strive to approach in teaching and writing about political theory. I am also fortunate to have as department colleagues Ellen Anderson, Brad Bauerly, Caroline Beer, Jonathan "Doc" Bradley, Matthew Carlson, Michele Commercio, Alec Ewald, Alex Garlick, Jack

Gierzynski, Deborah Guber, Pete Henne, Lisa Holmes, Leigh Raymond, Tom Sullivan, and Melissa Willard-Foster, soon to be joined by
Yujin Choi and Ahmed Khanani. Tom read the first three chapters of
the book and was the first scholar to cite *Answering to Us* in his book
with Richard Painter on the law of the presidency.[2] Leigh helped me to
thread the labyrinth of the literature on norm diffusion. I gained insight
from Alex on democratic responsibility and liberalism. Candace Smith
has worked as a peerless department administrator.

The UVM community has been wonderfully welcoming, including
Dean Pablo Bose in the Graduate College, Clayton Cafiero in Computer
Science, Alice Fothergill in Sociology, Dean David Jenemann at the Honors College, Bishop John McDermott and Father Scott Gratton at the
Catholic Center, Kate Nolfi in Philosophy, former President Patty Prelock,
Mark Usher in Geography, and Richard Watts and Meg Little Reilly at the
Center for Community News. The Center and Library helpfully hosted
my talk on a free press. I am especially grateful to Jack Pitblado, whose
philosophical discussions about the themes of the book were invaluable,
and Lindsey Papasian, who brilliantly taught me about Shakespeare and
advised on the art of the book cover. My students in Introduction to
Political Theory, Economic Justice, and Global Justice have been a privilege to teach and learn from as the next generation of political theorists
and democratic citizens. I thank in particular Theo Sternberg, who shed
light on Hegel and St. Augustine and served as an outstanding teaching
assistant. I am appreciative of the staff at the dining hall and YMCA, who
nourished my health. The keen comments from the students in the
Political Science Department honors seminar helped me in presentations
hosted by Jan and Jack. Dean Falls provided a research sabbatical and start-
up funding that allowed me to draft the core of the book. The Humanities
Center, directed by Ilyse Morgenstein Fuerst, granted a Publication Sub-
vention Award that supported the book's completion.

The book was refined at every turn by superlative research and editorial assistance from Philip Petrov, Jack Piblado, and Ian Walling. They

2. E. Thomas Sullivan and Richard W. Painter, *The U.S. Presidency: Power, Responsibility, and
Accountability* (Cambridge, UK: Cambridge University Press, 2025).

read the book in its entirety and contributed far-sighted comments, especially Philip on constitutional law, Jack on Locke, and Ian on Aristotle and ancient Greek political theory. Their friendship has flowed and refreshed as a fount of encouragement and insight.

Sonu Bedi hosted me at Dartmouth, where I presented a chapter from the manuscript to the Ethics Institute. I learned much from the comments and spirited conversation with Sonu, Luke Swaine, Julie Rose, and the talented Law & Ethics fellows.

I thank Graham Allison, who gave me the opportunity to work and reflect on government at the Belfer Center for Science and International Affairs at the Harvard Kennedy School.

I presented chapters at conference panels at the American Political Science Association. As my commentators, Corey Brettschneider, Melissa Schwartzberg, and Annie Stilz strengthened the book with their masterful feedback. My co-panelists have my gratitude, including Eric Beerbohm, Michael Blake, Tom Christiano, Paulina Ochoa Espejo, Dave Estlund, Katrina Forrester, Sam Freeman, Carol Gould, Anna Jurkevics, Jamie Mayerfeld, Steve Macedo, Josiah Ober, and Lucia Rafanelli. I thank my commentator, Eric Cheng, at the Western Political Science Association, where we were joined by Jamie Mayerfeld, Eric Mackey, and Sarah Rushing. The chapter on civic education was leavened with ideas from the Alliance for Civics in the Academy conferences at Stanford and the University of Colorado. I appreciate the conversations with Peter Berkowitz, Dave Campbell, Paul Carrese, Mary Clark, Brian Coyne, Dongxian Jiang, Michael Lamb, Peter Levine, Josh Ober, Avshalom Schwartz, R. Scott Smith, Alicia Steinmetz, Jenna Storey, and the other members.

I am grateful to the Princeton University Press reviewers and editorial board, whose comments greatly enhanced the book's argument and honed its message. Lisa Ellis worked as an excellent editor and early supporter of my work, publishing my article in the *Journal of Politics* on the human right to deliberative justification.

In writing the book, I thank Chris Perriello, who was a pillar of support in college and graduate school. I am in debt to his advice, loyalty, and friendship. Throughout the years, Andrew Braid, Gino Cheng,

Alejandro Fernandez, David Newman, Alex Umfrid, Devin Windham, and Rob Zahra have been steadfast, irrepressible friends. My neighbor Jennifer's cat, Mr. Moo (Whitepaw), oversaw the first chapters drafted outside in the California sun. My stylish allies Bill, David, Derek, Dov, Mitch, and Neil introduced me to the sartorial arts. Mr. Joseph Houdart was the first teacher to discern, on a distant horizon, the glimmers of a future academic career, and gifted me a copy of *A Brief History of Time*.

Stanley Hoffmann took me under his wing as my adviser in college. I thank him for educating me in ethics and international relations, which he always edified with literature and history. The impetus for the book's last chapter was Stanley's magisterial writing and teaching on Kant, human rights, and the possibilities of peace. Stanley showed me how a scholar can combine learning in the classics of political thought with a dedication to the morality of foreign policy. I deeply appreciate how Stanley encouraged me to become a professor. I am grateful to Nancy Rosenblum, who admitted me into her PhD political theory class, a model of how to conduct a seminar, when I was in college. Harvey Mansfield taught my first undergraduate political philosophy course, and demonstrated the importance of intellectual dialogue across diverse viewpoints. Eric Beerbohm extended with his characteristic graciousness an invitation to join an APSA workshop on democracy when I was a graduate student. His discussions have continued to prove a rich source of philosophical acuity and illumination.

Tennyson wrote his poem "Ulysses" to express his "feeling about the need of going forward and braving the struggle of life" in the face of grief and loss.[3] During the completion of the book, I lost the friend who I most wanted to read the manuscript. I reserve a special tribute to a professor who has helped me since my undergraduate days at Harvard. It was only because of Dennis Thompson's confidence and belief in me that I became a political theorist and philosopher. When we are young, we are unsure of ourselves and our abilities. It takes a great teacher and

3. Hallam Tennyson, *Alfred Lord Tennyson: A Memoir by his Son, Vol. 1* (New York: Macmillan, 1897), 196.

devoted mentor to inspire us to develop our talents and embark on the right course in life. I will always remember and be grateful to Dennis, who opened the world of scholarship to me. Dennis and my other teachers and colleagues have shown me how "to follow knowledge like a sinking star, beyond the utmost bounds of human thought."[4]

I want to express my deepest gratitude, above all, to my cherished family. I am grateful to Anna, Lisa, Rune, J.J., Pam, Gilles, Andrew, Laurel, Liana, Fred, Hugh, Guillaume, Kelly, Alexandre, Katherine, Genevieve, Mimi, Lily, Don, and my aunts and uncles for their thoughtfulness and constancy. I thank with special affection Barbara, who was my second mother and treated me as a son, and whom I miss dearly. Mimi, Richard, and Amy blazed a path as professors in the family. Dick and Suzanne have been the most delightful and generous hosts, with their gift of a beautiful environment to begin and finish my book on the coast of France. My grandparents, Le Van Thuy, Nguyen Thi Nhu, Ly Vinh Phu, and Nguyen Thi Bich Lien, abounded with love for us, and courageously sailed across a vast ocean to make a new life for their family. My nieces and nephews, Aki, Kira, Elizabeth, and Chloe, remind me daily of the importance of working for a better world.

My family has brought warmth to my life. This book is above all else the result of the love of Cam, Chung, and Theodora, who have offered a wellspring of kindness, support, and creative ideas. I am reminded of a passage from Corinthians—love always protects, always trusts, always hopes, always perseveres—every day when I think of their help and sacrifices.[5] Any success that I may have in life would have been impossible without all of their work. I dedicate this book with affection to Cam, Chung, and Theodora.

---

4. Tennyson, "Ulysses."

5. 1 Corinthians 13 (New International Version).

ANSWERING TO US

1

The Need for Democratic Accountability

THE CRISIS IN DEMOCRACY

> He [Dr. Martin Luther King Jr.] said we are all complicit when we tolerate injustice. He said it is not enough to say it will get better by and by. He said each of us has a moral obligation to stand up, speak up and speak out. When you see something that is not right, you must say something. You must do something. Democracy is not a state. It is an act, and each generation must do its part.
>
> —REPRESENTATIVE JOHN LEWIS[1]

Democratic Accountability Frees Us to Govern Ourselves

When Doris Hayashi graduated from college, she did not expect that she would soon be detained in a concentration camp ringed by a barbed wire fence and seven guard towers.[2] Yet, she was held captive in the Topaz War Relocation Center in Utah's Sevier Desert because of her ethnicity. Doris was one of 120,000 Japanese Americans incarcerated

1. John Lewis, "Together, You Can Redeem the Soul of Our Nation," *New York Times*, July 30, 2020, https://www.nytimes.com/2020/07/30/opinion/john-lewis-civil-rights-america.html.
2. Sandra C. Taylor, *Jewel of the Desert: Japanese American Internment at Topaz* (Berkeley: University of California Press, 1993); Patricia Wakida, "Doris Hayashi," *Densho Encyclopedia*, accessed March 11, 2025, https://encyclopedia.densho.org/Doris%20Hayashi; Niiya Brian, "Topaz," *Densho Encyclopedia*, accessed March 11, 2025, https://encyclopedia.densho.org/Topaz.

and subject to forced labor during World War II as the result of President Franklin Roosevelt's Executive Order 9066 in 1942.[3] Years later, in 1988, President Ronald Reagan signed the Civil Liberties Act, which provided compensation and apologized for the "fundamental injustice" of the mass internment.[4] The act declared, as one of its central purposes, the intent to "discourage the occurrence of similar injustices and violations of civil liberties in the future."[5]

The mass internment of Japanese Americans illustrates how discrimination and the denial of democratic rights are not new trends. They are long-standing problems, which are intensifying in today's crisis in democracy. These injustices raise three important questions, which this book sets out to answer.

First, how can citizens govern themselves freely in a representative democracy? I hold that to be self-governing means that as citizens, we are ultimately in charge of our government. We are the bosses.[6] Such a system contrasts with being governed by others, such as a dictator, a colonial power, or an otherwise discriminatory regime that excludes groups of the governed. Abraham Lincoln once said, "No man believed more than I in the principle of self-government; that it lies at the bottom of all my ideas of just government, from beginning to end."[7]

The puzzle about self-government is that, in reality, it seems that officials possess all the power. And yet citizens cannot be self-governing if they are powerless in their own government. A common reply to this

---

3. Stephanie Hinnershitz, *Japanese American Incarceration: The Camps and Coerced Labor during World War II* (Philadelphia: University of Pennsylvania Press, 2021), 2; Franklin D. Roosevelt, Executive Order 9066—Authorizing the Secretary of War to Prescribe Military Areas, American Presidency Project, accessed March 11, 2025, https://www.presidency.ucsb.edu/node/210838.

4. Civil Liberties Act of 1988, Pub. L. 100–383.

5. Civil Liberties Act of 1988.

6. Brook Manville and Josiah Ober define self-government as meaning that citizens are the bosses in *The Civic Bargain: How Democracy Survives* (Princeton, NJ: Princeton University Press, 2023).

7. Abraham Lincoln, "Speech of Hon. Abraham Lincoln at Springfield, June 17, 1858," in Abraham Lincoln and Stephen Douglas, *Political Debates between Abraham Lincoln and Stephen A. Douglas* (Cleveland: Burrows Brothers, 1894), 8. On Lincoln's principles, see George Kateb, *Lincoln's Political Thought* (Cambridge, MA: Harvard University Press, 2015).

dilemma is that we govern ourselves by electing our officials.[8] But the vote, though necessary, is not sufficient for self-government. Doris Hayashi was able to vote when she was held captive, but she was in other respects disempowered and relegated to the margins of the citizenry. She wrote in her diary, "I voted this afternoon. . . . I haven't been able to do any reading on these issues so it was rather blind voting for me."[9] Although Doris could vote, she was deprived of her democratic accountability right to freedom of the press to gather information about the candidates and public issues.[10] Behind the barbed wire of her camp, her right to freedom of speech was silenced. She could not participate in public deliberation about the election or canvass for candidates.[11] Aware that this deprivation of rights rendered the internees outcasts among their fellow citizens, Doris noted about one of her fellow inmates, "She is rather bitter about the treatment we are receiving—as non-citizens—when we are really citizens."[12]

I argue in this book that to be freely self-governing, we must be equally empowered to hold our officials democratically accountable,

8. Richard Tuck, *Active and Passive Citizens: A Defense of Majoritarian Democracy*, ed. Stephen Macedo (Princeton, NJ: Princeton University Press, 2024); Jeremy Waldron, *Political Political Theory* (Cambridge, MA: Harvard University Press, 2016).

9. Doris Hayashi Diary, November 2, 1942, available at University of California, Berkeley, Bancroft Library, Japanese American Relocation Digital Archives, p. 2, https://digicoll.lib.berkeley.edu/record/172733?v=pdf.

10. Freedom of speech and freedom of the press extend to the right of listeners and readers to receive information. Justice Hugo Black wrote, "The right of freedom of speech and press has broad scope. The authors of the First Amendment knew that novel and unconventional ideas might disturb the complacent, but they chose to encourage a freedom which they believed essential if vigorous enlightenment was ever to triumph over slothful ignorance. This freedom embraces the right to distribute literature . . . and necessarily protects the right to receive it." Martin v. City of Struthers, 319 U.S. 141, 143 (1943).

11. On deliberation as a key component of democracy, see Amy Gutmann and Dennis F. Thompson, *Democracy and Disagreement* (Cambridge, MA: Harvard University Press, 1996); Joshua Cohen, "Procedure and Substance in Deliberative Democracy," in *Deliberative Democracy*, ed. James Bohman and William Rehg (Cambridge, MA: MIT Press, 1997), 407–37; André Bächtiger et al., *The Oxford Handbook of Deliberative Democracy* (New York: Oxford University Press, 2018); Jürgen Habermas, *Between Facts and Norms* (Cambridge, MA: MIT Press, 1996); Robert E. Goodin, *Innovating Democracy: Democratic Theory and Practice after the Deliberative Turn* (New York: Oxford University Press, 2012); and James Fishkin, *Democracy When the People Are Thinking: Revitalizing Our Politics through Public Deliberation* (New York: Oxford University Press, 2018).

12. Hayashi Diary, 3–4.

and we must all be equally included in the citizenry.[13] Although officials use government power, this is compatible with self-government if they work as public servants and answer to us, the governed. I call this conception of democracy *equal accountability*. Equal accountability requires more than elections. It demands a host of rights and institutions that allow us to hold our public servants accountable during office. Throughout this book, I show that it is not enough to have democratic accountability rights only on paper. Equal accountability crucially demands that we be *empowered* with the material resources, civic education, legal aid, campaign finance reform, and voting access to exercise our democratic accountability rights equally, regardless of socioeconomic status or educational attainment.

Accountability stands against the helplessness implied in only being able to plead with officials, imploring them to act justly, like subjects to a king. I define democratic accountability as the *equal authority*, or set of rights, for the governed to impose the enforceable duties on officials. What makes the duties enforceable is that they can be upheld by the rule of law, which can only function if officials serve subject to the constraints of office.[14] For example, we should have recourse to independent courts to secure our democratic accountability rights to speak, protest, and vote against attempts by officials

13. I explain in chapter 5 how, in order to be self-governing, we must possess two types of rights: procedural democratic accountability rights and substantive human rights. While a procedural right relates to how government decisions are made, a substantive right pertains to the impact of those decisions. For instance, the rights to vote, run for office, and campaign for candidates are procedural rights to participate politically. The rights against discrimination and arbitrary imprisonment are substantive rights. Other rights, such as freedom of speech, contain both procedural and substantive elements. The denial of either type of right detracts from our democratic standing as equal citizens who are ultimately in charge of our government.

14. Melissa Lane elucidates how the ancient Athenians construed government positions as offices in *Of Rule and Office: Plato's Ideas of the Political* (Princeton, NJ: Princeton University Press, 2023). For the ancient Athenians, anarchy did not simply refer to the absence of government; it also applied to despotic regimes, where power is exercised without the constraints and duties of office. Daniel Carpenter sets out insightfully the evolution of the notion of "office" from ancient times to the Middle Ages, early modern era, and the American Founding. See Daniel Carpenter, "2023 John Gaus Award Lecture: Toward a Theory of Office: Ministry, Accountability, Authority," September 7, 2024, American Political Science Association Annual Meeting, Philadelphia, available at: https://dcarpenter.scholars.harvard.edu/sites/g/files/omnuum8536/files/gaus_lecture_20250207.pdf.

to restrict those rights. Democratic accountability grants us authority over our officials, empowering the governed and compelling officials to work not as kings, but as public servants who answer to the governed.

The second question this book addresses is: How can we stop the violations of rights aimed at denying citizens their freedom as self-government? These injustices are mounting in severity. For example, Asian Americans suffered 6,603 violent hate incidents during the first year of the COVID-19 pandemic.[15] It is tempting to believe that the solution lies in elite checks and balances, such as courts.[16] These institutions are indispensable to democracy. But they do not suffice on their own. Judicial review failed to stop the mass internment of Japanese Americans and the disenfranchisement of African Americans under Jim Crow laws. The Supreme Court upheld these discriminatory policies in *Korematsu* and *Plessy v. Ferguson*.[17] It took the democratic participation of citizens to dismantle the legal structure of racial segregation through the Civil Rights Movement.

Citizen action is needed to safeguard democracy from two threats. The first is the peril of *factions*, or a group of citizens who are, as James Madison says, "adverse to the rights of other citizens."[18] For instance, the instigators and accomplices of the Jim Crow regime of racial segregation comprised a faction. The second threat to democracy emanates from officials who exercise power unjustly. These officials act as *elected authoritarians*.[19] Factions and elected authoritarians strip citizens of

15. Barbara Sprunt, "Here's What the New Hate Crimes Law Aims to Do as Attacks on Asian Americans Rise," NPR, May 20, 2021.

16. On judicial review to protect minority rights, see Ronald Dworkin, *Freedom's Law: The Moral Reading of the American Constitution* (Cambridge, MA: Harvard University Press, 1996). I leave open whether democracies adopt strong judicial review that can strike down legislation. This is a question of institutional design that citizens must work out. Some democracies have not instituted it, such as The Netherlands and the United Kingdom. See Stephen Macedo, "Against Majoritarianism: Democratic Values and Institutional Design," *Boston University Law Review* 90 (2010): 1031.

17. Plessy v. Ferguson, 163 U.S. 537 (1896); Korematsu v. United States, 323 U.S. 214 (1944).

18. James Madison, "Federalist No. 10," in Alexander Hamilton, James Madison, and John Jay, *The Federalist*, ed. Terence Ball (Cambridge, UK: Cambridge University Press, 2003), 41.

19. The term "elected authoritarian" is fitting, since the officials who endanger democracy today are largely elected: "Since the end of the Cold War, most democratic breakdowns have

their freedom of self-government by extinguishing their rights and taking away their standing as the ones in charge. Throughout this book,
I refer to such actions as marginalization, and the targeted citizens as
the *marginalized*.[20]

I argue that as citizens, we should fulfill a vital set of *democratic duties*
necessary to end marginalization and other injustices.[21] The duties are
democratic in calling for the exercise of our democratic rights, and in
securing the inclusion of all citizens in democracy. I bring to the fore-
front the novel insight that our democratic duties are morally grounded
in self-government. If we are the bosses in charge of our government,
we have the duty to hold the public servants who work for us democratically accountable for exercising the power of our government justly
on our behalf.[22] As citizens, we bear what I call the democratic duty of
oversight. Like townspeople who have lent a gun to a sheriff, we should

---

been caused not by generals and soldiers but by elected governments themselves.... Democratic backsliding today begins at the ballot box." Steven Levitsky and Daniel Ziblatt, *How
Democracies Die* (New York: Crown, 2019), 5.

20. I thank Jan Feldman, Sonu Bedi, Lucas Swaine, and Julie Rose, as they contributed helpful discussion regarding whether to use the term *marginalized* or *minority*. There are two potential meanings of a minority: a group of citizens that is *numerically smaller* than the majority, or
a group of citizens *subject to injustice*. Marginalized is a clearer term. It acknowledges the possibility that citizens who are the victims of injustice can comprise either a numerical minority
or majority. Injustice is not just a subjective belief that one has been wronged, such as billionaires believing they have been slighted. Injustice occurs when people have been denied their
human rights, deprived of their equal authority in democracy, or afflicted with other forms of
oppression. See Iris Marion Young, *Justice and the Politics of Difference* (Princeton, NJ: Princeton
University Press, 1990). I benefited from conversation with Jan Feldman at the University of
Vermont and my Stanford PhD students on the work of Iris Marion Young.

21. I use "officials" neutrally to denote people who work in one of the three branches of
government. A "public servant" is a moralized role that officials ought to take, where they understand themselves as working for citizens and as having democratic duties of fidelity in public
office. The leaders of the East German Stasi or secret police were officials but not public
servants.

22. The duty to participate in democratic accountability may be morally attenuated for citizens who are marginalized, because they are not being treated as among the people in charge.
However, this marginalization should be rectified by other citizens and public servants acting
on their democratic duties. Citizens should be empowered to participate as equals in democratic accountability, so they can take full responsibility as the ones ultimately in charge of
government. Chapter 4 discusses how marginalized citizens may have prudential reasons to
participate in democratic accountability to protect their rights. I thank Kevin Elliott for discussion of this point at APSA.

hold our sheriff accountable for exerting that power to secure rights and not to abuse anyone, either citizens or noncitizens.

Alongside our duty of oversight, we should act on our duty of *solidarity* and harness our democratic accountability rights to protect our fellow citizens. When officials commit injustices, we should speak, write, protest, petition, organize associations, and vote for new public servants who will pursue justice with integrity. We should also urge public servants to enact and enforce laws that secure citizens from the danger of elected authoritarians and factions. Citizens acted in solidarity when they advocated the 1964 Civil Rights Act, which prohibits discrimination in public accommodations, public education, and federally assisted programs.[23] Solidarity secures our liberty in the form of self-government that is free from the threat of marginalization. The horizontal relation of solidarity between citizens protects the vertical relation of citizens holding their public servants democratically accountable.

Former attorney general Merrick Garland spoke eloquently of citizens' democratic duty of solidarity in a speech on the first anniversary of the January 6th attack on the Capitol:

> We are all Americans. *We must protect each other. . . .* [The] Justice Department—even the Congress—cannot alone defend the right to vote. The responsibility to preserve democracy—and to maintain faith in the legitimacy of its essential processes—lies with every elected official and with every American.[24]

The lesson that as citizens "we must protect each other" epitomizes the duty of solidarity. I explain that we protect one another by holding our public servants democratically accountable, ensuring that they pass and enforce laws to safeguard our fellow citizens from injustice. Public servants, in turn, owe us the democratic duty of *fidelity* to cooperate with democratic accountability and to aid us in stopping elected

23. Civil Rights Act of 1964, Pub. L. 88-352.

24. Merrick Garland, "Attorney General Merrick B. Garland Delivers Remarks on the First Anniversary of the Attack on the Capitol," Washington, DC, January 5, 2022, available at Archives, US Department of Justice, www.justice.gov/opa/speech/attorney-general-merrick-b -garland-delivers-remarks-first-anniversary-attack-capitol (emphasis added).

authoritarians and factions from trampling on rights. For example, the president and Congress acted on their duty of fidelity when they passed the COVID-19 Hate Crimes Act in 2021 to stanch the wave of violence by factions of citizens against Asian Americans.[25] Similarly, Attorney General Elliot Richardson fulfilled the duty of fidelity when he resigned to protest President Nixon's interference with the Watergate investigation.

The significance of democratic duties is thrown into sharp relief when we consider what our government would look like without them.[26] Citizens failed in their duties of solidarity and oversight when they did not oppose the mass detention of 120,000 innocent Japanese Americans in concentration camps, and when they faltered in speaking out against the near century of racial segregation during the Jim Crow era, from 1877 to the mid-1960s.[27] Representative John Lewis, a leader of the Civil Rights Movement, expressed the urgency of our democratic duties in the quote that opens this book: "Each of us has a moral obligation to stand up, speak up and speak out. When you see something that is not right, you must say something. You must do something. Democracy is not a state. It is an act, and each generation must do its part."[28]

The third question that this book addresses is whether to recognize a human right to democratic accountability. Suppose that other states are pursuing policies similar to the Japanese American internment or Jim Crow. Do we have duties to refrain from stoking authoritarianism and discrimination in other countries? When South Africa imposed a brutal regime of racial segregation, did we owe Black South Africans the commitment to avoid complicity with apartheid? Citizens of other countries, moreover, are sensitive to the inherent hypocrisy in US foreign policy that is at odds with a professed commitment to democratic

25. COVID-19 Hate Crimes Act, Pub. L. 117-13, https://www.congress.gov/bill/117th-congress/senate-bill/937/text.

26. I am grateful to Sonu Bedi, who made the valuable comment at my Dartmouth presentation suggesting that I demonstrate the importance of democratic duties by describing what a state would look like in their absence.

27. On Jim Crow, see Henry Louis Gates, *Stony the Road: Reconstruction, White Supremacy, and the Rise of Jim Crow* (New York: Penguin Press, 2019) and Margaret A. Burnham, *Hands Now Known: Jim Crow's Legal Executioners* (New York: Norton, 2022).

28. Lewis, "Together, You Can Redeem."

values. For example, in 2005, a Council of Foreign Relations poll asked Arabs what they think of the United States. The responses revealed that many Arabs "simply cannot understand why a country whose democratic institutions they so much admire provides political, economic and military aid to absolute monarchs and military dictators."[29]

Through this book, I seek to demonstrate that democratic accountability is morally owed as a human right. Respecting it prohibits overthrowing the government of a foreign democracy, as the United States did in Iran in 1953, Guatemala in 1954, and Chile in 1973.[30] It is undemocratic to depose another state's democratic government, even if a majority of citizens in our own country prefer we do so. The human right to democratic accountability further entails that we should respect democratic rights in other states by ceasing to send the means of repression to authoritarians.[31] Finally, since the duty of oversight includes the responsibility for citizens to hold their public servants accountable for respecting the human rights of noncitizens, we should ensure that our public servants do not inflict torture on anyone, undermine democracy in other states, or wage unjust wars.

To summarize the thesis of this book, I offer a new conception of democracy, and what makes democracy work well, called *equal accountability*. It affirms, *first*, that we freely govern ourselves when we are equally empowered to hold our officials democratically accountable, and we are equally included in the citizenry that governs together. Equal accountability requires not only elections but also a host of rights and institutions to hold our officials to account during office. We must be empowered with the resources and civic education to exercise our

29. Robin Wright, "Campaign to Change Mideast under Fire," *Washington Post*, June 9, 2005.

30. Stephen Schlesinger and Stephen Kinzer, *Bitter Fruit: The Story of the American Coup in Guatemala, Revised and Expanded* (Cambridge, MA: Harvard University Press, 2005); John Tirman, *The Deaths of Others: The Fate of Civilians in America's Wars* (New York: Oxford University Press, 2010); James Doubek, "The US Set the Stage for a Coup in Chile. It Had Unintended Consequences at Home," NPR, September 10, 2023, https://www.npr.org/2023/09/10 /1193755188/chile-coup-50-years-pinochet-kissinger-human-rights-allende.

31. Thomas Carothers and Benjamin Feldman, "Examining U.S. Relations with Authoritarian Countries," Carnegie Endowment for International Peace, December 13, 2023, https:// carnegieendowment.org/research/2023/12/examining-us-relations-with-authoritarian -countries?lang=en.

democratic accountability rights equally across the citizenry. *Second,* equal accountability emphasizes the democratic duties needed to secure our equal democratic rights. These duties of oversight, solidarity, and fidelity are essential for democratic accountability to work. Democratic duties are morally grounded in the value of self-government, or our standing as the ones in charge of our public servants. *Third,* all human beings are entitled to a democratically accountable government in their state so that they can govern themselves freely.[32] We bear the duty of oversight to hold our public servants democratically accountable for respecting the human rights of both citizens and noncitizens.

The Global Crisis of Democracy and the Lack of Democratic Accountability

My equal accountability theory of democracy helps us counter the rising democratic crisis. In many countries, governments are marginalizing minorities, attacking the rule of law, and cracking down on the freedom of dissent. Yet these governments claim to be democratic, because they hold elections said to represent the will of the people. But if the elected government represents the people's will, then criticism of the president or prime minister can appear undemocratic, because it opposes what the people want. This influential view makes protestors and the free press the "enemies of the people."[33] As Recep Tayyip Erdoğan, the president of

32. My theory of equal accountability contrasts with the work of high-profile critics of the human right to democracy, influential skeptics of self-government, and prominent majoritarians who focus on elections while overlooking the full range of rights, duties, and institutions required for democratic accountability. Critics of the human right to democracy include David Miller, "Is There a Human Right to Democracy?" CSSJ Working Paper Series, SJ032, April 2015, http://www.politics.ox.ac.uk/materials/publications/13731/sj032is-there-a-human-right-to -democracy-final-version.pdf; John Rawls, *Law of Peoples: With "The Idea of Public Reason Revisited"* (Cambridge, MA: Harvard University Press, 1999); and Charles Beitz, *The Idea of Human Rights* (New York: Oxford University Press, 2009). For skepticism about self-government, see Niko Kolodny, "Rule over None I: What Justifies Democracy?" *Philosophy and Public Affairs* 42, no. 3 (2014): 195–229 and Daniel Viehoff, "XIV—The Truth in Political Instrumentalism," *Proceedings of the Aristotelian Society*, 117, no. 3 (2017): 273–95. Examples of leading majoritarians are Tuck, *Active and Passive Citizens*, and Waldron, *Political Political Theory.*

33. Cristina Maza, "Just Like Richard Nixon, Hungary's Viktor Orban Has a List of Enemies," *Newsweek*, May 15, 2018, https://www.newsweek.com/richard-nixons-enemies-list-being-

Turkey, said to the opposition, "We are the people. Who are you?"[34] Meanwhile, at the global level, democracy is in decline as elected officials ally with and arm foreign dictators.

In short, at the root of the democratic crisis lies the widespread belief that democracy is about carrying out the people's will, defined by the majority and executed by the president.[35] This popular will theory of democracy ignores the people's diversity, stigmatizing marginalized citizens as not being part of the true people.[36] The popular will theory fuels the crisis of democracy by insisting that dissent against the elected government is undemocratic. The theory even allows a government to erode democracy in other countries if a majority prefers it.

We are at a critical juncture. Far from being limited to any one country, the fallacy is gaining ground internationally that all forms of accountability besides elections are undemocratic. From Hungary to Poland, Russia, and Turkey, a shadow is falling on democracy.[37] In India, the world's most populous democracy, the government has imprisoned opposition leader Rahul Gandhi for criticizing Prime Minister Narendra Modi.[38] This turn against accountability is the latest move in a "project

---

replicated-orbans-hungary-and-it-could-have-926784. Robert Dahl objects to the popular will–based presidential mandate in "The Myth of the Presidential Mandate," *Political Science Quarterly* 105 (1990): 355–72.

34. Jan-Werner Müller, *What Is Populism?* (Philadelphia: University of Pennsylvania Press, 2016), 3; Kim Lane Scheppele, "Autocratic Legalism," *University of Chicago Law Review* 85 (2018): 545–83.

35. Stephen Macedo and Josiah Ober incisively criticize the popular will theory, which they view as the most prevalent theory of democracy. See Macedo, "Against Majoritarianism." As Ober notes, "In modernity, democracy is often construed as being concerned, in the first instance, with a voting rule for determining the will of the majority." Josiah Ober, "The Original Meaning of 'Democracy': Capacity to Do Things, Not Majority Rule," *Constellations* 15, no. 1 (2008): 3.

36. Müller makes the important point that the popular will theory of democracy ignores the diversity of the people and treats the people as homogeneous. See *What Is Populism?* 57 and 77.

37. Larry Diamond, *Ill Winds* (New York: Penguin, 2019); Andrew Arato and Jean L. Cohen, *Populism and Civil Society: The Challenge to Constitutional Democracy* (New York: Oxford University Press, 2021); Müller, *What Is Populism?*; Jane Mansbridge and Stephen Macedo, "Populism and Democratic Theory," *Annual Review of Law and Social Science* 15 (2019): 59–77. There are some exceptions: In 2023, citizens in Poland voted against elected authoritarians. Jennifer Rubin, "Poland Offers Hope for Reclaiming Democracy," *Washington Post*, October 19, 2023.

38. Karan Deep Singh, "Leader of Indian Opposition Party Opposing Modi Is Sentenced in Defamation Case," *New York Times*, March 24, 2023. See also Martha C. Nussbaum, *The Clash*

to remake India's democracy unlike any in its 75 years of independence—stifling dissent, sidelining civilian institutions and making minorities second-class citizens."[39] The pretext for tightening the vise grip on dissent is that Modi was elected and represents the people, who are nearly 80 percent Hindu, making it undemocratic to oppose him. Democracy worldwide is being pushed to the brink and the marginalized are bearing the brunt of the attack, increasing the stakes of offering an alternative to the popular will theory.[40]

The Democratic Crisis Cannot Be Solved by Existing Approaches

A major reason why critics of this misguided vision of democracy have failed to make much headway is that they have not challenged the fundamental beliefs about democracy from which elected authoritarians draw so much strength. Until we take on that underlying view, we will find it far more difficult to defeat authoritarianism.[41]

The popular will theory is not limited to our era or any one political party. More than a century ago, Woodrow Wilson asserted about the president that "no one else represents the people as whole, exercising a national choice. . . . The nation as a whole has chosen him, and is conscious that it has no other political spokesman."[42] Wilson's words resemble former attorney general William Barr's portrayal of the presidency: it is "a remarkable democratic institution—the only figure

Within: Democracy, Religious Violence, and India's Future (Cambridge, MA: Harvard University Press, 2007).

39. Mujib Mashal, "The New India: Expanding Influence Abroad, Straining Democracy at Home," *New York Times*, September 25, 2022.

40. Not all popular will theorists are populists who view the president as the infallible representative of the people's will. "Popular will accountability" seeks to correct officials who deviate from the majority will. This approach, however, neglects the democratic duties of citizens, democratic accountability during office, and institutions for mediated accountability.

41. I am grateful to the anonymous reviewer of this work who trenchantly suggested this framing.

42. Woodrow Wilson, *Constitutional Government in the United States* (New York: Columbia University Press, 1911 [1908]), 68. Wilson at times moderated his views on this subject. For instance, he saw a role for courts to protect rights (see *Constitutional Government*, 143).

elected by the Nation as a whole."[43] Both Wilson and Barr cast opposition to the president as undemocratic, because it resists the voice of the entire people. Acting on this belief, President Wilson signed the Sedition Act of 1918, criminalizing speech and print critical of the government.[44]

Faced with the threat of elected authoritarianism, many writers have taken the misstep of ceding the authoritarians' claim to democratic legitimacy. Yascha Mounk, in the highly cited book *The People vs. Democracy*, considers elected authoritarians to be democratic precisely because they carry out the will of the people. Calling them "populists," he writes:

> In that sense, populists are deeply democratic: much more fervently than traditional politicians, they believe that the *demos* should rule. But they are also deeply illiberal: unlike traditional politicians, they openly say that neither independent institutions nor individual rights should dampen the people's voice.[45]

Mounk rebukes elected authoritarianism not for being undemocratic, but for being illiberal: "What sets it apart from the kind of liberal democracy to which we are accustomed is not a lack of democracy; it is a lack of respect for independent institutions and individual rights."[46] Writers like Mounk and Fareed Zakaria distinguish liberal rights and institutions from democracy, which is a system to "allow the people to rule" through elections.[47] "A *democracy*," says Mounk, "is a set of binding electoral institutions that effectively translates popular views into public policy."[48]

43. William Barr, "Attorney General William P. Barr Delivers the 19th Annual Barbara K. Olson Memorial Lecture at the Federalist Society's 2019 National Lawyers Convention," Washington, DC, US Department of Justice, November 15, 2019, https://www.justice.gov/opa /speech/attorney-general-william-p-barr-delivers-19th-annual-barbara-k-olson-memorial -lecture.

44. Wilson, *Constitutional Government*, 68.

45. Yascha Mounk, *The People vs. Democracy: Why Our Freedom Is In Danger and How to Save It* (Cambridge, MA: Harvard University Press, 2018), 8–9.

46. Mounk, *People vs. Democracy*, 11.

47. Mounk, *People vs. Democracy*, 27; Fareed Zakaria, "The Rise of Illiberal Democracy," *Foreign Affairs* 76, no. 6 (1997): 22–43 and idem, *The Future of Freedom: Illiberal Democracy at Home and Abroad*, rev. ed. (New York: W. W. Norton, 2007).

48. Mounk, *People vs. Democracy*, 27 (emphasis in original).

Later, Mounk makes the important point that economic opportunity must be made more available to ordinary citizens, so they are not lured into voting for illiberal democrats who promise them a better life in exchange for their freedoms. However, his earlier move of criticizing officials for being illiberal falls into a trap, handing the mantle of democracy over to authoritarians. Mounk grants too quickly that their "claim to being democratic need not be disingenuous. In the emerging system, the popular will reigns supreme (at least at first)."[49] This concession forces the citizens who resist elected authoritarians back on their heels. When the government assaults rights, theorists of illiberal democracy must surrender the point that the elected authoritarians are democratic. To undercut this source of authoritarian power, I maintain that rather than labeling these regimes "illiberal democracies," we should deem them elected *authoritarians*, taking away from them the mantle of democratic legitimacy.

Equal Accountability Addresses the Crisis in Democracy

I argue that elected authoritarians are undemocratic, because they are unaccountable to the people they govern. Resisting elected authoritarians requires that we overturn their underlying popular will theory of democracy, and replace it with a new theory of democracy: *equal accountability*. The purpose of a democratic theory is to define what democracy means and explain why it is valuable. Doing so shows us what the government must do to be fully democratic, and it clarifies our duties as citizens and public servants to sustain democracy.[50] Although

49. Mounk, 11.

50. It would be too high a bar to ask that any political theory completely solve, on its own, the crisis in democracy. The key question is whether the theory helps to move us in the right direction. Equal accountability contributes on three fronts to addressing the democratic crisis. First, countering elected authoritarians requires that citizens and officials act on their democratic duties. The equal accountability theory clarifies what those duties are. Second, citizens need to coordinate their actions in opposing elected authoritarians. Democratic norms lower the costs of collective action by providing coordination points that are common knowledge among citizens. Third, opposition to elected authoritarians is weakened by the widespread acceptance of populism, which views opposition as undemocratic, and popular will

democratic theory might seem abstract, it affords lessons of practical importance. We implicitly draw on claims of democratic theory when we contend that our officials' actions are undemocratic, or when we urge reforms that would make our government more democratic.[51]

Unlike existing democratic theories, equal accountability focuses on the essential role of ordinary citizens in holding their government accountable. I explain that to recover democracy, we must both *empower* citizens to participate in democratic accountability and defend the democratic value of *independent institutions*. Empowering citizens requires that we protect their democratic accountability rights to freedom of the press, speech, petition, protest, association, the vote, transparency, and the rule of law. These rights are not separate from democracy, as Mounk and Zakaria depict them.[52] They constitute democracy, giving us the authority to hold our public servants democratically accountable. Empowering citizens also requires that we equip each other with the material resources and civic education to exercise our democratic accountability rights equally.

Far from being undemocratic, institutions such as independent courts, law enforcement, impeachment, audit agencies, inspectors general, and congressional or parliamentary oversight can enhance democracy. They improve our capacity to investigate officials and uncover their misconduct. If they function properly, these institutions are not independent of democracy. They are independent of the president or prime minister so that he or she cannot warp our system of justice and evade accountability. Elected authoritarians are undemocratic for the very reason that they *disempower* citizens by clawing away the rights and

accountability, which is silent about the duties of citizens. Both versions of the popular will theory must be superseded by an improved understanding of democracy that emphasizes the democratic duties of citizens and the accountability of government. I thank Philip Petrov for discussion on this point.

51. I am offering one part of what must be a multipronged response to the democratic crisis. I seek to contribute a better understanding of the meaning of democracy and the democratic duties of citizens and public servants.

52. Zakaria splits rights from democracy when he says that "this latter bundle of freedoms— what might be termed constitutional liberalism—is theoretically different and historically distinct from democracy" ("Rise of Illiberal Democracy," 22–23).

independent institutions that citizens need to hold their officials accountable.

The question of whether we should ground democracy in accountability or the popular will is a persistent puzzle that has confronted democratic governments and its citizens. Nearly two and half thousand years ago, in Herodotus's *Histories,* Otanes hailed democracy as the best form of government, admiring how "it is accountable."[53] The ancient Athenians, who invented democracy in the sixth century BCE, created several institutions to hold their officials accountable. Before they could serve in office, officials underwent a scrutiny, or *dokimasia*, which examined whether the candidate had performed his duties as a citizen, paid his taxes, and served in the military.[54] While in office, government officials could be sued in a legal action, which the ancient Athenians called a *graphē paranómōn*, if they proposed decrees that violated the existing laws. After stepping down from office, officials were subject to a reckoning (*euthyna*) to investigate their financial integrity and uncover potential corruption in the spending of public funds. Many centuries later, this policy informed the 1789 French Declaration of the Rights of Man and the Citizen, which stated that "society has the right to require of every public agent an account of his administration."[55]

The ancient Athenians did not assume that their officials were exempt from accountability as infallible representatives who incarnate the popular will. Without accountability during office, an official would rule

53. Herodotus, *The Histories*, trans. Robin Waterfield (Oxford: Oxford University Press, 2008), 205. I appreciate Ian Walling's edifying discussion of Herodotus on democracy.

54. Melissa Lane, *The Birth of Politics* (Princeton, NJ: Princeton University Press, 2014), chaps. 3 and 5, esp. 364n23; Josiah Ober, *The Rise and Fall of Classical Greece* (Princeton, NJ: Princeton University Press, 2015), 167. Ober writes, "All officials, elected or lotteried, were subject to *ex ante* public scrutiny and held publicly accountable, on an annual basis, for their performance." On ancient Athenian mechanisms for accountability, see Matthew Landauer, *Dangerous Counsel: Accountability and Advice in Ancient Greece* (Chicago: University of Chicago Press, 2019); Bernard Manin, *The Principles of Representative Government* (Cambridge, UK: Cambridge University Press, 1997), chap. 1; and Daniela Cammack, *Demos: How the People Ruled Athens* (Princeton, NJ: Princeton University Press, forthcoming). On the *graphē paranómōn*, see Melissa Schwartzberg, "Was the Graphe Paranomon a Form of Judicial Review?" *Cardozo Law Review* 34 (2013): 1059 and Ober, *Rise and Fall*, 167.

55. I thank Dan Edelstein for an enlightening conversation about accountability in French political thought. *France: Declaration of the Right of Man and the Citizen*, August 26, 1789, article 15, https://www.refworld.org/docid/3ae6b52410.html.

for years with the absolutism of a king. But "how can monarchy be an orderly affair," asked Otanes in Herodotus's *Histories*, "when a monarch has the license to do whatever he wants, without being accountable to anyone?"[56] The popular will, however, is now ascendant in theory and pervasive in practice. We have forgotten the central place of accountability to democracy. When we do recall it fitfully, the meaning of accountability is distorted by restricting it to elections meant to induce officials to follow the preferences of the popular will.

Our self-governing standing as the ones in charge can only be preserved if our officials serve in *offices*, which are limited in powers and attached to duties.[57] If officials breached the restraints on power imposed by public office, they could escape accountability and terrorize citizens, who would no longer be the bosses but the captives of their government. To be freely self-governing, we must be able to hold our officials democratically accountable, not only during elections, but also in their years in office.

Citizen Participation and Institutions Are Both Needed to Remedy the Democratic Crisis

Equal accountability combines *citizen participation* guided by democratic duties, with *institutions* that strengthen democratic accountability to citizens. This strategy differs from the two most common approaches to mitigating elected authoritarians: elite checks and balances, and majoritarianism.[58] Each of these is missing key components for thwarting elected authoritarians. While checks and balances downplay empowered citizen participation, majoritarianism disregards the need for independent institutions.

Proponents of checks and balances recommend institutions and elites as roadblocks to an errant popular will. For example, Steven Levitsky and Daniel Ziblatt in *How Democracies Die* advise that party

56. Herodotus, *Histories*, 204.

57. Lane, *Of Rule and Office* and Carpenter, "2023 John Gaus Award Lecture."

58. I thank the second reviewer of this book, who asked about how my view differs from Waldron's majoritarianism and Dworkin's reliance on judicial review.

leaders should prevent authoritarian candidates from running for office. Jason Brennan and Bryan Caplan want to shift power away from citizen participation to experts. And many writers, led by Ronald Dworkin, pin their hopes on judicial review.[59]

These writers offer valuable insights, but they say little about the pivotal role of citizens in opposing elected authoritarians. Courts and other checks and balances are necessary but not sufficient safeguards, as we saw in the Supreme Court's failure to end the disenfranchisement of African Americans under Jim Crow and the mass internment of Japanese Americans.

James Madison was an eloquent exponent of the rights to free speech and the press. Madison, however, relied mainly on institutional checks and balances to avert the threat of elected authoritarianism: "In framing a government which is to be administered by men over men, the great difficulty lies in this," he says in Federalist 51. "You must first enable the government to controul [*sic*] the governed; and in the next place, oblige it to controul itself."[60] In his view, the government controls itself when it is divided into branches that stave off each other's attempts to accumulate excessive power.[61] While agreeing with the need for institutional checks and balances, equal accountability affirms that we, the *governed*, must control our government, so that we are freely self-governing as the ones in charge.[62]

59. Levitsky and Ziblatt, *How Democracies Die*; Jason Brennan, *Against Democracy* (Princeton, NJ: Princeton University Press, 2017); Dworkin, *Freedom's Law*; Bryan Caplan, *The Myth of the Rational Voter* (Princeton, NJ: Princeton University Press, 2008). Levitsky and Ziblatt focus on how political parties should work as "gatekeepers" against elected authoritarians: "Although mass responses to extremist appeals matter, what matters more is whether political elites, and especially parties, serve as filters" (*How Democracies Die*, 20).

60. Madison, "Federalist No. 51," in *The Federalist*, 252.

61. The "constant aim is to divide and arrange the several offices in such a manner as that each may be a check on the other," safeguarding "the public rights." Madison, "Federalist No. 51," 253.

62. Equal accountability bears a friendly affinity with republican theorists like Philip Pettit, Quentin Skinner, and Frank Lovett. We agree that democracy must include contestatory rights beyond the vote for citizens to control their government. Despite its great appeal, a worry about republicanism is that it may overstate the degree that individual citizens exercise power over their government. Equal accountability is more highly attuned than republicanism to the fact that individuals acting alone can be vulnerable and unfree, even when they possess contestatory rights to challenge government injustices. This individual vulnerability makes it crucial that as

In contrast to equal accountability theory, Madison did not sufficiently emphasize the value of *equality*. Indeed, he helped to draft a constitution that countenanced slavery and barred African Americans and
women from participating in democratic accountability.[63] In my theory
of equal accountability, all those subject to the jurisdiction of a government are entitled to citizenship and equal democratic accountability
rights.[64] Furthermore, citizens must be empowered with the resources
and civic education to exercise their democratic rights equally.

If checks and balances place too much stock in institutions to stop
elected authoritarians, then majoritarianism places too little stress on
those institutions. To better understand this point, we should distinguish between two versions of the popular will theory. One is associated
with elected authoritarians, and the other tries to resist elected authoritarians through democratic accountability based on elections.

The first, "populist" type, asserts that the president and other officials
represent the people's will without any need for accountability. Since
populism views presidents or prime ministers as closely representing
the popular will, criticizing them is considered undemocratic. The
bounds of office are seen as undemocratic barriers to the ability of the
chief executive to carry out the will of the people. This is the form of

---

citizens, we act on what I call our democratic duty of solidarity, using our democratic accountability rights to protect each other from injustice. While Thomas Simpson has written about
how republicanism needs a conception of democratic duties, I offer a theory of the democratic
duties of the offices of the citizen and public servant needed to sustain self-government. Leading
republicans include Philip Pettit, *On the People's Terms* (Cambridge, UK: Cambridge University
Press, 2012), Quentin Skinner, *Liberty before Liberalism* (Cambridge, UK: Cambridge University
Press, 1998), and Frank Lovett, *The Well-Ordered Republic* (New York: Oxford University Press,
2022). Cf. Thomas W. Simpson, "The Impossibility of Republican Freedom," *Philosophy and
Public Affairs* 45, no. 1 (2017): 27–53.

63. The Constitution's Fugitive Slave Clause ordered that slaves who escaped to another state
be "delivered up" to their human traffickers (U.S. Const. article IV, section 2, clause 3). Slaves
were counted as three-fifths of a person in apportioning a state's congressional representation,
which gave slave owners the preponderant power in the House of Representatives to block
emancipation (U.S. Const. article I, section 2, clause 3). The Slave Trade Clause restricted Congress from banning the international slave trade for twenty years, until 1808 (U.S. Const. article I,
section 9, clause 1). Article V entrenched the Slave Trade Clause by preventing it from being
altered even by constitutional amendment (U.S. Const. article V).

64. There is an exception for tourists and diplomats, since they are temporary visitors. I
elaborate this point in chapter 5 on my Inclusion Principle, which entitles the governed to equal
citizenship.

the popular will theory that elected authoritarians invoke. Populism claims to make us free, but it actually subordinates us to unaccountable power. When officials do not answer to us, we are no longer freely self-governing. Under the pretense of liberty, populism fastens the chains of servility.

The second, more subtle variant on the popular will theory attempts to combine accountability with the popular will.[65] "Popular will accountability" acknowledges that elected officials might act against the people's preferences. Although the choice of officials might reflect the people's will, what the officials do once in power may run afoul of what the people want. Officials can embezzle public money for private enrichment. Corrupt officials may do the bidding of the wealthy, instead of serving the majority of citizens.[66]

Given the danger of officials acting contrary to the will of the people, they must be incentivized to do what the citizens prefer. This is done by elections, which determine what voters want by weighing their

65. The popular will theory may seem to resemble Rousseau's approach to democracy. Rousseau thought that in a democracy, citizens are free because they only obey themselves. His theory depended on citizens making the law through a direct democracy. Since he was not writing about representative democracy, where laws are made through elected representatives, he lacked a full conception of democratic accountability. He did not explain how citizens can exercise equal authority over their elected public servants during office. Rousseau also sits as an uncertain ally of popular will theories. He did not believe that a morally legitimate democracy followed the raw preferences of citizens, or what he called the "will of all." For a democracy to be morally legitimate, or to have the right to make and enforce laws, it must follow the "general will." The general will comprises the preferences of citizens when they vote according to what they believe the public good requires, and when they are not biased against any group of citizens. Brettschneider persuasively points out that Rousseau's theory is susceptible to "the problem of false attribution." While in principle Rousseau distinguishes the general will from the will of all, he tends to conflate the outcome of actual, imperfect procedures with the ideal general will. This issue with Rousseau's proceduralism leads Brettschneider to propose a *value theory of democracy*, which holds that a morally legitimate government must respect the substantive values of equality of interests, autonomy, and reciprocity. The value theory regards these values as constitutive of democracy, because they respect the democratic status of citizens as free and equal. This approach avoids Rousseau's conundrum of how to locate an elusive general will or "true will of the people" that is separate from procedural outcomes. Corey Brettschneider, *Democratic Rights: The Substance of Self-Government* (Princeton, NJ: Princeton University Press, 2007). I thank Corey Brettschneider and Melissa Schwartzberg for asking about the relation between my theory and Rousseau's at an APSA conference.

66. This is the concern that Lawrence Lessig raises: "The great threat to our republic today," he says, is that "our government doesn't track the expressed will of the people." See *Republic, Lost: How Money Corrupts Congress—and a Plan to Stop It* (New York: Hachette, 2011), 7–8.

preferences through a majority vote.[67] Bernard Manin, Adam Przeworski, and Susan Stokes describe lucidly this election-centered approach to democratic accountability: "The standard view of how the accountability mechanism operates relies on 'retrospective voting.' In this view, citizens set some standard of performance to evaluate governments. . . . They vote against the incumbent unless these criteria are fulfilled."[68] Joseph Schumpeter takes a similar election-centric approach to democracy. In a book cited over sixty-seven thousand times, he defines "the democratic method" as "that institutional arrangement for arriving at political decisions in which individuals acquire the power to decide by means of a competitive struggle for the people's vote."[69] Popular will

67. In the social choice theory that prevails in economics and political science, voting aggregates citizens' preferences. The model compares citizens to consumers who have preferences for candidates in elections. See Anthony Downs, *An Economic Theory of Democracy* (New York: Harper & Row, 1957) and Kenneth Arrow, *Social Choice and Individual Values*, 2nd ed. (New Haven, CT: Yale University Press, 1963). The election-centric approach has been taken up more recently by "principal-agent" models of democratic accountability, discussed in chapters 2 and 4. See also Sean Gailmard, "Accountability and Principal-Agent Theory," in *The Oxford Handbook of Public Accountability*, ed. Mark Bovens, Robert E. Goodin, and Thomas Schillemans (New York: Oxford University Press, 2014), chap. 6. While social choice theorists regard elections as selecting officials based on majority preferences, they are sensitive to difficulties in the majority will. One problem is that cyclical majorities may arise when the electorate is given three or more choices. Arrow observes that the outcome can vary arbitrarily depending on the order of voting. None of the outcomes can be said to express exclusively the majority will. Another issue is that most citizens do not possess preferences regarding many public issues, which means that "they have no real 'will' regarding what should be done." Anthony Downs, "The Public Interest: Its Meaning in a Democracy," *Social Research* 29, no. 1 (1962): 12.

68. Bernard Manin, Adam Przeworski, and Susan C. Stokes, "Elections and Representation," in *Democracy, Accountability, and Representation*, ed. Bernard Manin, Adam Przeworski, and Susan C. Stokes (New York: Cambridge University Press, 1999), 41. Achen and Bartels refer to the standard view of democratic accountability as involving retrospective accountability through elections. See Christopher Achen and Larry Bartels, *Democracy for Realists* (Princeton, NJ: Princeton University Press, 2016), 98.

69. Joseph Schumpeter, *Capitalism, Socialism and Democracy* (New York: Taylor & Francis, 2003 [1947]), 269. According to Google Scholar, by June 5, 2025, this work had been cited 67,351 times. A more recent version of Schumpeter's theory is Ian Shapiro, *Politics against Domination* (Cambridge, MA: Harvard University Press, 2016). Schumpeter admits that it is difficult to impute a will to the people when they disagree, and that they have no preference when it comes to many policies. However, Schumpeter shares with the popular will theory the narrow focus on elections and believes citizens should be passive during their officials' terms in office. As he writes, "once they have elected an individual, political action is his business and not theirs" (*Capitalism, Socialism and Democracy*, 295). Amy Gutmann and Dennis F. Thompson view Schumpeter as a proponent of an "aggregative" or preference-based conception of democracy,

accountability gains credibility when we consider how Indian citizens handed Prime Minister Modi an electoral setback in 2024, when twenty of Modi's ministers were voted out of office.[70]

Despite the appeal of popular will accountability, it overlooks how institutions can augment the power of citizens to hold their officials democratically accountable.[71] For example, the Indian Supreme Court stayed the conviction of opposition leader Rahul Gandhi for criticizing Prime Minister Modi. Parliament then reinstated him as a lawmaker.[72] Constitutional rights, the rule of law, and independent courts raise a *shield* to defend the ability of citizens to participate in democratic accountability and self-government.

Independent institutions may appear undemocratic because they act as a counterweight to the elected chief executive. Elected authoritarians denigrate independent institutions as part of a "deep state" that opposes the will of the people. This view, however, ignores the democratic character of institutions that are independent of the officials being scrutinized. These institutions redress the disparity of power between citizens and officials that jeopardizes self-government. Although citizens should be able to exercise authority over their officials by holding them democratically accountable, this self-governing relationship is in constant peril of being reversed. The danger arises from how officials wield the coercive force of the police and imprisonment.[73] The accountability

which they criticize. See *Why Deliberative Democracy* (Princeton, NJ: Princeton University Press, 2004), 191.

70. Fareed Zakaria, "Narendra Modi and the Myth of the Strongmen," *Washington Post*, June 7, 2023, https://www.washingtonpost.com/opinions/2024/06/07/modi-election-rebuke-democracy/.

71. Admittedly, there are cases when institutions might weaken democratic accountability. The Supreme Court arguably did this in the 2024 immunity case, placing the president above the law (Trump v. United States, 603 U.S. 593). Institutions must be properly designed and enacted, and a key test is whether they enhance equal accountability. Sullivan and Painter present a convincing argument against the Supreme Court's decision in E. Thomas Sullivan and Richard W. Painter, *The U.S. Presidency: Power, Responsibility, and Accountability* (Cambridge, UK: Cambridge University Press, 2025), part 3, chap. 3, section c.

72. Associated Press, "India's Parliament Reinstates Opposition Leader Rahul Gandhi as a Lawmaker," NPR, August 7, 2023, https://www.npr.org/2023/08/07/1192481362/india-rahul-gandhi-parliament-modi.

73. Madison refers to government officials as "public servants" in "Federalist No. 57," in Hamilton, Madison, and Jay, *Federalist*, 280.

rights of citizens are more secure when the president cannot manipulate the judicial system to exact retribution. But to relieve this risk, the courts and law enforcement need to be sufficiently independent of the president, who should be subject to the duties and constraints of office.

Independent institutions play a further democratic role. They heighten the ability of citizens to discover what their public servants are doing. Independent institutions are not only the shield but the *eyes* of citizens. Congressional investigations, law enforcement, the courts, and the press uncovered President Nixon's malfeasance in Watergate. Their efforts informed citizens, who sent over 150,000 telegrams successfully urging the Senate to launch an impeachment inquiry.[74] The threat of impeachment then lifted the *sword* of citizens, sanctioning Nixon for his efforts to compromise the 1972 election. Without congressional oversight, law enforcement, and courts independent of the president, citizens would have been blinded to his crimes, vulnerable to his abuses, and powerless to sanction him during his years in office. Independent institutions fortify our democratic accountability rights with *mediated accountability*, where one set of public servants help us to hold other officials accountable.

Besides neglecting the democratic function of independent institutions as the eyes, shield, and sword of citizens, popular will accountability also tends to set aside forms of accountability other than elections. For example, Schumpeter believes that citizens should lapse into torpor between elections:

> The voters outside of parliament must respect the division of labor between themselves and the politicians they elect. They must not withdraw confidence too easily between elections and they must understand that, once they have elected an individual, political action is his business and not theirs.[75]

Schumpeter criticizes accountability between elections: "the practice of bombarding them [officials] with letters and telegrams for

74. Bob Woodward and Carl Bernstein, *The Final Days* (New York: Simon & Schuster, 1976), 71.
75. Schumpeter, *Capitalism, Socialism and Democracy*, 295.

instance—ought to come under the same ban.”[76] These are the same
letters and telegrams that had successfully urged Congress to start impeachment hearings against President Nixon. The tendency to truncate
accountability to elections is not limited to theorists, but has spread to
public officials. Chief Justice John Roberts wrote:

> The resulting constitutional strategy is straightforward: divide power
> everywhere except for the Presidency, and render the President di-
> rectly accountable to the people through regular elections. In that
> scheme, individual executive officials will still wield significant au-
> thority, but that authority remains subject to the ongoing supervision
> and control of the elected President.[77]

Chief Justice Roberts assumed that any abuses of presidential power
would be held accountable by citizens in elections. But the vital question is how elections can work if the president is unaccountable in the
years between voting. For example, a president with unlimited control
over the executive branch could subvert the independence of law enforcement and direct officials to arrest members of the opposition party
and judges.

While elections are crucial, we would be hardly self-governing if we
had no way of holding our officials democratically accountable for years
during office.[78] We do so through our democratic accountability rights

76. Schumpeter, 295.

77. Seila Law v. Consumer Financial Protection Bureau, 591 U.S. 197, 224 (2020). In *Seila*,
the court ruled in a 5–4 decision that the president may remove the director of the Consumer
Financial Protection Bureau, even if there is no cause to justify removal such as “inefficiency,
neglect of duty, or malfeasance” (591 U.S. 197, 207). The court added that Congress had violated
the separation of powers by protecting the director from being fired at will by the president.

78. On election-centered democracy, see Tuck, *Active and Passive Citizens*. A compelling
defense of elections is Emilee Chapman, *Election Day* (Princeton, NJ: Princeton University
Press, 2022). Melissa Schwartzberg upholds majority rule in *Counting the Many: The Origins and
Limits of Supermajority Rule* (Cambridge, UK: Cambridge University Press, 2013). Schumpet-
erians regard majoritarian elections as definitive of democracy. See Schumpeter, *Capitalism,
Socialism and Democracy*, 269, and Jeffrey Green, *The Eyes of the People* (New York: Oxford
University Press, 2011). Adam Przeworski takes a Schumpeterian, “minimalist” view that equates
democracy with elections, valuing voting as an alternative to violent contests for power. See
Przeworski, “Minimalist Conception of Democracy: A Defense,” in *Democracy's Value*, ed. Ian
Shapiro and Casiano Hacker-Cordón (Cambridge, UK: Cambridge University Press, 1999),
chap. 2. Economists and political scientists have largely adopted an election-centric approach

and mediated accountability. Our rights to free speech, press, petition, protest, association, transparency, and the rule of law enable us to govern ourselves freely in the long span of years between elections. It is precisely because these democratic accountability rights and institutions during office are so potent in restraining the malice and corruption of office-holders that elected authoritarians worldwide are bent on repudiating them. Citizens who are only awake in elections are liable to be suffocated in their sleep.

Despite their differences, the theories of popular will accountability and checks and balances share a similar flaw. They seldom pay attention to the democratic duties of citizens and public servants. Checks and balances rely on the structure of the constitution instead of citizen participation in accountability to contain elected authoritarians. Popular will accountability takes a more active approach to citizenship, but it tends to give short shrift to citizens' duties. It restricts democracy to responsiveness to majority preferences, regardless of their substantive content, detaching citizens from any duty to adopt just preferences when they impose government power through their public servants. The distinguished democratic theorist John Ferejohn equates democratic accountability with this type of neutral responsiveness to popular preferences: "responsiveness is a measure of how much accountability an institutional structure permits."[79] Ferejohn conditions the claim by sounding the cautionary note that "responsiveness is not an unmitigated virtue."[80] Responsiveness to preferences is desirable when the majority wants to pursue justice, but it is dubious when it aims at racial segregation or other injustices. Ferejohn concludes that "how much and what kind of accountability there should be is a delicate matter to be decided in view of how much popular responsiveness is desired."[81]

---

to democracy, beginning with Downs, *Economic Theory of Democracy*, and continuing with the principal-agent model of democracy (Gailmard, "Accountability and Principal-Agent Theory").

79. John Ferejohn, "Accountability and Authority: Toward a Theory of Political Accountability," in Manin, Przeworski, and Stokes, *Democracy, Accountability, and Representation*, 131.

80. Ferejohn, "Accountability and Authority," 132.

81. Ferejohn, 132.

Equal accountability instead reconciles democratic accountability with justice by according a more prominent place to the *democratic duties* of citizens and public servants. The central idea of this book is that democratic accountability makes us freely self-governing. But an essential component of my position is that democratic accountability is premised on *duties* related to how citizens should exercise their democratic accountability rights. When we meet these duties as citizens, we work together to protect the inclusion of our fellow citizens in democracy. When we shirk these duties, we abandon other citizens, like Doris Hayashi, to be excluded.

A skeptic might say that citizens do not always meet their democratic duties. But I am not providing solely an empirical theory limited to predicting how citizens will behave. I am presenting a moral or normative theory of democracy that explains how citizens *should* act to sustain democratic government and protect the inclusion of their fellow citizens in self-government. Just as the moral requirement to shun slavery is not invalidated by the existence of servitude, the duty of citizens to hold their public servants democratically accountable is morally valid even if citizens might fall short of fulfilling that responsibility. It is possible and important for citizens to fulfill these duties, as shown when citizens acted to ban slavery in the Constitution's Thirteenth Amendment.[82] At the same time, the moral duties matter empirically. As the Nobel laureate in economics Elinor Ostrom has written, norms coordinate citizens to overcome collective action problems.[83] In my theory of equal accountability, the duty of oversight is a norm that coordinates citizens to stop the injustices committed by their public servants. The duty of solidarity is a norm that coordinates citizens to fend off the injustices inflicted by officials or groups of other citizens. The duty of fidelity constitutes a norm coordinating public servants to cooperate with democratic accountability, and to aid citizens in guarding against

82. U.S. Const. Amend. XIII. I thank the PhD students in Corey Brettschneider's graduate class in political theory at Brown University who contributed thoughtful discussion on the empirical and normative distinction and how norms can overcome collective action problems.

83. Elinor Ostrom, "A Behavioral Approach to the Rational Choice Theory of Collective Action," *American Political Science Review* 92, no. 1 (1998): 1–22.

elected authoritarians and factions. Whether we fulfill our democratic duties lies in our hands. Our choice will determine whether we will continue to live in a democracy.

For example, if citizens abdicated their democratic duty of solidarity, we would be forsaken by our fellow citizens when we are preyed upon by factions and elected authoritarians. Consider a group of friends beset by a bully. Suppose that the friends are apathetic and stand aside when the bully degrades and humiliates one of them. The abused person would be left in the lurch, the sense of friendship would atrophy, and the bully could pick off the rest one by one. But consider the case if the friends put up a united front and protect each other in solidarity. No longer left isolated and vulnerable, the friends would combine their forces, steadfastly come to each other's aid, and fend off the bully. When citizens fulfill their democratic duty of solidarity, they mutually support each other, forming a more perfect union so as to overcome elected authoritarians and factions. Citizens acting in solidarity secure one another's equal authority, so that they are all freely self-governing.

Equal Accountability Is Properly Responsive to Citizens

Proponents of popular will accountability may claim their approach is more responsive than my theory to the preferences of citizens. I reply that equal accountability offers a better understanding of *why* democracy should be responsive to citizens. Equal accountability discerns that the lack of responsiveness by public servants to ordinary citizens is a problem. Majorities of both Republicans (53 percent) and Democrats (77 percent) back a wealth tax, yet the policy has not passed Congress, which is beholden to rich voters.[84] Equal accountability agrees with

---

84. Howard Schneider and Chris Kahn, "Majority of Americans Favor Wealth Tax on Very Rich: Reuters/Ipsos Poll," *Reuters*, January 10, 2020, https://www.reuters.com/article/us-usa -election-inequality-poll/majority-of-americans-favor-wealth-tax-on-very-rich-reuters-ipsos -poll-idUSKBN1Z9141. I agree with the political scientists Levitsky and Ziblatt that the government is insufficiently responsive to the majority of citizens in the United States. See Steven

popular will accountability that Congress should be more responsive to the ordinary citizens who endorse a wealth tax. Unlike popular will accountability, however, equal accountability can shed greater light on why the government should not enact discriminatory preferences, such as the demand for the Japanese American internment. I argue that officials should listen to citizens due to the *standing* of citizens as the equal authorities or bosses in democracy.

Equal standing is what I call a *bounded ground*: the reason that morally justifies an entitlement can also limit that entitlement. For instance, equal standing is a bounded ground, because it explains why our public servants should be responsive to our preferences, and it limits when it is appropriate to implement those preferences. Our public servants work for us, so they should listen to us. At the same time, counting preferences is downstream of our equal authority. Securing our standing as equal authorities mandates that the government refuse to coercively execute plurality preferences that are inimical to our standing, including the desire to enslave or disenfranchise our fellow citizens.

The idea of standing being a bounded ground is akin to how friendship justifies why we should listen to our friends' preferences when deciding what to do together. At the same time, friendship gives us the duty of respect, which requires us to refrain from carrying out abusive preferences. Our standing as friends is the reason to consider each other's preferences when we make plans together. But our standing forms a *bounded ground*, because the moral reason why we should listen to preferences also limits when it is proper to carry out those preferences. Abuse would be anathema to one another's standing as friends. The preference for it must never be inflicted. Similarly, public servants should refuse to blot out the rights of a racial group, even if a majority demands it. Our public servants' recognition of our rights protects democracy by guaranteeing our equal standing as citizens. Our equal standing to hold our government democratically

Levitsky and Daniel Ziblatt, *Tyranny of the Minority* (New York: Crown, 2023). Martin Gilens and Benjamin Page confirm this lack of citizen influence in "Testing Theories of American Politics: Elites, Interest Groups, and Average Citizens," *Perspectives on Politics* 12, no. 3 (2014): 564–81.

accountable is the bedrock of democracy: it shows why government should be responsive to our preferences, and it regulates that responsiveness to protect our equal authority, which makes us self-governing.[85]

Popular will accountability is partially correct in calling for greater responsiveness to citizens. But it suffers from a larger structural defect that has gone unnoticed. It reverses the proper relation between democratic standing and responsiveness. Popular will accountability takes responsiveness to preferences, no matter how malicious they may be, as the basis for democracy. This inverts the proper relation between democratic standing and responsiveness. It holds hostage our democratic standing to the vagaries of plurality preferences, which can disenfranchise or discriminate. Popular will accountability's reversal of the proper relation between democratic standing and preferences makes it self-defeating. A plurality can exclude other citizens from democracy and deny them both responsiveness and the democratic value of self-government. By contrast, equal accountability explains that citizens freely govern themselves when they are equally included in the citizenry, and they are empowered with the equal authority to hold their public servants democratically accountable. We should protect the inclusion of all citizens in democracy through the democratic duties of solidarity, oversight, and fidelity.

85. A philosophical precursor for my bounded grounds argument is Locke's justification for private property. Locke derives the right to private property from the precept to "preserve" oneself and "the rest of mankind" (see his "Second Treatise of Government," in *Two Treatises of Government*, ed. Peter Laslett [Cambridge, UK: Cambridge University Press, 1988], 271). The right of private property preserves humanity by protecting each person's possession of food, shelter, and other necessities from interference. The crucial point is that "the same law of nature, that does by this means give us property, does also *bound* that property too" (290). Since the purpose of property is to preserve humanity, the right to property can be curtailed when it contradicts that end. For example, Locke qualifies the right to private property with the right to charity, which entitles the poor to food from people who possess a surplus (170). Whether or not we accept Locke's argument for property can be bracketed. The key is that Locke provides an example of what I call *bounded grounds*: the reason that morally justifies an entitlement can limit that same entitlement.

Missed Opportunities in the Absence
of the Equal Accountability Theory

How have opportunities to avert elected authoritarians and marginalization slipped through our grasp in the absence of equal accountability? Consider two key cases. First, many commentators and officials
oppose impeachment because they believe that removing a president
would be undemocratic. They claim that impeachment would stymie
the will of the people. As one congressional representative said, "The
effect of impeachment is to overturn the popular will."[86]

If equal accountability had been central to our understanding of democracy, an impeachment would not have been perceived as undemocratic, provided there was a sound basis for it. Impeachment is a form
of mediated accountability through our elected representatives. It holds
the president democratically accountable during office, and it protects
the integrity of elections. For example, the House of Representatives
Judiciary Committee held impeachment hearings against President
Nixon. The Committee investigated Nixon's attempt to disrupt the integrity of the 1972 election when his subordinates broke into the Democratic National Committee headquarters at the Watergate Hotel and
covered up his involvement.[87]

Other writers approve of impeachment, but at times they focus only
on Congress and do not back up the impeachment process with enough
active citizen support. Equal accountability would place at center stage
the need for citizens to participate in democratic accountability. They
should have launched a grass-roots campaign, contacted members of
Congress, submitted petitions, organized civic associations in favor of
impeachment, and assembled mass protests.[88] Citizens would then have

86. CNN. "Transcript: Rep. Jerrold Nadler on Impeachment." CNN.com. December 11, 1998.
https://www.cnn.com/ALLPOLITICS/stories/1998/12/11/transcripts/nadler.html.

87. John R. Labovitz, *Presidential Impeachment* (New Haven, CT: Yale University Press,
1978), ch. 3.

88. A petition circulates to the government and the public a statement of grievances with a
list of signatories. This gives voice to citizens and identifies injustices to be corrected. On the
importance of the right of petition to democracy, see Daniel Carpenter, *Democracy by Petition*
(Cambridge, MA: Harvard University Press, 2021). On the democratic role of civic associations,

been acting on their democratic duty of oversight, as they did when they sent a record number of telegrams to Congress advocating the impeachment of President Nixon. Within days, representatives introduced twenty-two bills that "called for an impeachment investigation."[89] Equal accountability combines empowered citizen participation with independent institutions as bulwarks of democracy.

Consider a second consequential missed opportunity when citizens and public servants operate on the popular will theory instead of equal accountability. A study found that racial justice protests are three times more likely to be confronted by police in riot gear compared to other demonstrations, even when controlling for the protestors' behavior.[90] Other research has found that Black infant mortality is nearly twice the national average, and African Americans are "over twice as likely to die from diabetes, kidney disease, or infectious disease."[91] Researchers from the University of Michigan report that "from 1970–2004, there were *2.7 million excess black deaths* due to racial inequality, which led to *1 million lost black votes* in the 2004 election."[92] African American excess deaths have swung elections. Researchers "estimate that between 1970 and 2004 the outcomes of 7 close senate elections and 11 close gubernatorial races could have been reversed" if African Americans had lived as long as whites.[93] African Americans cannot equally hold their government democratically accountable when their peaceful protests are suppressed

---

see Robert Putnam and Shaylyn Romney Garrett, *The Upswing: How America Came Together a Century Ago and How We Can Do It Again* (New York: Simon & Schuster, 2020).

89. Woodward and Bernstein, *Final Days*, 71.

90. Sandhya Kajeepeta and Daniel K. N. Johnson, "Police and Protests: The Inequality of Police Responses to Racial Justice Demonstrations," Thurgood Marshall Institute, November 2023, https://tminstituteldf.org/wp-content/uploads/2023/10/Police-and-Protests_PDF-3.pdf.

91. Elizabeth Anderson, *The Imperative of Integration* (Princeton, NJ: Princeton University Press, 2010), 23.

92. Chloe L. Brown, Danyaal Raza, and Andrew D. Pinto, "Voting, Health and Interventions in Healthcare Settings: A Scoping Review," *Public Health Review* 41, no. 16 (2020): 16, citing Javier M. Rodriguez et al., "Black Lives Matter: Differential Mortality and the Racial Composition of the U.S. Electorate, 1970–2004," *Social Science & Medicine* 136–37 (2015): 193–99 (emphasis added).

93. Rodriguez et al., "Black Lives Matter," 197.

by police action, and when they are fatally excluded by poor health. Focusing only on the formal right to vote in elections would miss these restrictions on democracy.

My *Equal Accountability Principle* requires that the equal capability to exercise democratic accountability must not be hindered by membership in a marginalized group. Citizens should fulfill their democratic duty of solidarity and leverage their democratic accountability rights to protect African Americans and other marginalized groups from injustice. Public servants should abide by their democratic duty of fidelity and empower all citizens with the material resources and conditions to participate in democratic accountability.

The Plan of the Book

Chapter 2 charts the democratic accountability rights that constitute our equal authority over our public servants. To govern ourselves as citizens, we must possess equal democratic accountability rights to evaluate and sanction our public servants during office, to authorize and remove them from office, and to run for office and campaign for candidates in elections. We exercise these core elements of democratic accountability through free speech, the press, protest, petition, association, transparency, deliberative justification, and the rule of law. Our authority over public servants should be reinforced by the mediated accountability offered in independent institutions.

Chapter 3 lays out the democratic duties of citizens and their public servants necessary to secure the equal authority and rights that make us self-governing. I propose an innovative *citizen–public servant model*, which recasts the prevailing principal-agent model of popular will accountability by linking *democratic duties* to the offices of public servant and citizen. The positions of citizen and public servant are *offices* with three attributes: they wield the coercive power of government; their power must be regulated instead of being arbitrary or absolute; and that power must be guided by duties to accomplish just or morally legitimate purposes. In the office of the citizen, we collectively own the power of government and employ our public servants to use it on our behalf. We should shoulder the duty of oversight and participate in democratic accountability to ensure that our public servants are using the coercive power of government justly. In the office of the public servant, our officials should heed their duty of fidelity. They should use power justly, cooperate with democratic accountability, and equally empower citizens.

Chapter 4 answers potential criticisms of democratic duties. One objection claims that citizens are exempt from any duties when they select the standard of democratic accountability that their officials must satisfy.[94] If the plurality of voters prefers to discriminate against other citizens, it would, paradoxically, be *undemocratic* if officials respected women and racial minorities. The pitfall of this purely subjective standard of democratic accountability is that it fails to explain why it could ever be morally legitimate or permissible for the government to inflict coercion. Acting as an agent following a principal's or boss's subjective preferences can no more legitimate coercion by itself than the orders a capo carries out issued by a mafia don. Nor does it suffice to hold an election. Coercion would not be morally excused if a cartel held an election, with equal votes, to select a kingpin.

I put forward the principle that government power must satisfy the standard of *justice*. Justice consists of the requirements for coercive power to be morally legitimate, rather than morally prohibited brute force.[95] The meaning of justice is not limited to majority preferences in an election. The concept of tyranny of the majority presupposes that there are standards of justice independent of majority preferences. If there were

---

94. The chapter also rebuts the objection that democratic duties are at odds with the freedom of citizens. I show how democratic duties are needed to secure freedom. Drawing on John Stuart Mill, I develop a typology of the enforcement of democratic duties. In addition, the chapter outlines how civic associations and civic education can promote compliance with democratic duties, which reviewer 2 helpfully suggested that I clarify.

95. This is not the only definition of justice, but it is the aspect of justice that I concentrate on in the context of presenting standards of democratic accountability. I welcome the possibility that justice may contain additional requirements. I thank reviewer 1, who raised the important point that justice may also apply to the treatment of the environment, animals, and future generations. I agree that justice requires action to save current and future generations from the massive loss of life and human rights violations caused by climate change. These further requirements deserve volumes of their own to explicate more fully.

no such standards, then the majority could simply vote to abolish rights in its definition of justice, and there would be no more rights for it to tyrannically violate.

I suggest that *deliberation* enables us to question majority preferences and identify principles of justice. Citizens may disagree with each other about the meaning of justice or have mistaken views of justice. They should then test their beliefs about justice in discussion with diverse other citizens. The more inclusive and open the deliberation, the greater confidence we can place in its conclusions, keeping in mind the findings are provisional or subject to revision with further deliberation.[96]

It is important that the power of government be guided by justice, because government coercion can injure, imprison innocents, and kill human beings on a vast scale if misused. The Harvard political theorist Judith Shklar wrote from her own experience escaping the forces of Nazi Germany and the Soviet Union, "While the sources of social oppression are indeed numerous, none has the deadly effect of those who, as the agents of the modern state, have unique resources of physical might and persuasion at their disposal."[97]

Chapter 5 proposes requirements of justice that can serve as standards of democratic accountability and guide the duties of oversight, solidarity, and fidelity. The first requirement draws internally from the value of freedom as self-government itself. To assess whether citizens have equal authority, I present the *Equal Accountability Principle*: the ability of citizens to rectify injustices must not be impeded by their membership in a marginalized group. The second requirement that public servants should satisfy is the *Equal Human Rights Principle*: public servants should secure the equal human rights of all citizens, while not violating the human rights of noncitizens. A human right is a moral right that is morally owed to human beings and protects urgent human

96. The findings of public discussion are provisional in being "open to revision in an ongoing process of moral and political deliberation" (Gutmann and Thompson, *Why Deliberative Democracy*, 97). I thank Philip Petrov, who asked perceptively about the justification of human rights and how it differs from mere consensus. I am also grateful to Lucia Rafanelli and Jack Pitblado who offered helpful suggestions on this subject.

97. Judith Shklar, "The Liberalism of Fear," in *Political Thought and Political Thinkers*, ed. Stanley Hoffmann (Chicago: University of Chicago Press, 1998), 3.

interests against threats, especially the danger of state oppression or neglect. As President James Madison proclaimed in his 1815 Message to Congress, "our political institutions" are "founded in human rights, and framed for their preservation."[98]

The Equal Accountability and Equal Human Rights Principles may seem overly demanding as standards of democratic accountability. But if the Equal Human Rights Principle were violated, marginalized citizens would suffer more abject denials of their human rights. If officials disrespected the Equal Accountability Principle, the marginalized citizens afflicted with the harshest injustices would be least able to remedy them using their democratic accountability rights. The citizens consigned to the lowest pit of abuse would be left with the steepest climb to escape. That condition cannot possibly be justifiable to the marginalized.

It might be thought that democratic duties of citizens do not cover respect for the human rights of *noncitizens*. Against this view, I set forth the *Delegation Principle*: citizens can only delegate the use of powers that it would be morally legitimate for the citizens to collectively own and exercise. Just as people cannot delegate to their real estate agent the right to sell a house they do not own, citizens cannot delegate to their public servants the right to use the coercive power of government to degrade human rights. No one owns or can delegate the power to assault human rights and dehumanize others, either noncitizens or citizens. Consequently, while public servants can prioritize securing the human rights of the citizens they work for by protecting and empowering their human rights, they must do so while respecting, or not abusing, the human rights of noncitizens.

The Declaration of Independence offers an implicit standard for who is entitled to citizenship: "That to secure these rights, Governments are instituted . . . deriving their just powers from the consent of the

---

98. James Madison, "Annual Message to Congress, 5 December 1815," Founders Online, National Archives, https://founders.archives.gov/documents/Madison/03-10-02-0061. Chap. 4 distinguishes accountability from consent.

governed."[99] My *Inclusion Principle* states that the governed should be entitled to equal citizenship, so that they freely govern themselves. The governed are the people subject to the jurisdiction of the government in its territory to enact and enforce laws. The Inclusion Principle stands in opposition to views such as those expressed in *Dred Scott*. In that case, the Supreme Court ruled that African Americans could never be citizens of the United States.[100] The decision subjected African Americans to government, while denying them citizenship. Asian-American permanent residents were governed, but they were barred from citizenship under the Chinese Exclusion Act.[101] The Inclusion Principle instead provides that the people who are governed should be citizens, so they are freely self-governing. The Inclusion Principle also entitles the governed to equal democratic accountability rights, enabling the governed as citizens to participate in democracy in defense of their human rights.

Chapter 6 lays the basis for a human right to democratic accountability, which advances three urgent interests. By showing that democratic accountability promotes these urgent interests, I challenge the critics of democracy who have grown more vocal and influential.[102] First, democratic accountability liberates the governed to be *freely self-governing*, as declared in the Freedom Charter of Nelson Mandela's African National Congress. Second, democratic accountability *respects our human dignity* as free and equal persons capable of reason and conscience, a value that Frederick Douglass proclaimed. The third urgent interest is that democratic accountability *protects our other human rights* from state oppression and neglect. I marshal evidence that the human right to democratic accountability has been vindicated by deliberation across cultures in the drafting and ratification of a remarkable array of

---

99. "Declaration of Independence: A Transcription," National Archives, accessed June 6, 2025, https://www.archives.gov/founding-docs/declaration-transcript (emphasis added).

100. Dred Scott v. Sandford, 60 U.S. 393, 405 (1857).

101. Chinese Exclusion Act, 22 Stat. 58, chap. 126 (1882).

102. Prominent critics of democracy include Brennan, *Against Democracy*, Caplan, *Myth of the Rational Voter*, and Daniel A. Bell, *The China Model: Political Meritocracy and the Limits of Democracy* (Princeton, NJ: Princeton University Press, 2015).

human rights treaties. This right is further attested by the claiming of democratic accountability by people within diverse states.

In chapter 6, I defend a peacefully promoted human right to democratic accountability against the popular will theory, which resurfaces in a new guise. In popular will self-determination, a plurality of voters can select any type of government it wants. The plurality can choose an authoritarian government that denies equal political rights to marginalized citizens. For example, South Africa held a referendum on a new constitution in 1960. The government banned Black South Africans from voting on the referendum, denying them the act of self-determination.[103] The result of the referendum was a notorious apartheid regime.

In place of popular will self-determination, I contribute a new conception of *democratic self-determination*: the values of nondiscrimination and self-government call for equal democratic accountability rights for all the governed, who should be recognized as equal citizens under the Inclusion Principle. Self-determination is not prior to democracy, allowing a plurality to select an authoritarian or racist form of government. Rather, the standing of all citizens as equal authorities is the *bounded grounds* for listening to preferences regarding the form of government. Democracy must be made integral to the procedures or *input of self-determination*, entitling the governed to equal democratic rights of free speech, the press, protest, association, the rule of law, and the vote to debate and select the proposed government and constitution. Democracy should also be secured in the *output of self-determination, or* the constitution that is created. The constitution should guarantee equal rights for women and men all races. Democratic self-determination is a precondition for the choice of government to be morally legitimate, and not an imposition of brute force. Democratic self-determination is vital given the internal diversity of states and the human right to

---

103. T.R.H. Davenport and Christopher Saunders, *South Africa: A Modern History*, 5th ed. (New York: St. Martin's Press, 2000), 416. Chapter 6 draws on ideas I discuss in Minh Ly, "Democratic Self-Determination and the Need for Deliberation," *European Journal of Political Theory* 24, no. 3 (2025): 462–70.

nondiscrimination that stands at the core of international human rights treaties.

This book grounds democratic government in equal accountability instead of the popular will. In place of elected authoritarians who are unaccountable domestically and who support dictators globally, the equal accountability theory requires that government power must respect human rights and answer to us, the people who are governed. To be free to govern ourselves, we must be equally included in the citizenry and equally empowered to hold our government democratically accountable.

John Adams, writing to Thomas Jefferson, reflected on the meaning of the American Revolution. Adams wrote in 1815 to his fellow Framer:

> What do We mean by the Revolution? The War? That was no part of the Revolution. It was only an Effect and Consequence of it. The Revolution was in the Minds of the People . . . in the course of fifteen Years before a drop of blood was drawn at Lexington. The Records of thirteen Legislatures, the Pamphlets, Newspapers in all the Colonies ought be consulted . . . to ascertain the Steps by which the public opinion was enlightened and informed.[104]

At the heart of the American Revolution is the conviction, in the minds of the people, that government ought to be accountable to the governed. Democratic accountability requires more than elections. As James Madison said, quoting Jefferson, "An elective despotism was not the government we fought for."[105] Democratic accountability demands that officials work as our public servants and answer to us.

104. "John Adams to Thomas Jefferson, 24 August 1815," Founders Online, National Archives, https://founders.archives.gov/documents/Jefferson/03-08-02-0560. [Original source: *The Papers of Thomas Jefferson*, Retirement Series, vol. 8, *1 October 1814 to 31 August 1815*, ed. J. Jefferson Looney (Princeton, NJ: Princeton University Press, 2011), 682–84.]

105. James Madison, "Federalist No. 48," in Hamilton, Madison, and Jay, *The Federalist*, 243. Madison is quoting from Thomas Jefferson's *Notes on the State of Virginia*.

2

The Rights of Democratic Accountability

All power residing originally in the people, and being derived from them, the several magistrates and officers of government, vested with authority, whether legislative, executive, or judicial, are their substitutes and agents, and are *at all times accountable* to them.

—MASSACHUSETTS CONSTITUTION,
DRAFTED BY JOHN ADAMS, ARTICLE V[1]

IN DECEMBER 1955, a twenty-six-year-old pastor who had just earned his doctorate in theology moved to Montgomery, Alabama. A woman named Rosa Parks had just been arrested for sitting in a bus. The Alabama law mandated "separate accommodations on each vehicle for the white and colored races."[2] The City of Montgomery Code directed the drivers to enforce racial segregation, granting them "the powers of a police officer of the city while in actual charge of any bus."[3] Parks was seated at the middle of the bus when the driver

1. Massachusetts Constitution, part 1, article V (emphasis added). The Massachusetts Constitution, ratified in 1780, provided a model for the US Constitution ratified in 1788. Martha Davis, "The Massachusetts Constitution: The Oldest in the United States, and Often Ahead of Its Time, *State Court Report*, April 18, 2025, https://statecourtreport.org/our-work/analysis -opinion/massachusetts-constitution-oldest-united-states-and-often-ahead-its-time.
2. Alabama Motor Carrier Act of 1939, cited in Browder v. Gayle, 142 F. Supp. 707, 721 (1956).
3. Section 10, chapter 6, Code of the City of Montgomery, 1952, cited in *Browder v. Gayle*, 721.

brusquely demanded that she move to the back. It was just three months after Emmett Till, a fourteen-year-old African American, had been abducted and murdered. Parks bravely refused and was arrested.

Hearing about Parks's case, the young pastor gave a speech that galvanized the members of the Holt Street Baptist Church. He persuaded the parishioners to embark on a citywide bus boycott. Members volunteered in droves to organize carpools for their neighbors. The parishioners assembled peacefully, but assailants firebombed the pastor's home and the police jailed him along with dozens of drivers. The arrests riveted the attention of the country and attracted national media coverage. After the pastor was released, the US District Court for the Middle District of Alabama ruled that racial segregation in busing had violated the Fourteenth Amendment's Equal Protection Clause, which prohibits a state from denying "to any person within its jurisdiction the equal protection of the law."[4] The Supreme Court affirmed the district court's ruling, and the city of Montgomery passed a law desegregating its bus system.[5] Years later, Congress awarded Rosa Parks its highest honor. Congress expressed its gratitude for how Parks's "dignity ignited the most significant social movement in the history of the United States." She "symbolizes all that is vital about nonviolent protest . . . from which the Nation has benefited immeasurably."[6] Parks's friend, the twenty-six-year-old pastor, was Dr. Martin Luther King Jr.

I set out in this chapter the democratic accountability rights that we require to govern ourselves freely. As discussed in chapter 1, democratic accountability is often thought to revolve narrowly around voting. While embracing elections, my theory of equal accountability seeks to broaden democratic accountability to encompass a wider range of rights and institutions, such as free speech and protest. This more expansive conception offers two prime advantages. First, equal accountability contributes

4. U.S. Const. Amend. XIV; *Browder v. Gayle*, 717.

5. The Supreme Court upheld the district court's decision in *Gayle v. Browder*, 352 U.S. 903 (1956).

6. "An Act to Authorize the President to Award a Gold Medal on Behalf of Congress to Rosa Parks in Recognition of Her Contributions to the Nation," Public Law 106-26, https://www.govinfo.gov/content/pkg/PLAW-106publ26/html/PLAW-106publ26.htm.

a more compelling explanation of how we can be self-governing, or the ones ultimately in charge of our government. Popular will accountability, which fixates narrowly on voting, struggles to explain how citizens can be in charge *between elections*. This is a crucial omission, since the years between elections are when officials are actually in power and in a position to subvert the integrity of the next election. Equal accountability aims to make us self-governing by entitling us to democratic accountability rights *during office*, as well as through elections.

Second, equal accountability is better placed than popular will accountability to counter elected authoritarians. Equal accountability emphasizes the democratic accountability rights and institutions that elected authoritarians attack, from freedom of protest, press, and petition, to courts, congressional oversight, and impeachment. When these institutions are independent of the control of the president, they strengthen the control of the president by citizens. We depend on these institutions as our *eyes* to reveal what our officials are doing, our *shield* to protect our rights from our officials' power, and our *sword* to sanction our officials during office.

This chapter sets out the five core elements of equal accountability that make us self-governing, or the ones in charge of our public servants. The first core element is *authorization*. As citizens, we authorize our public servants when we elect them to public office, giving them our permission to work for us. The second is *evaluation*. We evaluate our public servants by morally judging their conduct during office. For example, we can use our freedom of speech and the press to discuss the justice of our public servants' actions. The third core element is *sanctioning*, or stopping injustices committed by our public servants during office. We can sanction them through the naming and shaming of public criticism, the pressure of protest, and the penalties of the rule of law. The fourth core element is *removal from office*, where we vote public servants out of office. Fifth is *running for office* or *campaigning for candidates*.[7] Opposition parties can field candidates without facing

7. I am grateful to Annie Stilz, who helpfully suggested the importance of the democratic accountability right to run for office in her comments at one of my talks at the American Political Science Association Annual Meeting.

violence or a rigged election. To campaign, we canvass in person, knock on doors, send mail, raise funds, phone bank, hold rallies, organize political parties, and get out the vote for our candidates. With the five core elements of equal accountability in hand, we are the bosses in charge of our government.

In this chapter, I dispel the notion that it is undemocratic to constrain the power of elected officials. The prevailing view is that accountability rights during office and independent institutions allegedly hamper officials from carrying out the popular will.[8] By contrast, I argue that *authorization* is the permission to hold an *office*. A public office limits the power of officials, so that they do not reverse the self-governing relationship and transform themselves from public servants into our masters. Officials wielding force heedless of the limits and duties of office would overpower citizens and end freedom as self-government. I emphasize that public office is a trust attached to *democratic duties of fidelity*, which requires officials to cooperate with democratic accountability and to recognize the equal authority of citizens as the ones in charge. The bounds of public office and democratic accountability during office avert what Madison and Jefferson call "elective despotism."[9]

This chapter draws on examples from history and the US Constitution to demonstrate how democratic accountability is premised on rights in addition to elections. Elected authoritarians aim to abolish these accountability rights. For instance, King exercised his right to free speech to rally the members of the Holt Street Baptist Church. The

---

8. The majority decision in *Trump v. United States* lost sight of the fundamental principle that the president serves in an office bounded in power. The decision gave the president, even after he or she leaves office, immunity from criminal prosecution for acts involving official powers, such as the police or military. This would entail that the president could not be prosecuted for directing the military to arrest members of the opposition party. Justice Sonia Sotomayor warned in her dissent, "The relationship between the President and the people he serves has shifted irrevocably. In every use of official power, the President is now a king above the law. . . . Never in the history of our Republic has a President had reason to believe that he would be immune from criminal prosecution if he used the trappings of his office to violate the criminal law. Moving forward, however, all former Presidents will be cloaked in such immunity. If the occupant of that office misuses official power for personal gain, the criminal law that the rest of us must abide will not provide a backstop. With fear for our democracy, I dissent." Trump v. United States, 603 U.S. 593, 685–86 (2024) (Sotomayor, J., dissenting).

9. Hamilton, Madison, and Jay, *Federalist*, 243.

Women's Political Council and the Montgomery Improvement Association organized a bus boycott, relying on their freedom of association.
The boycotters marched against segregation under the aegis of the
right to protest. When King and Parks were arrested, they secured their
release through rights to the rule of law. Their cause roused the conscience of citizens as it was publicized through freedom of the press. The
NAACP petitioned the US District Court for the Middle District of
Alabama, arguing against the constitutionality of segregation. These
democratic accountability rights mobilized citizens against the injustice
of discrimination and informed their votes. The Civil Rights Movement, according to Congress itself, "led to the Civil Rights Act of 1964,
which broke down the barriers of legal discrimination against African
Americans."[10] My argument in this chapter begins with a defense of the
value of freedom as self-government. I then specify the five core elements of equal accountability that enable us to govern ourselves freely.

Freedom as Self-Government Is Valuable as a Relationship

Democracy has long been linked to the kindred value of freedom as
self-government. James Madison, Alexander Hamilton, and John Jay
declare the "honorable determination which animates every votary of
freedom, to rest all our political experiments on the capacity of mankind
for self-government."[11] After the Civil War, Frederick Douglass addressed an audience at Arlington, including President Ulysses Grant,
esteeming the sacrifices of the soldiers for "our great Republic, the hope
of freedom and self-government throughout the world."[12]

Despite this close association with democracy, the concept of self-
government has recently fallen on hard times. Jean Hampton takes the
skeptical position on self-government: "Our elected 'representatives'
don't represent us in any literal sense. This is nonsense. They rule and

10. Pub. Law 106-26.
11. Madison, "Federalist No. 39," in Hamilton, Madison, and Jay, *Federalist*, 182.
12. Frederick Douglass, *The Life and Times of Frederick Douglass: His Early Life as a Slave, His Escape from Bondage, and His Complete History* (Mineola, NY: Dover, 2003 [1892]), 301.

we don't."[13] Joseph Schumpeter, one of the most influential democratic theorists, wrote, "democracy does not mean and cannot mean that the people actually rule. . . . Now one aspect of this may be expressed by saying that democracy is the rule of the politician."[14] This notion is plausible given that citizens can be left powerless if they are marginalized or subject to injustice. But my response to this challenge is not to be resigned to remaining powerless. My strategy is to empower all of us as citizens to govern ourselves. In this chapter, I demonstrate how we can strengthen and expand our rights to hold our public servants democratically accountable. The fact that democratic accountability rights are powerful is attested by how elected authoritarians consistently fear and restrict them.[15]

It is commonly believed that citizens govern themselves, because they can select and replace their public servants in elections.[16] But reducing self-government to elections runs into a problem noted by Jean-Jacques Rousseau. Relying on elections alone would leave us devoid of self-government in the years between voting: "The English people thinks it is free; it is greatly mistaken, it is free only during the election of Members of Parliament; as soon as they are elected, it is enslaved, it is nothing."[17] Even if elections are held, it is unclear how all citizens, and not simply the plurality, can be self-governing. John Stuart Mill put

13. Jean Hampton, quoted in Eric Beerbohm, *In Our Name* (Princeton, NJ: Princeton University Press, 2012), 28.

14. Schumpeter, *Capitalism, Socialism and Democracy*, 284–85.

15. I make this point in my *revealed preferences argument* in chapter 4.

16. Schumpeter contends that "democracy means only that the people have the opportunity of accepting or refusing the men who are to rule them" (*Capitalism, Socialism and Democracy*, 284–85). Green (*Eyes of the People*) and Przeworski ("Minimalist Conception") are contemporary Schumpeterians.

17. Jean-Jacques Rousseau, *The Social Contract and Other Later Political Writings*, ed. Victor Gourevitch (Cambridge, UK: Cambridge University Press, 1997), 114. It might be asked why self-government does not require direct democracy, where citizens vote on all the laws directly. Indeed, it may seem that direct democracy comports more closely with the idea of citizens being in charge of their government. My response is that representative democracy offers the advantage of providing greater democratic accountability. If public servants act unjustly, they can be criticized, sanctioned, and voted out of office. However, if citizens made all the laws directly, it would be difficult to hold them accountable for injustices. It would be objectionable to remove their right to vote on the laws as punishment for voting unjustly, since they would no longer be treated as equal citizens. I thank the PhD students in Corey Brettschneider's graduate political theory class at Brown University for raising this question.

the point memorably: "The 'people' who exercise the power are not always the same people with those over whom it is exercised; and the 'self-government' spoken of is not the government of each by himself, but of each by all the rest."[18] The danger of citizens being excluded is exacerbated by marginalization. Marginalized citizens are not self-governing when they suffer from discrimination and their rights are trampled by factions or elected authoritarians. Nelson Mandela rebuked apartheid for excluding Black South Africans from government: "The African people were not part of the Government and did not make the laws by which they were governed."[19] Popular will accountability does not explain how the marginalized can be made self-governing.

I argue that self-government must be grounded in the inclusion of the governed as equal citizens in government. This means, in a representative democracy, that all citizens should be equally empowered to hold their government officials democratically accountable. In a pioneering speech before Parliament, John Stuart Mill advocated political rights for women:

> But allow me to ask, what is the meaning of political freedom? Is it anything but the control of those who do make their business of politics, by those who do not? Is it not the very essence of constitutional liberty, that men come from their looms and their forges and decide, and decide well, whether they are properly governed, and whom they will be governed by?[20]

Mill was a proponent of expanding the freedom to participate in government to women: "We ought not to deny to them, what we are conceding

18. John Stuart Mill, "On Liberty," in *The Collected Works of John Stuart Mill*, vol. 18, *Essays on Politics and Society Part I*, ed. John M. Robson (Toronto: University of Toronto Press, 1977), 219. I thank Jamie Mayerfeld who offered valuable philosophical discussion of this passage, clarifying that I define self-government as the inclusion of all citizens in government as equal authorities. Self-government is not merely casting a ballot in a majoritarian procedure that can do anything to citizens, even excluding them from democracy.

19. Nelson Mandela, *In His Own Words* (New York: Back Bay Books, 2003), 30.

20. John Stuart Mill, "The Admission of Women to the Electoral Franchise," May 20, 1867, House of Commons, in *Collected Works of John Stuart Mill*, vol. 23, *Public and Parliamentary Speeches*, ed. John M. Robson and Bruce L. Kinzer (Toronto: University of Toronto Press, 1988), 154.

to everybody else."[21] Indeed, political freedom is a real form of liberty, one that women are entitled to possess just as much as men.

Two key attributes of freedom as self-government emerge from Mandela and Mill. The first is that all the governed should be *included* as equal citizens in government. Second, inclusion in a representative democracy means that the governed participate in the "*control* of those who do make their business of politics," as Mill writes. Political liberty implies that the governed, as equal citizens, can decide "whether they are properly governed, and whom they will be governed by."[22]

I hold that we can be freely self-governing if we possess the equal authority to hold our public servants democratically both during office and through elections. In defining freedom as self-government, I adopt the triadic concept of freedom.[23] It contains three parts: the *person* who is free, the *obstacles* she is free from, and the *act* or condition she is free to achieve. In freedom as self-government, the persons who are free are the persons who are governed. The main obstacles to self-government are powerlessness and interference from elected authoritarians and factions of rights-violating citizens. I offer an original definition of *freedom as self-government*: it is the liberty of the governed to be included as equal authorities in the citizenry that is governing together by holding its public servants democratically accountable.

Democratic accountability is exercised both individually and collectively.[24] As individuals, citizens voice their opinions about government and cast their ballots. Citizens wield their democratic accountability rights collectively when they deliberate with each other to evaluate and sanction their public servants, and when they collectively authorize and remove public servants in elections where citizens are free to run for office and campaign.

21. Mill, "Admission of Women," 161.

22. Mill, "Admission of Women," 161 (emphasis added).

23. Gerald MacCallum proposes a triadic definition of freedom in "Negative and Positive Freedom," *Philosophical Review* 76, no. 3 (1967): 312–34. An accessible introduction to the same concept is Adam Swift, *Political Philosophy* (Malden, MA: Polity Press, 2014), part 2.

24. I thank Annie Stilz, who asked me during one of my APSA talks whether democratic accountability is exercised individually or collectively.

Since democratic accountability contains both individual and collective aspects, two conditions must be met for citizens to have equal authority. First, citizens must possess *equal democratic accountability rights*. These must be formally equal in the laws, and citizens must be empowered with the civic education and material resources needed to apply those rights as substantive freedoms. Second, citizens must be *included as equal authorities in the citizenry* or collective body that is governing together. Citizens must not be marginalized in the citizenry by the denial of their human rights, which the government has the duty to secure for all its citizens.

Democratic accountability rights are necessary but not sufficient to be included as an equal authority in the citizenry. Marginalized citizens may be granted free speech, the vote, and other democratic accountability rights, but if they live in terror of the government, they lack the *standing* of being equal authorities in the citizenry. As we saw in the opening of the book, the US government imprisoned 120,000 innocent Japanese Americans in concentration camps during World War II. In many cases, like that of Doris Hayashi, they retained the right to vote. Although Doris could vote, she could not deliberate freely with other citizens to evaluate her public servants and learn about their conduct. She could not campaign or canvass for her favored candidates, or join the associations that organize democratic participation. The first facet of freedom as self-government was missing, in the form of her equal democratic accountability rights. At the same time, the government effaced Doris's human rights. She suffered discrimination and detainment without a trial in a concentration camp and was thereby denied the second facet of freedom as self-government, her equal standing in the citizenry as a member with equal human rights. In this way, she was not treated as an equal authority, but as a second-class citizen and outcast.

It might be asked why freedom as self-government, as Mandela sought for Black South Africans and Mill for women, is one of the reasons why democracy is valuable or choice-worthy. Why not base the value of democracy only on the instrumental reason that it protects citizens from abuses?[25] Many widely cited theorists of democracy believe that the value of democracy is purely instrumental, and does not involve self-government. Jason Brennan writes that "the choice between democracy and epistocracy is instrumental."[26] I will invoke the instrumental argument for democracy in supporting a human right to democratic accountability in chapter 6. But we should not limit the value of democracy to the idea that it is a mere tool that yields beneficial consequences.

Self-government is needed to explain *who should be included in the government*. It is a democratic value that condemns racially discriminatory regimes or foreign colonialism. These types of government impose undemocratic *external rule*. The intuitive problem with external rule is that we do not govern ourselves freely when we are driven out of government, as occurred under South African apartheid. External rule denies us the authority to hold our officials democratically accountable. But that potent argument against external rule is foreclosed if we deny the value of freedom as self-government.

A further issue with relying on the instrumental argument alone is that it would leave the value of democracy too contingent, or dependent on the circumstances. If a benign authoritarian government could deliver the same, or slightly better benefits than a democracy, there would be no reason to choose democracy if its value were only instrumental. Many critics of democracy have asserted that an authoritarian or colonial regime can deliver high economic growth.[27] Other opponents want to shift power away from democracy to the market or to technocratic

25. I am grateful to Melissa Schwartzberg, who raised this question as my commentator at the American Political Science Association Annual Meeting.

26. Brennan, *Against Democracy*. An epistocracy is a government of experts enacting and enforcing laws without being democratically accountable. Unlike Brennan, Achen and Bartels favor democracy, but they give purely instrumental arguments for it, such as avoiding corruption, permitting political opposition, providing "authoritative, widely accepted agreement about who shall rule," and preventing any one party from being entrenched in power. Achen and Bartels, *Democracy for Realists*, 317.

27. Bell, *China Model*; Lee Kuan Yew and Fareed Zakaria, "Culture Is Destiny: A Conversation with Lee Kuan Yew," *Foreign Affairs* 73, no. 2 (1994): 109–26. Against Bell and Lee, I defend the human right to democratic accountability in chapter 6. An incisive criticism of Bell is Stephen Macedo, "The Self-Sustaining Virtue of the Powerful? A Critique of the China Model," *Politics and Religion* 11, no. 4 (2018): 884–88.

elites who can purportedly deliver better results.[28] It should concern us that an exclusively instrumental argument is ambivalent between democracy and authoritarianism when the results are similar.

By contrast, I regard democracy as choice-worthy in the kind of relationship that it constitutes or creates among citizens. Democracy should not be reduced to an instrumentally valuable tool interchangeable with undemocratic forms of government that generate similar results. Democracy offers an irreplaceable intrinsic value that is *noninstrumental*, in that it allows for the creation of a *relationship* among citizens wherein they govern themselves. A human relationship is valuable for reasons beyond its mere expediency.[29]

Several prominent scholars agree that democracy constitutes a valuable relationship. However, these "social egalitarians" view the democratic relationship as one of social equality, where citizens share the same social rank, unlike a hierarchical, caste society. While social egalitarianism is in many respects attractive, it is susceptible to a levelling-down objection. The trouble is that citizens can be social equals while lacking any right to participate democratically. Niko Kolodny concedes that social egalitarianism "would be satisfied equally well by one's having no influence at all—so long as no one else had any influence either."[30] Citizens would be social equals in being equally powerless.

Unlike social egalitarianism, equal accountability requires the positive presence of equal authority for citizens. Equal accountability foregrounds the rights and duties of citizens to participate democratically, framing democracy as a vertical *relationship of equal authority*, where citizens possess the positive authority to hold their public servants democratically accountable. When it is fulfilled, equal accountability

---

28. Caplan, *Myth of the Rational Voter*; Bell, *China Model*; Brennan, *Against Democracy*.

29. Here I agree with Beerbohm that democracy has a noninstrumental value in the relationship it forms (Beerbohm, *In Our Name*, chap. 1). In his agenda-setting book, Beerbohm insightfully contrasts theories that ground democracy in self-government with those that found it on accountability. I endeavor here to unite the two previously divided democratic values of democratic accountability and self-government.

30. Niko Kolodny, "Rule Over None II: Social Equality and the Justification of Democracy," *Philosophy and Public Affairs* 42, no. 4 (2014): 325. On social egalitarianism, see also Viehoff, "Truth in Political Instrumentalism" and Niko Kolodny, *The Pecking Order: Social Hierarchy as a Philosophical Problem* (Cambridge, MA: Harvard University Press, 2023).

also constitutes a horizontal *relationship of solidarity*, where citizens participate in democratic accountability to secure each other's equal authority from the threats of elected authoritarians, factions, and powerlessness. These relationships of equal authority and solidarity are missing from the social egalitarian approach, which regards democracy as satisfied by equal powerlessness and passive indifference, as long as all citizens share the same social rank.

When we act on its duties, democracy as equal accountability constitutes an intrinsically valuable relationship where citizens are free and equal in solidarity with one another. During the French Revolution, citizens striving for democracy linked it with three values: liberty, equality, and fraternity.[31] Equal accountability demands that citizens should be *free* in being self-governing. To be self-governing, citizens must be included in democracy as *equal authorities* with both equal procedural rights to hold their government democratically accountable and equal substantive human rights in how they are treated by the government. Fraternity, or what I call *solidarity*, is the mutual commitment of citizens to respect, protect, and empower each other's equal authority. Solidarity contrasts with being aloof and apathetic when other citizens are being marginalized. Citizens who act in solidarity participate in democratic accountability to secure one another's freedom and equality.

When we constitute a relationship, its value is not reducible to the instrumental outcome of maximizing beneficial results. The democratic relationship instead *embodies* and lives by the values of freedom, equality, and solidarity. A relationship embodies a value by *respecting* and *protecting* the participants in a relationship, rather than maximizing a result by sacrificing them.[32] As Tim Scanlon notes, it would not respect the value of friendship to betray "one friend in order to make several

31. These three values comprise the national motto of France and the Republic of Haiti. Rawls notes that liberty, equality, and fraternity are the three values that have been associated with democracy since the French Revolution. See John Rawls, *Theory of Justice*, rev. ed. (Cambridge, MA: Harvard University Press, 1999), 90. On the values of the French Revolution, see further Dan Edelstein, *On the Spirit of Rights* (Chicago: University of Chicago Press, 2019).

32. There are also rights that we possess as human beings aside from any relationship. For example, we should respect the human rights of all human beings, as I write in chapter 5.

new ones, or in order to bring it about that other people had more friends."[33] The betrayal may multiply the total number of friends, but it would fail to embody the intrinsic value of the relationship.

The democratic relationship gives rise to both negative duties to respect other citizens, and positive duties to protect and empower our fellow citizens in solidarity with them.[34] I argue that when it is fulfilled, democracy as equal accountability creates a profoundly valuable relationship that is intrinsically choice-worthy. In the democratic relationship, we look after one another in solidarity, we are included as equal authorities, and we govern ourselves freely in the pursuit of justice with public servants who answer to us.

The Democratic Accountability Right to Authorize: The First Core Element

Equal accountability contains five core elements that constitute our equal authority over our public servants, enabling us to govern ourselves freely. The first core aspect, *authorization*, is the democratic accountability right to collectively give permission for officials to work as our public servants in office. Officials are *directly* authorized when they are elected by citizens in free and fair elections. Other officials are *indirectly* authorized when they are appointed by the directly authorized, elected officials.

I challenge the widespread misconception that democratic authorization involves citizens giving officials unlimited power through

---

33. T. M. Scanlon, *What We Owe Each Other* (Cambridge, MA: Harvard University Press, 1998), 89.

34. Robert Nozick holds that rights are "side-constraints" that prohibit certain ways of treating others, even if that treatment might generate in greater overall benefits. In contrast to Nozick, I defend positive rights that require duties to act, along with negative rights with duties of restraint. Cf. Robert Nozick, *Anarchy, State, Utopia* (New York: Basic Books, 1974), 30–33. Restricting the rights in a relationship to only negative rights and duties would ignore the importance of solidarity, which protects other people. Nozick came to accept this view: "The libertarian position I once propounded now seems to me seriously inadequate." With its purely negative rights, libertarianism "truncate[s] the reality of our social *solidarity* and humane concern for others." See Robert Nozick, *The Examined Life: Philosophical Meditations* (New York: Simon and Schuster, 1989), 287–88 (emphasis added).

elections. I recast authorization to reflect how citizens are equal authorities who together own the power of government to make and enforce the law.[35] The authorization that occurs in elections gives permission to serve as public servants in offices that are limited in power and bound by important duties. Citizens continue to own government power after the election, and can demand accountability from the public servants who work for them.

The authority of officials to legislate and enforce the law is *derived* or originates from the higher authority of citizens, who are the owners of the power of government. As Madison writes in Federalist 46, "the ultimate authority, wherever the derivative may be found, resides in the people alone."[36] The Declaration of Independence proclaims that citizens are the source of the legitimate power of government: "Governments are instituted among Men, deriving their just powers from the consent of the governed."[37] The constitution or Basic Law of Germany similarly reads, "All state authority is derived from the people. . . . The legislature shall be bound by the constitutional order, the executive and the judiciary by law and justice."[38]

Equal accountability entitles citizens to the democratic accountability right to *authorize* public servants to work for them. When unelected dictators, insurrectionists, or colonial regimes seize control, they are unauthorized. They were never given permission to rule by citizens in elections. The Framers call this unauthorized theft of power from

---

35. However, the citizens' collective ownership right over the power of government is not unlimited. Nor does it have all of the "incidents" or rights of ordinary property ownership. Democratic accountability rights are inalienable, unlike the ownership of ordinary property. For instance, citizens do not have the right to alienate their democratic accountability rights by selling their votes. I explain that government power requires a more responsible type of ownership, attached to the democratic duties of the office of the citizen, because government power coerces by making and enforcing laws. This coercive power risks inflicting death or injury if misused.

36. Madison, "Federalist No. 46," in Hamilton, Madison, and Jay, *Federalist*, 228.

37. Declaration of Independence.

38. Germany, Basic Law for the Federal Republic of Germany, May 23, 1949, as amended in June 2008, art. 20, available at https://www.refworld.org/docid/4e64d9a02.html.

citizens a "usurpation."[39] The word usurpation descends from the Latin verb *usurpare*, meaning "taking possession without a legal claim."[40]

In Federalist 39, Madison articulates how it is central to the meaning of a republic, or what we would call a constitutional representative democracy, that officials must derive the authority of their public offices from the more fundamental authority of citizens:

> We may define a republic to be, or at least may bestow that name on, a government which derives all its powers directly or indirectly from the great body of the people; and is administered by persons holding their offices during pleasure, for a limited period, or during good behavior.[41]

I interpret authorization as taking place when citizens vote in elections. In his dissent from the Sedition Act of 1798, Madison says that "the right of electing the members of the Government constitutes more particularly the essence of a free and responsible government."[42]

While the power of officials in a representative democracy must derive from a direct or indirect appointment by citizens, not all officials need to be directly elected. It is not feasible to elect all the officials working in government, who number in the millions.[43] The citizens can

39. According to Alexander Hamilton, the federal design of the constitution, with power divided between the state and federal levels, counteracts the threat of usurpation: "Were he to subdue a part, that which would still remain free might oppose him with forces, independent of those which he had usurped, and overpower him before he could be settled in his usurpation." Hamilton, "Federalist No. 9," in Hamilton, Madison, and Jay, *Federalist*, 38.

40. *Merriam-Webster Online*, s.v. "usurp," https://www.merriam-webster.com/dictionary/usurp.

41. Madison, "Federalist No. 39," 182 (emphasis in original). Madison argues that for a government to be a republic, officials must derive their authority from the "great body of the society," and not "an inconsiderable proportion, or favored class of it." In chapter 5, I show how this argument supports my Inclusion Principle that citizenship should extend to all residents within a country's jurisdiction.

42. James Madison, "Report on the Resolutions," in *The Writings of James Madison*, vol. 6, *1790–1802*, ed. Gaillard Hunt (New York: G. P. Putnam, 1906), 395.

43. On the number of people who work in local, state, and federal government, see Fiona Hill, "Public Service and the Federal Government," Brookings Institution, May 27, 2020, https://www.brookings.edu/policy2020/votervital/public-service-and-the-federal-government/. The number of government employees has fallen as a proportion of the population over the last half

delegate the selection of lower-ranking officials to their directly authorized, elected officials in a process of indirect appointment.

Madison's distinction between direct and indirect derivation of
power leads us to ask: Which officials should be directly authorized, and
by what standard? In the Constitution ratified in 1788, senators were
originally chosen by state legislatures, and not directly by citizens.[44] The
Electoral College, not citizens voting in a direct election, was intended
to select the president. Indeed, the Supreme Court has ruled that a state
legislature "may, if it so chooses, select the electors itself," contrary to
the election by the state's citizens.[45]

I clarify that for citizens to be equal authorities who govern themselves freely, they must be able to collectively select and replace their
highest officials, who wield the power to make and enforce the law.
Abraham Lincoln in his first inaugural address said that the president
originates the authority of public office from citizens: "The Chief Magistrate derives all his authority from the people."[46] But for this principle
to be realized fully, I add that the president must be elected by citizens.
It would not be democratic if only minor clerks were elected, while the
legislators and president were exempt from election. The laws that legislators enact and the president enforces form the basic structure of
society. The freedom as self-government of citizens would be severely
diminished if the framework of their government were shaped by officials who are not directly authorized by citizens.[47]

---

century. Eight million people work for the federal government, and sixteen million serve in state
and local government.

44. This reasoning for this was given in Madison, "Federalist No. 63" and Jay, "Federalist
No. 64," in Hamilton, Madison, and Jay, *Federalist*, 305–12 and 312–17.

45. Bush v. Gore, 531 U.S. 98, 104 (2000).

46. Abraham Lincoln, "First Inaugural Address, March 4, 1861," in *The Complete Works of
Abraham Lincoln*, vol. 6, ed. John G. Nicolay and John Hay (New York: Tandy-Thomas, 1905),
183.

47. The decision of whether to directly or indirectly authorize judges is ultimately accorded
to citizens. But one broad guideline is that if judges are not subject to democratic accountability,
they should show greater deference to the democratically accountable branches. If judges instead exercised more extensive powers of judicial review enabling them to strike down laws,
then citizens should consider offsetting that more formidable power by enhancing democratic
accountability for judges. This is the approach taken by Germany, where the justices on the
Federal Constitutional Court wield powers of abstract review that surpass judicial review. But
the German justices are elected indirectly by a two-thirds vote of both houses of the legislature,

Both elected and appointed officials must work as the public servants of citizens. This foundational principle is why US officials do not swear an oath of fealty to the president, but an oath of office to the Constitution, which considers citizens to be the ultimate authorities.[48] A democracy differs from a monarchy, where officials take an oath of personal loyalty to the king. In the Roman Republic, the soldiers once swore an oath (*sacramentum militare*) to the Roman Senate and the people. Following the fall of the Republic, the oath was altered, the people and Senate were forgotten, and the imperial legions transferred the object of their oath and loyalty to the emperor.[49] In contrast, Chairman of the Joint Chiefs of Staff General Mark Milley reminds us that in a democracy, "We do not take an oath to a king or queen, or tyrant or dictator, we do not take an oath to an individual." Rather, "we take an oath to the Constitution, and every soldier . . . every sailor, airman, marine, coastguard—each of us protects and defends that document, regardless of personal price."[50]

The tenet that officials work as the authorized public servants of citizens, and not the president, entails a crucial corollary. If the president issues an unconstitutional or unlawful order to other officials, such as

with eight justices elected by the Bundestag, and eight justices elected by the Bundesrat. Justices serve a limited twelve-year term with a mandatory retirement age of sixty-eight. In Japan, the Supreme Court holds the power of judicial review, but Japanese justices can be removed in national elections that take place soon after their appointment and every decade afterward, until the mandatory retirement age of seventy. I am grateful to Rob Reich, who perceptively raised this question about the authorization of judges. I thank Ian Walling for helpful discussion on this subject. On Germany's Federal Constitutional Court, see Georg Vanberg, *The Politics of Constitutional Review in Germany* (Cambridge, UK: Cambridge University Press, 2005), 81–86. On Japan's judicial system, see Christopher P. Banks and David M. O'Brien, *The Judicial Process: Laws, Courts, and Judicial Politics* (Thousand Oaks, CA: CQ Press, 2016), 128.

48. Madison, "Federalist No. 46," 228: "The ultimate authority, wherever the derivative may be found, resides in the people alone." On the oath of office, see Corey Brettschneider, *The Oath and the Office: A Guide to the Constitution for Future Presidents* (New York: W. W. Norton, 2018).

49. On this change in the Roman oath from the Republic to the Empire, see William Whewell, *The Elements of Morality, Including Polity*, vol. 2 (London: John W. Parker, 1845), 238–39. The analogy to the Roman case is partial. A notable difference is that the Romans took a dual oath to the people and the Senate. The Senate was not a representative body for the people but represented the wealthy patrician class.

50. James Walker, "Top General Says Military Doesn't Take Oath to Any Individual amid Pentagon Shakeup," *Newsweek*, November 13, 2020, https://www.newsweek.com/top-general-military-oath-individual-pentagon-shakeup-1547167.

to interfere with an election, to launch a politically motivated prosecution, or to inflict violence on peaceful protestors, officials should oppose the order and prioritize the ultimate authority of citizens. They should inform citizens of the attempted unlawful order through Congress and their department's inspector general. The authority of citizens commands primacy and must be protected from lawless elected authoritarians.

For example, the US Uniform Code of Military Justice states that members of the military are to obey the lawful and constitutional orders of their superiors. But military personnel should staunchly refuse to execute unlawful and unconstitutional orders, including commands to commit war crimes, subvert elections, or overthrow democracy. In the Iran-Contra hearings, Congress investigated the Reagan administration for selling arms to Iran, which was under an arms embargo enacted by Congress. The administration was accused of diverting the proceeds from the Iranian arms sales to the Contra rebels in Nicaragua, in breach of Congress's express ban on funding the Contras.[51] Senator Daniel Inouye, a World War II veteran, chaired the Senate Select Committee on Iran-Contra. During a hearing, he admonished an officer for following unlawful orders: "The uniform code makes it abundantly clear that it must be the lawful orders of a superior officer," said Senator Inouye. "In fact, it says, 'Members of the military have an obligation to disobey unlawful orders.' This principle was considered so important that we, we the Government of the United States, proposed that it be internationally applied in the Nuremberg trials."[52] The officials who work in government are not the minions of the president, but the public servants of citizens.

51. Congress forbade funding the Contras in Public Law 98-473, 98 Stat. 1935–1937 (1984).
52. Senate Select Committee on Secret Military Assistance to Iran and the Nicaraguan Opposition and the House Select Committee to Investigate Covert Arms Transactions with Iran, *Joint Hearings on the Iran-Contra Investigation, part I, July 7, 8, 9, and 10, 1987* (Washington, DC: US Government Printing Office, 1988), 201. The Nuremberg trials laid down the principle that soldiers can only obey lawful and constitutional orders. The court did not consider it a valid excuse that the defendants were executing orders when they committed atrocities. I thank Scott Sagan and Allen Weiner for discussion of the duties of soldiers.

Democratic Authorization Gives Permission
to Hold Office as an Accountable Trust

I frame the right to authorize as an *accountable, fiduciary authorization* and not a permanent transfer of power. In a democratic authorization, citizens continue to own the power of government and give their permission for their public servants to use it on their behalf in a democratically accountable public office. This contrasts with a Hobbesian authorization where citizens surrender the ownership of government power to an unaccountable sovereign.[53] A democratic authorization instead gives permission to serve in a *public office* with a limited extent and term of power. The Framers regarded usurpation not only as unelected persons seizing public office but also as the unauthorized annexation of power by elected officials beyond the limits of their offices. As I interpret authorization, we give permission for officials to exercise government power as a *trust*, while we continue to own that power collectively, with the right to hold our officials democratically accountable during office. Government officials must work for us as fiduciaries. A fiduciary is a person authorized to administer a trust, or a property other people own, for the benefit of the owners, subject to strict duties that the fiduciary always pursue the owners' interest. In a democracy, the ultimate owners of government power are the citizens as a collective body.

To illustrate an accountable authorization, suppose that we hire financial advisers to invest our savings. Their work is a trust, as they are investing money that other people own. At the outset, we possess authority over the advisers, who are accountable to us. We have authorized

---

53. Thomas Hobbes views authorization as permanently transferring the ownership of government power to the sovereign. A sovereign is a government, which can consist of one person, a part of the people, or the entire people voting directly on the laws, that wields unaccountable, absolute power with no separation of powers between the branches of government. As Hobbes states the agreement establishing the sovereign, "I authorise and give up my right of governing myself to this man, or to this assembly of men, on this condition: that thou give up, thy right to him, and authorise all his actions in like manner" (*Leviathan*, ed. Richard Tuck [Cambridge, UK: Cambridge University Press, 1996], 120). Once the ownership of government power is alienated by the subjects, they no longer have any right to hold the sovereign accountable for how that power is exercised. See *Leviathan*, 120.

them to invest our savings. We can demand that our advisers justify or give reasons for their handling of our money. We can compel them to transparently disclose accurate and accessible information about their investments of our funds. Based on our evaluation of their performance, we can choose whether to remove them from their positions as our financial advisers. If they attempt to embezzle from us, we can sanction them in court.

One day our financial advisers cease being accountable to us, following the pattern of elected authoritarians in government. The advisers hide from us how they invest our money. They do not justify or give reasons for their decisions regarding our funds. The advisers threaten us with violence if we ask what they are doing with our money, talk about their actions, form associations with other investors, or protest. Their lack of accountability would be unjust in repudiating our authority, even if their management of our money remained profitable.

Instead of having a relationship where we freely govern our own financial affairs with advisers who are accountable to us, we would be the subjects of masters who control our money. We would no longer be the authorities in the relationship with our advisers. The injustice of the advisers' conduct is not fully captured by the instrumental argument, because their financial returns stay the same. The injustice is that they have stolen our freedom in governing our own financial lives. Instead of working as our democratically accountable servants or agents, they have forced upon us an authoritarian relationship of unaccountable rule.

The Framers frequently describe public office as a fiduciary trust.[54] Madison says in Federalist 46, "The Federal and State Governments are in fact but different agents and trustees of the people, instituted with different powers, and designed for different purposes."[55] Citizens are the authorities in this relationship, because they are the "common

<hr>

54. A philosophical forerunner of my view that citizens authorize their officials to serve in a trust is the work of John Locke: "The Legislative being only a Fiduciary Power to act for certain ends . . . there remains still in the People a Supreme Power to remove or alter the Legislative, when they find the Legislative act contrary to the trust reposed in them." "Second Treatise of Government," 367, §149.
55. Madison, "Federalist No. 46," 228.

superior" of government officials.[56] The Constitution characterizes "Office" at several points as a "public Trust."[57]

The Framers draw an important parallel between public servants and other types of fiduciaries, such as a banker who is managing our money, or a real estate agent handling the sale of our home. The Framers refer to public office as a fiduciary trust to express how officials are subject to strict duties in handling public funds and government power. These stringent duties are grounded in how fiduciaries are using something owned by other people.

A fiduciary duty is the highest standard of care in law, with three sets of responsibilities. The *duty of loyalty* demands that the fiduciaries act in the best interest of the beneficiary and avoid any conflict of interest. Second, fiduciaries shoulder the *duty of care* to pursue the interest of the beneficiary prudently, not recklessly or negligently. Third, the *duty of good faith* dictates that fiduciaries be dedicated in their responsibilities, and not derelict in their duties.[58] Fiduciaries must always act with probity in the best interests of the beneficiary.

The Code of Federal Regulations endorses this conception of public office as a fiduciary trust: "Public service is a public trust. Each employee has a responsibility to the United States Government and its citizens to place loyalty to the Constitution, laws and ethical principles above private gain."[59] As a public trust, an office must not be abused for the officials' own enrichment. Corruption in office would betray their duty of loyalty to citizens.[60] An accountable authorization gives

56. Madison, "Federalist No. 46," 228. In "Federalist No. 57," Madison calls officials "public servants" (280).

57. U.S. Const. Art. VI, clause 3; Art. II, sect. 1, clause 2; Art. I, sect. 3, clause 7; Art. I, sect. 9, clause 8. On how officials are fiduciaries of citizens, see Ethan J. Lieb and Jed Shugerman, "Fiduciary Constitutionalism: Implications for Self-Pardons and Non-Delegation," *Georgetown Journal of Law & Public Policy* 17 (2019): 463–48.

58. On these sets of duties, see Ethan J. Lieb and Stephen R. Galoob, "Fiduciary Principles and Public Offices," in *The Oxford Handbook of Fiduciary Law*, ed. Evan J. Criddle, Paul B. Miller, and Robert H. Sitkoff (New York: Oxford University Press, 2019), chap. 16.

59. 5 CFR § 2635.101 - Basic Obligation of Public Service, available at Cornell University, Legal Information Institute, accessed March 12, 2025, https://www.law.cornell.edu/cfr/text/5/2635.101.

60. This requirement is expressed in the Constitution's Foreign Emoluments Clause (Art. I, sec. 9, clause 8), Domestic Emoluments Clause (Art. II, sec. 1, clause 7), and the Sinecure

permission to hold the power of public office as a temporary trust that the official fulfills in a spirit of stewardship for citizens. Officials must heed their duties of loyalty, care, and good faith in the trust of public office, as part of the public servants' democratic duty of fidelity.

I argue that the *democratic duty of fidelity* vests public servants with responsibilities that include, but are also more demanding than, the duties of ordinary fiduciaries. The duty of fidelity sets a higher bar because public servants wield the coercive power of government, unlike other fiduciaries, such as a lawyer, accountant, or financial adviser. Government coercion is necessary to secure rights against anarchy, but it poses the danger of injuring, innocently imprisoning, or killing others. Since government power potentially jeopardizes life and liberty, and it is collectively owned by citizens, public servants owe to citizens the more stringent *democratic duty of fidelity*, which requires public servants to accept the principle of democratic accountability, to recognize the equal authority of all citizens, and to use government power justly. Attorney General Garland distilled the essence of the duty of fidelity for public servants in his speech to the Department of Justice:

> We will protect the cornerstone of our democracy: the right to every eligible citizen to cast a vote that counts. And we will do all of this in a manner that adheres to the rule of law and honors our obligation to protect the civil rights and civil liberties of everyone in this country.[61]

Garland recalled how President Ulysses S. Grant and Congress founded the Department of Justice to preserve the rights of African Americans from the violence of factions: "the department's first principal task was to secure the civil rights promised by the 13th, 14th and 15th Amendments. This meant protecting Black Americans seeking to exercise their right to vote from acts and threats of violence by white

---

Clause (Art. I, sec. 6, clause 2). Hamilton defends the Domestic Emoluments Clause in "Federalist No. 73" (*Federalist*, 356–62). He justifies the Foreign Emoluments Clause in "Federalist No. 22" (*Federalist*, esp. 103), where he writes, "One of the weak sides of republics, among their numerous advantages, is that they afford too easy an inlet to foreign corruption."

61. Garland, "Remarks on the First Anniversary."

supremacists. The framers of the Civil War Amendments recognized that access to the ballot is a fundamental aspect of citizenship and self-government."[62] Public servants who act in fidelity, like the founders of the Department of Justice, stand as sentinels against elected authoritarians, factions, and powerlessness.

The conception of office as a democratically accountable fiduciary trust opposes what Max Weber called "patrimonial rule."[63] In patrimonial rule, the ruler owns the power of government as a personal possession for self-enrichment. A striking example of patrimonial rule may be found in the first census of Russia in 1897. Czar Nicholas II listed his occupation in the census questionnaire not as a public servant, but as the "owner" of all of Russia's lands.[64] Many elected authoritarians have followed in the czar's footsteps, imposing what Francis Fukuyama refers to as "neopatrimonial rule."[65] These despots govern behind a modern veneer of law and elections, but their regimes are brazenly corrupt. The US Constitution's bans on emoluments or self-enrichment can be seen as upholding the fiduciary duties of public office against the specter of neopatrimonial rule. Officials must act as public servants for citizens with incorruptible integrity.

Officials Are Authorized to Serve in a Public Office with Limited Powers

The office of the public servant is a position limited in its extent and duration of power and subject to democratic accountability. Madison declared in an April 1796 speech before Congress that accountability and the bounds of public office distinguish the president from a king. He drew the line between a "hereditary Sovereign, not accountable for his conduct, and a Magistrate like the President of the United States,

---

62. Garland.

63. Max Weber, *Economy and Society: An Outline of Interpretive Sociology*, ed. Guenther Roth and Claus Wittich (Berkeley: University of California Press, 1978), 1006–69.

64. J. Arch Getty, *Practicing Stalinism: Bolsheviks, Boyars, and the Persistence of Tradition* (New Haven, CT: Yale University Press, 2013), 83.

65. Francis Fukuyama, *Political Order and Political Decay* (New York: Farrar, Straus and Giroux, 2014), esp. 287–88.

elected for four years, with limited powers, and liable to impeachment for abuse of them."[66] The powers of the presidency and other public offices are regulated to oblige officials to fulfill their morally legitimate purposes without betraying their fiduciary trusts.[67]

Unlike the position of a king, a public office limits how much power officials wield and how long they can possess it. In Federalist 48, Madison writes that "in a representative republic," the "executive magistracy is carefully limited; both in the extent and the duration of its power."[68] These limits on office, remarks Hamilton in Federalist 69, evince a "total dissimilitude" between the President "and a king of Great Britain."[69] There is a stark difference, says Hamilton, between a king and the president, who is subject to the rule of law and constraints of office: "The President of the United States would be liable to be impeached, tried, and, upon conviction of treason, bribery, or other high crimes or misdemeanors, removed from office; and would afterwards be liable to prosecution and punishment in the ordinary course of law."[70]

I locate an additional reason, rooted in democratic accountability, for limiting the power of public office. The limits of office preserve the *equal authority* of citizens to hold their public servants democratically accountable. Even if the officials were benevolent, their power must be confined to a public office for citizens to be freely self-governing. If there were no limits to public office, then the equal authority of citizens could be stripped away by officials wielding unlimited power, leaving citizens no longer free to govern themselves.

The following analogy illustrates how the power of office must be limited to respect the equal authority of citizens. Suppose that you live in a condominium. You and the other tenants decide to authorize, or collectively give permission, for one of the residents to serve as the

66. James Madison, "The Jay Treaty, Speech in Congress, April 6, 1796," in *Writings of James Madison*, 273.
67. Madison says in Federalist 52, "It is a received and well-founded maxim, that . . . the greater the power is, the shorter ought to be its duration" (*Federalist*, 259).
68. Madison, "Federalist No. 48," 241–42. Madison argues that both the executive and the legislative branches must be checked when they attempt to impose tyrannical power.
69. Hamilton, "Federalist No. 69," in *Federalist*, 335.
70. Hamilton, "Federalist No. 69."

condo chair, who can levy fees and make binding rules. What would happen if the chair claims to be authorized to possess unrestricted power, instead of holding an office? The chair insists that he can enter your home in the middle of the night. You are prohibited from publicly questioning anything the chair does, and you are banned from demanding a justification for the chair's decisions or calling for transparent financial records. When you finally demand that the chair's power be reined in, he deigns to reply, "I was selected by a majority vote of the condo's tenants. Because you had an equal vote in the decision to select me, you are freely self-governing. My power must not be limited, for that would interfere with my carrying out the will of the tenants, as declared in my election."

The condo chair's claim would echo the line taken by elected authoritarians, but it would be morally myopic for three reasons. First, you are not freely self-governing when you are subject to an official wielding overwhelming limitless force. Nor are you freely self-governing when you are powerless to hold the chair accountable during office, or when the chair abuses your human rights. You do not govern yourself but are subjugated to the external rule of elective despot.

Second, your ability to hold the chair accountable depends on the official's power being regulated by the duties and limits of office. Democratic accountability means that you can impose enforceable duties on your officials both during their terms in office and in elections. When the officials' powers are absolute, the duties of democratic accountability are no longer enforceable through the rule of law. If citizens sued to stop a violation of their rights, officials with unlimited power could blatantly ignore the court order or replace the judges with complicit confederates. The duties imposed by democratic accountability rights on public servants ought to be *enforceable*. A duty that is enforceable offers a remedy when it is violated. A canon of law, dating to ancient Rome, states that there is no right without a remedy, *ubi jus, ibi remedium*.[71] The

71. William Gardiner Hammond, the chancellor of the University of Iowa Law School, stated the principle, "The true meaning of *ubi jus, ibi remedium* is that the two things are necessary complements of each other. As every remedy implies a right, so every right requires a remedy, and is not fully and practicably a right until the remedy for its breaches is given." William

correlative duties imposed on officials by democratic accountability rights can only be enforceable if their power is limited to an office subject to the rule of law. Even if the officials had benign intentions, their power must be limited to constitute the democratic relationship where citizens are freely self-governing. Officials who hold unbridled power would not be the servants but the owners of the public, like the czar.

A third reason why the power of public office must be regulated is that an authorization gives permission for an official to carry out just or morally legitimate purposes. "Justice is the end [the aim] of government. It is the end of civil society," said Madison in Federalist 51.[72] It would be just for the condo chair to maintain the building in sound condition. It would be unjust, or morally prohibited, to invade your rights. If we acknowledge this in the case of the condo chair, it is even more urgent that public servants be bound to pursue justice, since they wield far greater coercive force in government.

Elected authoritarians oppose the belief that officials must hold public office with limited powers. They contend that public office fetters their ability to carry out the popular will. But they are committing the same error as the condo chair, on a more perilous scale. It would be futile for ordinary citizens to attempt to hold accountable an implacable ruler who has aggrandized vast power that surpasses any office. The autocrat can censor the press, control the courts, and cancel elections without facing any constraints or consequences.

Absolute power that exalts itself above the law and exempts itself from the law reverses the *relationship of equal authority*. For citizens to be freely self-governing, the democratic relationship of equal authority must run in the proper direction, from citizens as the bosses down to officials as their accountable public servants. A federal district court ruling in 2019 marked the difference between democracy and unaccountable autocracy. The case involved former White House counsel Don McGahn seeking to avoid having to testify to Congress. Judge Ketanji

Blackstone, *Commentaries on the Laws of England, Book the Third*, ed. William G. Hammond (San Francisco: Bancroft-Whitney, 1890), 43–44.

72. Madison, "Federalist No. 51," 254.

Brown Jackson, before her accession to the Supreme Court, ruled that McGahn had to testify, because "Presidents are not kings."[73] Judge Jackson reminded McGahn that officials are public servants: "It is indisputable that current and former employees of the White House work for the People of the United States, and that they take an oath to protect and defend the Constitution of the United States."[74] The Constitution embodies the principle that "no one is above the law."[75] In democracy as equal accountability, presidents must not be kings, but they must answer to us as democratically accountable public servants, who must adhere to the rule of law and their office's limits on power.

Evaluation and Sanctioning: The Second and Third Core Elements of Equal Accountability

While elections are a mainstay of democratic accountability, the rights to evaluate and sanction officials *during office* are also essential to democratic accountability.[76] President Richard Nixon's chief counsel during the Watergate hearings, James St. Clair, tried to dismiss democratic accountability during office, saying to the US District Court for the District of Columbia, "The President wants me to argue that he is as powerful a monarch as Louis XIV, only four years at a time, and is not subject to the processes of any court in the land except the court of impeachment."[77] Nixon and St. Clair overlooked that without democratic accountability during office, we would lack authority over our officials until the next time we vote. We would not be freely self-governing for years between elections.

73. Committee on the Judiciary of the U.S. House of Representatives v. McGahn, No. 19-cv-2379 (Ketanji Brown Jackson), Slip Op. at 114 (Nov. 25, 2019), available at https://ecf.dcd .uscourts.gov/cgi-bin/show_public_doc?2019cv2379-46.

74. *Committee on the Judiciary v. McGahn*, 114.

75. *Committee on the Judiciary v. McGahn*, 117.

76. The right to run for office is a democratic accountability right exercised both during and between elections. Candidates do not run only on Election Day, but for an extended time beforehand as they organize supporters.

77. Quoted in Barry Sullivan, "FOIA and the First Amendment: Representative Democracy and the People's Elusive 'Right to Know,'" *Maryland Law Review* 72, no. 1 (2012): 53.

Democratic accountability occurs during office through the second and third core aspects of equal accountability, the evaluation of officials and their sanctioning. *Evaluation* examines whether the officials are using their entrusted power justly. *Sanctioning* corrects our officials when they commit injustices. In the following sections, I will outline how as citizens, we evaluate and sanction our public servants during office using the democratic accountability rights to free speech, the press, protest, association, deliberative justification, transparency, and petition. I will also show how democratic accountability during office is facilitated through the separation of powers and institutions for mediated accountability, such as impeachment.

The Democratic Accountability Rights to Freedom of Speech and the Press

Citizens *evaluate* public servants by deliberating about their actions using our rights of free speech and the press. Madison put the point lucidly: "The executive magistrates are not held to be infallible, nor the legislatures to be omnipotent; and both being elective, are both responsible."[78] To hold our public servants accountable or "responsible," we must have the "right of freely discussing public characters and measures."[79]

I refer to public discussion among citizens as *horizontal deliberation*.[80] Citizens need to be able to deliberate with each other due to the collective nature of elections. An individual alone does not decide whether to authorize or remove an elected official. Citizens collectively

---

78. James Madison, "Report on the Resolutions," in *Writings of James Madison*, vol. 6, 388.

79. *Writings of James Madison*, vol. 6, 396.

80. Jürgen Habermas views deliberation among citizens as taking place in the "public sphere" of civil society. In interpreting Habermas, I have benefited greatly from Simone Chambers, *Reasonable Democracy: Jürgen Habermas and the Politics of Discourse* (Ithaca, NY: Cornell University Press, 1996). Jane Mansbridge highlights how citizens engage in "everyday deliberation" in their daily lives. See Habermas, *Between Facts and Norms*, and Jane Mansbridge, "Everyday Talk in the Deliberative System," in *Deliberative Politics: Essays on Democracy and Disagreement*, ed. Stephen Macedo (New York: Oxford University Press, 1999), chap. 15. On deliberation, see Gutmann and Thompson, *Democracy and Disagreement* and *Why Deliberative Democracy*.

make that choice in free and fair elections. Citizens must have democratic accountability rights to free speech and the press to deliberate together as they *evaluate* whether their officials have acted justly. "Information and communication among the people," according to Madison, are thus "indispensable to the just exercise of their electoral rights."[81] After evaluating their public servants, citizens can decide how to vote, exercising the core elements in equal accountability of *authorizing* and *removing* our public servants.

Free speech and the press also contribute to the third core element of equal accountability, *sanctioning* or correcting the injustices of officials. Hamilton says in Federalist 70 that the "two greatest securities [citizens] can have for the faithful exercise of any delegated power" are "first, the restraints of public opinion," and "second, the opportunity of discovering with facility and clearness the misconduct of the persons they trust."[82] Citizens rely on free speech and the press both to discover the misdeeds of their public servants and to sanction them through the shame and opprobrium of public criticism. As Madison points out, citizens need freedom of speech and the press to bring officials "into contempt or disrepute" for their injustices and "control them by the censorship of the public opinion."[83]

The Democratic Accountability Rights to Protest and Free Association

The democratic accountability right to protest is pivotal to both the evaluation and sanctioning core aspects of equal accountability. When citizens protest, they communicate with each other about injustices,

81. *Writings of James Madison*, 395. Madison questions whether elections can be fair if officials can selectively censor criticism of themselves but not of their electoral opponents: "Will not those in power derive an undue advantage for continuing themselves in it, which, by impairing the right of election, endangers the blessings of the Government founded on it?" (397–98).

82. Hamilton, "Federalist No. 70," in *Federalist*, 346.

83. *Writings of James Madison*, 394. A valuable book on freedom of speech is Len Niehoff and E. Thomas Sullivan, *Free Speech: From Core to Current Debates* (New York: Cambridge University Press, 2022). There is a strong case to include freedom of thought among the array of democratic accountability rights needed to be feely self-governing. On freedom of thought, see Lucas Swaine, "Freedom of Thought as a Basic Liberty," *Political Theory* 46, no. 3 (2018): 405–25.

evaluate their public servants, and impose the sanctions of public pressure. In his 1963 "Letter from a Birmingham Jail," Martin Luther King Jr. advocated the right of citizens to participate in marches, boycotts, demonstrations, and other forms of nonviolent protest or direct action. Protest challenges the "tragic effort to live in monologue rather than dialogue," he wrote.[84] Protest dispels the complicity of silence that shrouds injustices. The "injustice must be exposed," said King, "with all the tension its exposure creates, to the light of human conscience and the air of national opinion before it can be cured."[85]

The democratic accountability right to free association magnifies the power of protests and voices of citizens. John Stuart Mill observes that "to make these various elements of power politically influential, they must be organized."[86] I frame freedom of association as a democratic accountability right that protects citizens when they organize together in civil society to hold their public servants accountable. Civil society groups, such as the Southern Christian Leadership Conference, trained volunteers in nonviolent protest during the 1963 Birmingham campaign. Lawyers for the NAACP provided legal assistance for citizens to petition the courts under the rule of law. The chief counsel, Thurgood Marshall, argued in *Brown v. Board of Education* against the policy of racial segregation in public schools. Marshall later served with distinction as

84. Martin Luther King Jr., "Letter from Birmingham Jail," April 16, 1963, University of Pennsylvania African Studies Center, https://www.africa.upenn.edu/Articles_Gen/Letter_Birmingham.html.

85. King, "Letter from Birmingham Jail." On how protest can influence presidents and Congress, see Daniel Q. Gillion, *The Political Power of Protest: Minority Activism and Shifts in Public Policy* (New York: Cambridge University Press, 2013).

86. John Stuart Mill, *Considerations on Representative Government*, in *Collected Works of John Stuart Mill*, vol. 19, ed. J. M. Robson (Toronto: University of Toronto Press, 1977), 381. Freedom of association is essential to the health of a democracy for two additional reasons. First, citizens learn to work together and to trust one another in associations. They then apply the cooperative habits and skills they practice in associations when they participate in government. See Robert Putnam with Robert Leonardi and Raffaella Nonetti, *Making Democracy Work* (Princeton, NJ: Princeton University Press, 1993) and Putnam and Garrett, *Upswing*. Second, freedom of association allows the formation of organizations independent of the government. These organizations can better resist abuses of power than isolated individuals, who would be more vulnerable to tyranny. See Alexis de Tocqueville, *Democracy in America*, trans. Harvey C. Mansfield and Delba Winthrop (Chicago: University of Chicago Press, 2000). It is telling that authoritarian governments, such as the Soviet Union and East Germany, suppressed freedom of association to maintain their unaccountable rule.

the first African American Supreme Court Justice.[87] Using their right to free association, citizens register voters, form political parties, and act on their democratic accountability rights to run for office and campaign for candidates. Freedom of association coordinates citizens in holding their officials accountable during office and in elections.[88] It is easier to hold officials democratically accountable when citizens work together and combine their powers. As Alexis de Tocqueville wrote of civic associations, "It is clear that if each citizen, as he becomes individually weaker and consequently more incapable in isolation of preserving his freedom, does not learn the art of uniting with those like him to defend it, tyranny will necessarily grow with equality."[89]

Democratic Accountability Rights to Deliberative Justification and the Rule of Law

One of the distinguishing features of democracy as equal accountability, compared to Madison's constitutional democracy, is that officials must actively support the democratic participation of citizens, facilitating the evaluation process in deliberative justification and transparency. *Deliberative justification* is a type of vertical deliberation held between citizens and their officials.[90] Through this process, public servants must provide moral reasons that explain why they are wielding the government power that the citizens collectively own. The democratic accountability right

87. Brown v. Board of Education of Topeka, 347 U.S. 483 (1954).

88. On the important role of political parties, which are protected by freedom of association, see Russell Muirhead, *The Promise of Parties in a Polarized Age* (Cambridge, MA: Harvard University Press, 2014) and Nancy Rosenblum, *On the Side of the Angels: An Appreciation of Parties and Partisanship* (Princeton, NJ: Princeton University Press, 2008).

89. Tocqueville, *Democracy in America*, 489.

90. On deliberative justification, see Minh Ly, "A Human Right to Deliberative Justification," *Journal of Politics* 80, no. 4 (2018): 1355–68. I am grateful to Lisa Ellis, whose editing of the article was as helpful as it was philosophically illuminating. The original article implied that other democratic accountability rights were derived from the more fundamental right to deliberative justification. I take the position here that democratic accountability is the overarching right and deliberative justification is one of its constitutive rights. It should be noted that vertical and horizontal deliberation interact. For instance, citizens can deliberate with each other to discuss a ruling given by the Supreme Court or the findings of a congressional hearing.

to *transparency* entitles citizens to accurate and accessible information about the actions of their public servants.

We cannot evaluate our public servants if we have no justification to explain their use of power and lack information about their actions. Transparency alone is not enough. We need an explanation of the reasons for those policies to understand why they are being pursued. The question answered by transparency—"What did you do?"—must be followed up with the question answered by deliberative justification: "Why did you do it?" Once we know what our public servants are doing and why, we can evaluate their actions and sanction their injustices.

In *deliberative justification*, officials give moral reasons for their policies, and we can challenge injustices through independent institutions that the officials being evaluated do not control. The independence of institutions for democratic accountability prevents the officials under evaluation from acting as biased judges in their own case. Madison cautions against this type of bias in Federalist 10: "No man is allowed to be a judge in his own cause; because his interest would certainly bias his judgment, and, not improbably, corrupt his integrity."[91] Deliberative justification is vested in several independent institutions. Executive officials must give moral reasons to justify their policies when they appear before our representatives. Congressional oversight committees review the conduct and control the budget for executive agencies. Congress can also convene investigative committees, as seen in the Senate Select Committee on Iran-Contra. When it conducts oversight, Congress holds hearings where citizens can offer testimony and argue against government policies. In the United Kingdom, the government engages in

91. Madison, "Federalist No. 10," 42. Madison remarks in "Federalist No. 49" that an institution for oversight should not be "composed chiefly of men who had been, who actually were, or who expected to be, members of the department whose conduct was arraigned. They would consequently be parties to the very question to be decided by them" (248). Locke writes that persons should not be judges in their own case in *Two Treatises of Government*, 326, §90 and 275, §13. Dennis Thompson invokes this principle in support of independent institutions to investigate congressional ethics charges, in "Statement of Dennis F. Thompson," *Hearings on Reform of Congressional Disciplinary Procedures, Joint Committee on the Organization of Congress, February 25, 1993* (Washington, DC: US Government Printing Office, 1993), 111–12. According to Thompson, the rule that officials should not act as judges in their own case sustains public trust and confidence in officials.

deliberative justification when it gives moral reasons for its policies and opens them to challenge in the Prime Minister's Question Time and parliamentary debates.

The executive branch in the United States must justify its appointment of officials in Senate confirmation hearings. Hamilton drew attention to the need for such hearings when he objected to how the state of New York selected officials through a Council of Appointments that met in private.[92] He wrote in Federalist 77, "This small body, shut up in a private apartment, impenetrable to the public eye, proceed to the execution of the trust committed to them."[93] Without the transparency of public deliberation, an "unbounded field for cabal and intrigue lies open," and "all idea of responsibility is lost."[94]

Officials must also justify their use of government power in the courts under the rule of law. The US judiciary defines the rule of law as "the principle under which all persons, institutions, or entities are accountable to laws that are: publicly promulgated, equally enforced, independently adjudicated, and consistent with international human rights principles."[95] I will discuss in chapter 5 human rights as standards of democratic accountability, which officials must satisfy for their use of the power of government to be just. Here I note that the rule of law raises a shield to protect the equal authority of citizens from officials. It also provides access to courts where citizens can exercise their democratic accountability rights.

The courts hold at least three types of deliberative justification. First, during criminal trials, prosecutors must give reasons for proposing to use the government's coercive power to punish. These reasons are critically reviewed by judges and juries independent of the prosecutor and police. The defendants can then challenge the executive's proposed use

92. Hamilton, "Federalist No. 69," 339. The Council of Appointment was later abolished by the 1821 New York constitution, which transferred the power of appointment to the state legislature. J. M. Gitterman, "The Council of Appointment in New York," *Political Science Quarterly* 7, no. 1 (1892): 80–115.

93. Hamilton, "Federalist No. 77," in *Federalist*, 374.

94. Hamilton, "Federalist No. 77."

95. United States Courts, "Overview—Rule of Law," accessed March 12, 2025, https://www .uscourts.gov/educational-resources/educational-activities/overview-rule-law#:~:text=Rule %20of%20law%20is%20a,with%20international%20human%20rights%20principles.

of power against them. This form of deliberative justification safeguards citizens from arbitrary imprisonment, as we saw with Martin Luther King Jr. and Rosa Parks. A second form of deliberative justification in courts takes place when officials break the law. The officials must give reasons in court for their actions, and they can be punished if found criminally liable. For example, Spiro Agnew was prosecuted as a criminal for bribery committed when he was governor of Maryland and later Nixon's vice president.[96] A third type of deliberative justification occurs when citizens sue the government. These civil trials force officials to provide reasons to justify their conduct and to release information through the legal discovery process. The court can issue an injunction directing the wrong to be repaired, as it did in the Montgomery busing case. Higher level courts, like the circuit courts of appeal and the Supreme Court, can review laws or executive orders in a process of deliberative justification, where officials must give reasons for their policies, and citizens can challenge those policies. This third form of deliberative justification corrects injustices suffered by citizens. For instance, citizens sued to challenge gender discrimination against LGBT citizens. In response, the Supreme Court extended the 1964 Civil Rights Act to LGBT citizens in *Bostock v. Clayton County* (2020).[97]

The moral reason-giving of deliberative justification informs us of why our public servants are using power, so that we can understand, evaluate, and sanction their conduct. If officials from one branch of government are remiss in their duty to correct injustices, they can be compelled by an order from another branch of government, such as by a congressional subpoena or a court order, in a process of mediated accountability. Since deliberative justification takes place publicly, it informs other citizens of injustices. Our fellow citizens can then act in solidarity by speaking out against the injustice and voting out the officials responsible.

96. Ben A. Franklin, "Court Says Agnew Took Bribes; Orders Repayment," *New York Times*, April 28, 1981.

97. Bostock v. Clayton County, 590 U.S. 644 (2020). Pamela Karlan argued the case successfully before the Supreme Court.

The Democratic Accountability Right to Transparency

The evaluation of officials demands transparency, or accurate and accessible information about their conduct.[98] The US Freedom of Information Act (FOIA) enjoins the government to release federal agency records to citizens. The Federal Court of Appeals closely connects FOIA with democratic accountability.[99] The act grants "citizens access to the information on the basis of which government agencies make their decisions, thereby equipping the populace to *evaluate* and criticize those decisions."[100]

More than ninety states around the world have codified the democratic accountability right to transparency in right-to-information laws.[101] Japan's freedom of information law declares that the purpose of transparency is to ensure that "the government is *accountable* to the people for its various operations, and to contribute to the promotion of

98. Views of accountability that focus on transparency include Allen Buchanan and Robert Keohane, "The Legitimacy of Global Governance Institutions," *Ethics and International Affairs* 20 (2006): 405–37; Jeremy Waldron, "Accountability: Fundamental to Democracy," April 1, 2014, NYU School of Law, Public Law Research Paper No. 14–13, https://ssrn.com/abstract =2410812; and Ferejohn, "Accountability and Authority." Although some government information might arguably be kept secret for national security, there is a danger of officials using security as a pretext to cover up misconduct. The standards of classification ought to be transparent and subject to democratic deliberation. Classification decisions should be independently reviewed outside of the classifying agency, such as by Congress. See Gutmann and Thompson, *Why Deliberative Democracy*, 5, and Rahul Sagar, *Secrets and Leaks* (Princeton, NJ: Princeton University Press, 2014).

99. 5 U.S.C. § 552. Jeremy Bentham holds that transparency contributes to accountability "by bringing to light, and thus exposing to the law and of public opinion . . . every instance of contravention." Quoted in James E. Crimmins, "Bentham and Utilitarianism," in *The Cambridge Companion to Utilitarianism*, ed. Ben Eggleston and Dale E. Miller (Cambridge, UK: Cambridge University Press, 2014), 43. On Bentham's thought, see Nancy Rosenblum, *Bentham's Theory of the Modern State* (Cambridge, MA: Harvard University Press, 1978).

100. McGehee v. CIA, 697 F.2d 1095 (D.C. Cir. 1983), 1108–9 (emphasis added).

101. Japan, Law Concerning Access to Information Held by Administrative Organs, Law No. 42 of 1999, English translation available from the Japanese Ministry of Internal Affairs and Communications, https://www.soumu.go.jp/main_sosiki/gyoukan/kanri/translation4.htm. On the number of states with freedom of information laws, see Roy Peled and Yoram Rabin, "The Constitutional Right to Information," *Columbia Human Rights Law Review* 42 (2011): 357. The preface in the Japanese law explaining its aim is an apt example of Plato's recommendation in the *Laws* that legal rules be introduced with remarks on their purpose. This type of justification respects the citizens' capacity for reason. See Lane, *Of Rule and Office*, 94.

a fair and democratic administration that is subject to the people's accurate understanding and criticism."[102]

Our public servants should impart information about their conduct that is accessible, in a form that is readily understood and easily found by citizens.[103] Without accessibility, officials could escape accountability as they formally release information about their actions, only to obscure it in a bureaucratic labyrinth or cryptic language that citizens can scarcely navigate. The democratic accountability right to transparency charges our officials with the duty to release *accessible* and accurate information, so that we know about what our public servants are doing with the power that we collectively own.[104] The right to transparency should be extended beyond existing laws and made an active responsibility of officials, as part of their democratic duty of fidelity to comply with democratic accountability.[105]

Inspectors General and the Government Accountability Office

One of the functions of congressional oversight, courts, inspectors general, and other independent institutions is to compel officials to give moral reasons for their conduct and transparent information about it. For instance, Congress enacted the Inspector General Act of 1978 after the Watergate scandal.[106] Inspectors general serve as "independent, nonpartisan officials who prevent and detect waste, fraud, and abuse within federal departments and agencies."[107] They investigate government agencies, receive reports from whistleblowers, and inform law

102. Japan, Law Concerning Access to Information, art. 1 (emphasis added).

103. According to Buchanan and Keohane, "Legitimacy of Global Governance Institutions," the accessibility of information is a prerequisite for accountability (425). Beerbohm, *In Our Name*, chap. 10, notes that transparency alone does not suffice; rather, the information must be accessible or readily available and understandable for citizens.

104. Fuller argues that legal rules must be publicly promulgated, as well as clear and intelligible. See Lon Fuller, *The Morality of Law*, rev. ed. (New Haven, CT: Yale University Press, 1969).

105. Waldron stresses that officials bear the duty of transparency in "Accountability: Fundamental to Democracy."

106. 92 Stat. 1101.

107. Kathryn A. Francis, *Statutory Inspectors General in the Federal Government: A Primer* (Washington, DC: Congressional Research Service, 2019), 1. On the role of whistleblowers, see Sagar, *Secrets and Leaks*.

enforcement, the courts, and Congress of violations. There are now seventy-three Offices of Inspectors General with over fourteen thousand employees. Their work has "resulted in recommendations for hundreds of billions of dollars in potential savings, [and] tens of thousands of successful prosecutions."[108] The inspectors general promote deliberative justification and transparency, as they conduct investigations that force officials to give reasons to explain their conduct and keep us apprised about their actions.

A long established independent institution for democratic accountability is the Government Accountability Office (GAO), founded by Congress in 1921. The GAO audits government agencies and can order the disclosure of documents and information.[109] It also reports on the performance of government agencies in meeting their declared goals.[110] The GAO's investigations seek to uncover "violations of federal criminal law, particularly conflict of interest or procurement and contract fraud."[111] To prevent interference with its investigations, Congress established the GAO to be "independent of the executive departments."[112] Internationally, a total of 195 countries have created supreme audit institutions, similar to the GAO, to examine government expenditures.[113] The GAO, inspectors general, the courts, congressional and parliamentary oversight, and other independent institutions are the *eyes* of citizens. They increase transparency and enhance the ability of citizens to *evaluate* their public servants.

108. Council of the Inspectors General, "Building on 40 Years of Excellence in Independent Oversight," May 8, 2018, https://www.ignet.gov/sites/default/files/files/IGAct40_Press _Release_05-08-18.pdf.

109. Congressional Research Service, "CRS Report for Congress, GAO: Government Accountability Office and General Accounting Office" (Washington, DC: Congressional Research Service, 2008), p. CRS-7, https://fas.org/sgp/crs/misc/RL30349.pdf. The GAO was called the General Accounting Office until 2004.

110. Government Performance and Results Act of 1993, Pub. L. 103–62 (1993) and GPRA Modernization Act of 2010, P.L. 111-352 (2010). These laws direct government agencies to compile annual performance plans that track whether the agencies are meeting their goals. Congressional Research Service 2008, p. CRS-5-6.

111. Congressional Research Service 2008, pp. CRS-1-2.

112. Congressional Research Service 2008, pp. CRS-1-2.

113. This is the number of state members in the International Organization of Supreme Audit Institutions. See International Organization of Supreme Audit Institutions, "INTOSAI— Members," https://www.intosai.org/about-us/members.html.

The Democratic Accountability Right to Petition

After evaluating their public servants, citizens should not have to wait years until the next election to rectify misconduct. The third core aspect of equal accountability is the right to *sanction* or correct public servants during their term in office. Citizens can impose sanctions through public criticism and pressure expressed through the rights of free speech, press, protest, and association. They can further sanction officials through the democratic accountability right to *petition* the courts. Justice Anthony Kennedy made clear the importance of the right of petition in his ruling for *Borough of Duryea v. Guarnieri*. The First Amendment's Petition Clause, said Justice Kennedy, "protects the right of individuals to appeal to courts and other forums established by the government for resolution of legal disputes. The right of access to courts for redress of wrongs is an aspect of the First Amendment right to petition the government."[114] Kennedy distinguished the roles of the rights to petition and free speech:

> The right to petition allows citizens to express their ideas, hopes, and concerns to their government and their elected representatives, whereas the right to speak fosters the public exchange of ideas that is integral to deliberative democracy as well as to the whole realm of ideas and human affairs.[115]

In my terms, the right to petition initiates deliberative justification between officials and citizens who seek "a redress of grievances."[116] One type of petition appeals to courts, as Justice Kennedy points out. Another form circulates to the government and the public a statement of grievances with a list of signatories. This second type of petition gives voice to citizens and identifies injustices to be corrected, as Daniel Carpenter has written.[117]

114. Borough of Duryea v. Guarnieri, 564 U.S. 379, 388 (2011). The Duryea case concerned whether public employees can file lawsuits against their government employers under the First Amendment's Petition Clause.

115. 564 U.S. 379, 388.

116. U.S. Const. Amend. I.

117. Carpenter, *Democracy by Petition*, 2021.

Rights to free speech, press, and protest protect horizontal deliberation among citizens. With horizontal deliberation silenced, citizens cannot evaluate their public servants or sanction them through the pressure
of public criticism. If independent institutions for deliberative justification were eliminated, citizens could not petition courts or congressional
committees to help them remedy injustices. In the absence of deliberative justification or vertical deliberation between citizens and public
servants, citizens would be left in darkness about the reasons why their
public servants are using government power. They would cast their
votes in a vacuum, unaware of injustices committed by their officials.

Democratic Accountability and the Separation of Powers

Independent institutions have come under fire for opposing the popular
will represented by elected officials. In Poland, President Andrzej Duda
signed legislation in 2020 granting him the power to fine and dismiss
judges when he disagrees with their decisions.[118] However, this criticism
of independent institutions ignores the democratic role of courts, law
enforcement, inspectors general, audit agencies, and congressional hearings. They provide *mediated accountability*, allowing citizens to appeal to
one branch of government in holding the other branches accountable.

The separation of powers between three independent branches of
government is advocated by writers as diverse as Sun Yat-Sen, who
founded the Republic of China, and Polybius, the Greek historian of
the Roman Republic. These authors, along with Montesquieu, Madison, and Kant, understood that the separation of powers keeps at bay
a tyrannical concentration of force that would threaten the liberty of
citizens.[119] In a 1792 article, Madison counsels that power must be

118. Fryderyk Zoll and Leah Wortham, "Judicial Independence and Accountability: With-
standing Political Stress in Poland," *Fordham International Law Journal* 42 (2019): 875, 902–3;
Associated Press, "In Poland, Controversial Legislation Restricting Judiciary Is Signed into
Law," *New York Times*, February 4, 2020, https://www.nytimes.com/2020/02/04/world/europe
/Poland-judiciary-law.html.

119. Madison, "Federalist No. 47," in *Federalist*, 234: "The accumulation of all powers, legislative, executive, and judiciary, in the same hands . . . may justly be pronounced the very definition
of tyranny"; Polybius, *The Histories*, trans. W. R. Paton, rev. F. W. Walbank and Christian Habi-
cht (Cambridge, MA: Harvard University Press, 2011), book 6:345; Immanuel Kant, "Perpetual

separated into different branches of government to prevent misconduct: "Power being found by universal experience liable to abuses, a distribution of it into separate departments, has become a first principal [*sic*] of free governments."[120] These divisions of power head off the usurpation of unauthorized force: "The portion entrusted to the same hands being less, there is less room to abuse what is granted," says Madison, "and the different hands being interested, each in maintaining its own, there is less opportunity to usurp what is not granted."[121] Justice Kennedy explains the purpose of the separation of powers: "The Framers' inherent distrust of governmental power was the driving force behind the constitutional plan that allocated powers among three independent branches. This design serves not only to make Government *accountable* but also to secure individual liberty."[122]

I incorporate the separation of powers as a key component of democratic accountability. If the legislative, executive, and judicial branches were instead amassed into a single juggernaut, the government would be able to crush every effort to hold it democratically accountable. No institutions would be independent of the officials being evaluated. But

---

Peace," in *Political Writings*, 2nd ed., ed. Hans Reiss, trans. H. B. Nisbet (Cambridge, UK: Cambridge University Press, 1991), 101; and Madison, "Federalist No. 51," 251–55. Sun Yat-Sen argued that the power of government should be divided between five branches or "yuan." Besides the legislative, executive, and judicial branches, the accountability or "Control Yuan" investigates government corruption, audits the budget, and censures officials. The "Examination Yuan" scrutinizes the conduct of the civil service. Audrey Wells, *The Political Thought of Sun Yat-Sen* (New York: Palgrave Macmillan, 2001). This system has been implemented by Taiwan.

120. Madison, "Government of the United States," in *Writings of James Madison*, 91. To be precise, the separation of powers involves different branches of government exercising distinct powers. For instance, the House of Representatives, and not the president, has the power of the purse, or authority to levy taxes and spend money. The House can exert this authority to curb the usurpation of other branches of government, which depend on the House for their finances: "The power over the purse may, in fact, be regarded as the most complete and effectual weapon with which any constitution can arm the immediate representative of the people, for obtaining the redress of every grievance, and for carrying into effect every just and salutary measure." Madison, "Federalist No. 58," in *Federalist*, 285. Checks and balances, on the other hand, characterize how different branches of government can mitigate each other's abuses in a shared sphere of power. For instance in the United States, the president can check Congress by vetoing legislation, and Congress can check the president by overriding the veto by a two-thirds majority of both the House and the Senate. I thank Ian Walling for discussion of this point.

121. *Writings of James Madison*, 91.

122. Boumediene v. Bush, 553 U.S. 723, 742 (2008) (emphasis added).

when power is divided into three separate, independent branches, citizens can avail themselves of one or more of the branches to hold another branch accountable in mediated accountability. In short, there would be more entry points for democratic accountability. For example, citizens discovered President Nixon's misconduct through congressional hearings and the special prosecutor's investigation. Independent institutions are not undemocratic for opposing officials who represent the popular will. They are democratic for protecting the authority of citizens and fortifying their ability to hold their public servants democratically accountable. Independent institutions serve as the *eyes* of citizens by investigating the conduct of officials, they are the *shield* of citizens in protecting their democratic accountability rights, and they are the *sword* of citizens in helping them to sanction their officials' misconduct during office.

Democratic Accountability and the Sanction of Impeachment

Citizens can sanction an official during office with the assistance of other officials through impeachment. Presidents who face impeachment accuse the process of overriding the choice of citizens in the previous election and preempting the choice of citizens in the next one. However, if the removal of presidents who have committed rank injustices were deferred until the next election, they would be free to corrupt the voting process. This threat is greatly intensified by the power of the president, who heads federal law enforcement and the military. In an essay published in 1800, Madison relates how officials must be removable by elections, in cases where they violate their fiduciary trusts. But the power of the president necessitates the greater margin of safety that impeachment affords while she or he is on office: "The Constitution supposes that the President, the Congress, and each of its Houses, may not discharge their trusts, either from defect of judgment or other causes." Since public officials may betray the trusts of their public offices, "they are all made responsible to their constituents, at the returning periods of election; and the President, who is singly intrusted [*sic*] with very great powers, is, as a further guard, subjected to an intermediate impeachment."[123] Impeachment is a sanction available in the vulnerable years "intermediate" or between elections. At the Constitutional Convention, the Framer George Mason pressed the need for impeachment: "No point is of more importance than that the right of impeachment should be continued. Shall any man be above Justice? Above all shall that man be above it, who can commit the most extensive injustice?"[124] Mason sounded the alarm that without impeachment, an incumbent could corrupt the election, usurp the power of the presidency, and rule with impunity.

Impeachment provides mediated accountability through citizens' elected representatives. The elected House of Representatives impeaches, and the Senate, which has been popularly elected since the passage of the Seventeenth Amendment, convenes the trial and can remove the official for high crimes and misdemeanors. In Federalist 65, Hamilton defends the democratic credentials of impeachment. Impeachment is a "method of national inquest into the conduct of public men," he writes, and "who can so properly be the inquisitors for the nation as the representatives of the nation themselves?"[125]

Equal accountability sees impeachment as exerting citizens' democratic accountability rights to *evaluate* and *sanction* their officials through mediated accountability. To evaluate the actions of their public servants, citizens must know about their conduct. A justified impeachment uncovers the malfeasance of officials. The Senate has the power to sanction, forcing the malefactors to step down and barring them from serving in the future. Impeachment protects the integrity of elections. This necessary safeguard was highlighted when President Nixon's team broke into the opposition party headquarters at the Watergate hotel.

123. *Writings of James Madison*, 394. See also Hamilton, "Federalist No. 65," in *Federalist*, 317.
124. Max Farrand, ed., *Records of the Constitutional Convention of 1787*, vol. 2 (New Haven, CT: Yale University Press, 1911), 65. George Mason's speech was from July 20, 1787.
125. Hamilton, "Federalist No. 65," 318.

The Democratic Accountability Right
to Remove from Office: The Fourth Core Element

Evaluation forms the basis for citizens to decide how to exercise the fourth core aspect of democratic accountability to *remove from office* officials through elections. For citizens to freely authorize or remove their officials, the elections should act as independent institutions for democratic accountability. Institutions that are independent are not subject to the manipulation of the officials being evaluated.[126] Officials must not subvert the election's independence by disenfranchising citizens, suppressing the vote, rigging the procedures, or unjustly undercutting public confidence in the election. The independent administration of elections can help to guard elections from these threats. To govern ourselves as equal authorities, we must be able to authorize and remove our highest public servants in free and fair elections.

The democratic accountability right to remove from office reflects how the authority of officials must *depend on* citizens to continue in office. As Madison writes in Federalist 51, "A dependence on the people is, no doubt, the primary controul [*sic*] on the government."[127] I define dependence to mean that the highest officials are subject to being elected and removed by citizens. Madison maintains in Federalist 57 that regular elections enable citizens to judge whether their public servants have fulfilled their duties in the trust of public office. Officials in elections "must descend to the level from which they were raised; there forever to remain unless a faithful discharge of their trust shall have established their title to a renewal of it."[128] The Framers valued the

126. An independent official, the chief electoral officer, administers Canadian elections. The officer is usually appointed by unanimous consent from the House of Commons. Jean-Pierre Kingsley, "The Administration of Canada's Independent, Non-Partisan Approach," *Election Law Journal* 3, no. 3 (2004): 406–11. The United Kingdom, South Africa, and other countries have adopted independent election administration. Thompson supports independent election administration in Dennis F. Thompson, *Just Elections: Creating a Fair Electoral Process in the United States* (Chicago: University of Chicago Press, 2004), 177–78.

127. Madison, "Federalist No. 51," 252.

128. Madison, "Federalist No. 57," 279. Lincoln in his first inaugural address said that public servants should depend on reelection to continue in office: "By the frame of the Government under which we live this same people have wisely given their public servants but little power

dependence of officials on reelection by citizens as instrumentally preventing abuses of power. Hamilton stresses in Federalist 70 that "the
circumstances which constitute safety in the republican sense" are first,
"a due dependence on the people," and "secondly, a due responsibility."[129]

In democracy as equal accountability, the intrinsic value of the democratic relationship grounds three further reasons for why citizens should
possess the democratic accountability right to remove their officials
from office. First, citizens can only be self-governing if they have the
authority to select and replace the public servants who work for them.
Second, for citizens to be *equal* authorities, no one can possess unequal
authority in perpetually holding public office. If presidents held a lifelong appointment, they would wield permanently greater authority
than other citizens.[130] Presidents would then be enthroned over us as
kings. Third, citizens bear the democratic duty of oversight to evaluate
whether their public servants are acting justly. For citizens to be able to
act on that evaluation, they must possess the democratic accountability
right to remove their public servants from office.

The Democratic Accountability Right to Run
for Office: The Fifth Core Element

The fifth core aspect of equal accountability is the right to *run for office
and campaign for candidates.* These rights give citizens the free choice of
officials besides the incumbent's party and allow citizens to appeal for
each other's votes. The right to vote is not sufficient for a free and fair
election. Without the right to run for office and campaign, citizens
would be unable to canvass in person, knock on doors, send mail, raise

---

for mischief, and have with equal wisdom provided for the return of that little to their own
hands at very short intervals" (*Complete Works of Abraham Lincoln,* 184).

129. Hamilton, "Federalist No. 70," 342.

130. A reform ending permanent, lifetime appointments to the US Supreme Court would
be consistent with equal accountability's requirement that government officials hold public
offices limited in duration and power. This is the practice of almost every other democracy. For
instance, Australia and Japan have a mandatory retirement age of seventy for judges. Swiss and
South African justices serve terms of six years and twelve years respectively. See the US Government's Federal Judicial Center, "Judicial Tenure," accessed March 12, 2025, https://
judiciariesworldwide.fjc.gov/judicial-tenure.

funds, phone bank, hold rallies, organize political parties, and get out the vote for the candidate they support. These actions exert the democratic accountability right to run for office. For example, political science field experiments have shown that personal canvassing is the most effective measure to increase voter turnout.[131]

If citizens lacked the right to run for office, there would be two injuries to democracy. In the first case, if citizens were not allowed to run for office based on their race, gender, or ethnicity, they would lack recognition as equal authorities. For instance, the European Court of Human Rights ruled that Bosnia's constitution had discriminated by barring Jews and Roma from running for the presidency and the upper house of the legislature.[132] Similarly, the apartheid regime in South Africa forbade Black South Africans from running for office. To ensure the democratic accountability right to run for office, the new constitution for South Africa's multiracial democracy, signed by President Nelson Mandela, closely couples the right to vote with the democratic right to run for office. Article 19 provides that "every adult citizen has the right— (a) to vote in elections . . . and (b) to stand for public office and, if elected, to hold office."[133]

A second consideration is that if citizens were restricted from running for office, it would prevent the incumbent officials from being removed, nullifying our authority over them and our freedom as self-government. Madison warned during the Constitutional Convention that "a Republic may be converted into an aristocracy or oligarchy as well by limiting the number capable of being elected, as the number authorized to

131. Gerber and Green conducted a randomized field experiment of thirty thousand voters in Connecticut. They found that "voter turnout was increased substantially by personal canvassing, slightly by direct mail, and not at all by telephone calls." See Alan S. Gerber and Donald P. Green, "The Effects of Canvassing, Telephone Calls, and Direct Mail on Voter Turnout: A Direct Experiment," *American Political Science Review* 94, no. 3 (2000): 653 and Donald P. Green and Alan S. Gerber, *Get Out the Vote*, 5th ed. (Washington, DC: Brookings Institution Press, 2023).

132. Human Rights Watch, "Second Class Citizens: Discrimination against Roma, Jews, and Other National Minorities in Bosnia and Herzegovina," April 4, 2012, https://www.hrw.org /report/2012/04/04/second-class-citizens/discrimination-against-roma-jews-and-other -national.

133. South Africa, Constitution of the Republic of South Africa, December 10, 1996, https:// www.refworld.org/docid/3ae6b5de4.html.

elect."[134] In Russia, President Vladimir Putin banned Alexei Navalny, the most popular opposition candidate, from running for president.[135] Over twenty-two thousand Russians demonstrated against Putin in July 2019, protesting for the right of independent candidates to run in elections. Citizens cannot authorize or remove officials when opponents of the regime are banned from campaigning for office, losing their right to democratic accountability.

Conclusion

Martin Luther King Jr. launched the Montgomery bus boycott with a speech at the Holt Street Baptist Church. King proclaimed, "We are here in a general sense because first and foremost we are American citizens and we are determined to apply our citizenship to the fullness of its meaning."[136] He heralded our democratic right as citizens to protest: "The great glory of American democracy is the right to protest for right."[137]

A long-standing debate in democratic theory divides scholars stressing the right to vote and elections and those emphasizing other rights along with nonelectoral institutions. I argue that these two aspects of democracy must be combined. They both spring from the equal authority of citizens. Equal accountability entitles citizens to democratic accountability rights over their officials during office and in elections. King and his allies in the civil right movement held their officials

134. Max Farrand, ed., *The Records of the Federal Convention of 1787*, vol. 2 (New Haven, CT: Yale University Press, 1911), 250. The quote is from Madison's speech to the Convention on August 10, 1787.

135. Vladimir Kara-Murza, "Protests Return to Moscow as Opposition Candidates Are Banned from a Crucial Election," *Washington Post*, July 22, 2019, https://www.washingtonpost.com/opinions/2019/07/22/protests-return-moscow-opposition-candidates-are-banned-crucial-election/.

136. Martin Luther King Jr., speech at Montgomery Improvement Association Meeting at Holt Street Baptist Church, Montgomery, AL, December 5, 1955, available at the Martin Luther King, Jr. Research and Education Institute, Stanford University, https://kinginstitute.stanford.edu/king-papers/documents/mia-mass-meeting-holt-street-baptist-church.

137. King, speech at Montgomery Improvement Association Meeting.

democratically accountable *during office* through the rights of free speech, press, petition, protest, association, and the rule of law. They drew the nation's attention to racial injustice, informing how citizens cast their votes and campaigned *in elections*.

The complete set of democratic accountability rights is necessary for citizens to be freely self-governing. I offered in this chapter an original definition of freedom as self-government: *it is the liberty to be included as equal authorities in the citizenry that is governing together by holding its public servants democratically accountable.*

I specified the five core elements of equal accountability that we require to freely govern ourselves: the rights to *authorize* our public servants to hold office, the rights to *evaluate* and *sanction* their conduct during office, the rights to *remove from office* our public servants, and the rights to *run for office and campaign for candidates.* Our authority over our public servants is enhanced by mediated accountability and the separation of powers. Democratic accountability is not only instrumentally valuable in protecting us. It is also intrinsically valuable in constituting a relationship where we govern ourselves freely as the ones in charge of our government.

Through elections, we authorize officials to serve in public office. Democratic authorization gives permission for public servants to work for us in an *office* with temporary and limited powers. Public office is a trust, where the public servants use the power of government on behalf of the citizens who collectively own it. Public servants must fulfill with integrity their fiduciary duties of loyalty, care, and good faith. They must also hew to their democratic duty of fidelity to cooperate with democratic accountability and to recognize our equal authority. Their powers are limited to secure our standing as the ones ultimately in charge of our government. The limits of power in public office prevent officials from reversing the relationship of equal authority, and towering over us as unaccountable kings and masters.

Although officials exercise the authority of public office, they must *derive* that authority from the more fundamental authority of citizens to authorize their officials. To continue in office, public servants must *depend on* the authority of citizens in elections where citizens can re-move their officials, run for office, and campaign for candidates. During office, public servants must be *subject to* the authority of citizens to hold them democratically accountable by evaluating their actions and sanc-tioning their injustices. To be freely self-governing citizens, we must possess the full array of our democratic accountability rights.

3

The Duties of Democratic Accountability

The most important office, and the one which all of us can and should fill, is that of private citizen. The duties of the office of private citizen cannot under a republican form of government be neglected without serious injury to the public.

—SUPREME COURT JUSTICE LOUIS BRANDEIS[1]

IN 1780 ELIZABETH FREEMAN attended a public gathering in Massachusetts that changed the course of her life and the history of her state. Freeman, who was known then as Mum Bett, was an African American woman enslaved by John and Hannah Ashley. Colonel Ashley had hosted the signing of the Sheffield Resolves in 1773. The Resolves opposed British colonialism, proclaiming that "mankind in a state of nature are equal, free, and independent of each other, and have a right to the undisturbed enjoyment of their lives, their liberty and property."[2] These words professed a right to freedom and equality, but they were

1. Quoted in Alpheus Thomas Mason, *Brandeis: A Free Man's Life* (New York: Viking Press, 1946), 122.
2. Xiomara Santamarina, "Freeman, Elizabeth," in *African American Lives*, ed. Henry Louis Gates Jr. and Evelyn Brooks Higgenbotham (New York: Oxford University Press, 2004), 317. On the Sheffield Resolves or Sheffield Declaration, see Mark Somos, *American States of Nature* (New York: Oxford University Press, 2019), 236–37.

signed in the Ashley house, the site of human enslavement and degrada-
tion. Bett carried a deep scar on her arm after she was burned shielding
her sister from a fire-heated shovel swung by Hannah Ashley.[3]

After the Revolutionary War, Bett listened to the Declaration of
Independence and the new Massachusetts Constitution read publicly
in the town of Sheffield.[4] The Massachusetts Constitution set forth
that "all men are born free and equal, and have certain natural, essential,
and unalienable rights."[5] Hearing the new state constitution and the
Declaration of Independence sparked an epiphany in Bett. She contacted two lawyers, Theodore Sedgwick, who had signed the Sheffield
Resolves, and Tapping Reeve, the founder of the first law school in the
United States. "I heard that paper read yesterday, that says, all men are
created equal," said Bett. "Won't the law give me my freedom?"[6]

Sedgwick and Reeve sued in court for the emancipation of Bett and
her fellow slave Brom. The County Court of Common Pleas in Great
Barrington heard their case, *Brom and Bett v. Ashley*, in August 1781.[7]
More than one in fifty state residents were enslaved at the time.[8]
Standing before the court, Sedgwick and Reeve argued that the Massachusetts Constitution had ended slavery when it proclaimed that "all
men are born free and equal."[9]

In a transformative decision, the citizens serving on the jury set Bett
and Brom free, awarding compensation for their unpaid labor. The *Brom*

3. Santamarina, "Freeman, Elizabeth," 317.
4. James Oliver Horton and Lois E. Horton, *Slavery and the Making of America* (New York: Oxford University Press, 2005), 66.
5. Massachusetts Constitution, part 1, article I, accessed March 12, 2025, https://malegislature .gov/laws/constitution.
6. Sari Edelstein, "Good Mother, Farewell: Elizabeth Freeman's Silence and the Stories of Mumbet," *New England Quarterly* 92, no. 4 (2017): 584–614.
7. Brom and Bett v. Ashley, May 28, 1781, Inferior Court of Pleas, Great Barrington, MA, *Supreme Judicial Court Record Books*, Massachusetts Archives, Boston; Massachusetts Court System, "Massachusetts Constitution and the Abolition of Slavery," March 11, 2025, https://www .mass.gov/guides/massachusetts-constitution-and-the-abolition-of-slavery.
8. Edgar Allan Toppin, *A Biographical History of Blacks in America since 1528* (New York: McKay, 1971), 45.
9. Massachusetts Constitution, part 1, article I. Reeve went on to serve as the chief justice of the Supreme Court of Connecticut. Theodore Sedgwick later became a US senator, speaker of the House of Representatives, judge on the Massachusetts Supreme Judicial Court, and ances-
tor of the actress Kyra Sedgwick.

and Bett case laid the basis for the Massachusetts Supreme Judicial Court's ruling that abolished slavery throughout the state in 1783.[10] To celebrate her emancipation, Bett chose a new name for herself: Elizabeth Freeman. After her liberation, Freeman raised a family. One of her descendants was the renowned civil rights advocate and writer, W.E.B. Du Bois. Born in the same town, Great Barrington, Massachusetts, where *Brom and Bett* was decided, he later cofounded the NAACP.[11]

The Freeman case raises the question of whether citizens have duties in democratic accountability. Do citizens bear any responsibilities regarding how they use their democratic accountability rights? Should they hold their public servants democratically accountable for recognizing the freedom and equality of all citizens? For example, Massachusetts citizens prevailed upon their state representatives in 1865 to ratify the Thirteenth Amendment to the US Constitution prohibiting slavery nationwide.

The duties of democratic accountability are often overlooked, because writers focus on democratic rights, especially the vote. In chapter 2, we saw that to be freely self-governing, we must possess a more expansive set of rights and institutions. For example, Freeman sought her liberty using the democratic accountability right to the rule of law, and Du Bois relied on the freedom of association to establish the NAACP.

In this chapter, we will explore how democratic accountability depends on *duties*. These are democratic in protecting our democratic rights and our ability to participate in self-government. Rights alone are not sufficient for democracy. The question is: How can our democratic accountability rights be protected when they are endangered by officials or other citizens? These are the threats to self-government from elected authoritarians and factions. How can we use our rights when we lack the resources or education to exercise them? This is the threat to self-government from powerlessness.

---

10. *Commonwealth of Massachusetts v. Nathaniel Jennison* (1783), reprinted in Paul Finkelman, *The Law of Freedom and Bondage: A Casebook* (New York: Oceana, 1986), 35–37.

11. "Freeman, Elizabeth," 318. W.E.B. Du Bois worked closely with his colleagues Ida B. Wells, Mary White Ovington, and Moorfield Storey to found the NAACP.

This chapter brings to light three sets of duties that are vital to democratic accountability. First, we bear the *democratic duty of oversight* to hold our public servants democratically accountable for using the power of our government justly. This duty applies to the *vertical relation* that flows downward from us to our public servants. As self-governing citizens, we collectively own the power of government to enact and enforce laws and employ public servants to use that power. Since our public servants work for us, we should make sure they are exercising power justly on our behalf. When they commit injustices, we should speak up, protest, petition, organize associations, campaign for candidates, and vote for new public servants who will pursue justice with integrity.

The second democratic responsibility is the *duty of solidarity*. When we act in solidarity, we *recognize* the equal authority of our fellow citizens by respecting it in our actions, protecting it from threats, and empowering it with the resources to participate in democracy. Solidarity applies to the horizontal relation among citizens. We should *respect* our fellow citizens by not committing direct injustices in our own actions. We should also respect our fellow citizens by not perpetrating the mediated injustice of inducing our officials into violating rights. To *protect* our fellow citizens from elected authoritarians and factions, we should hold our public servants democratically accountable for passing and enforcing laws that defend the marginalized.

I offer three arguments for the duty of solidarity, where we come to the aid of citizens facing injustice. First, solidarity *secures rights* for all citizens. Second, citizens who act in solidarity create a democratic relationship where all citizens *freely govern themselves*. The third argument for solidarity is that when we protect one another, we *support the self-respect* of our fellow citizens.

The empowerment component of solidarity contrasts markedly with Madisonian views. I emphasize that formal democratic accountability rights in the Constitution and laws are important but not enough. No one should be excluded from democracy by the powerlessness of poverty or the lack of education. For example, prior to the ratification of the Twenty-Fourth Amendment in 1964, African Americans who had the right to vote on paper could not cast a ballot if they could not pay a poll tax.[12] They cannot participate today if they cannot afford transportation to the voting booth, or if they are denied a civic education to know about their democratic rights and duties. I explain in this chapter that we should *empower* citizens with a strong civic education, campaign finance reform, legal aid, access to the vote, and a social minimum, all so that we have the resources to wield our democratic accountability rights as substantive, real freedoms.

Alongside the duties of solidarity and oversight, the third democratic responsibility is the *duty of fidelity*. It requires public servants to cooperate with democratic accountability and to recognize our equal authority. The duty of fidelity is vertical and flows upward from public servants to citizens. They should use the power of their office to guard us against the threats to self-government from elected authoritarians, factions, and powerlessness. When officials are derelict in this duty, they allow injustices to run rampant against vulnerable citizens. A tragic example is the lynching of more than four thousand African Americans since the late nineteenth century.[13] Congress abdicated its duty of fidelity, failing more than two hundred times to enact anti-lynching legislation until 2022.[14] Our public servants should heed their duty of fidelity and pass legislation, like the Emmett Till Antilynching Act, to protect the marginalized.[15] When we fulfill our duties of oversight and solidarity and ensure that our public servants act with fidelity, we free all citizens to govern themselves, including Elizabeth Freeman and her descendants.

12. U.S. Const. amend. XXIV. The amendment prohibited poll taxes in federal primaries or elections.

13. Steven Inskeep and Kelsey Snell, "Congress Passes an Anti-Lynching Bill after More than a Century of Trying," NPR, March 8, 2022, https://www.npr.org/2022/03/08/1085099926/congress-passes-an-anti-lynching-bill-after-more-than-a-century-of-trying.

14. Erin B. Logan, "Why Congress Failed Nearly 200 Times to Make Lynching a Federal Crime," *Washington Post*, July 5, 2018, https://www.washingtonpost.com/news/retropolis/wp/2018/07/05/how-congress-failed-nearly-200-times-to-make-lynching-a-federal-crime/. The Senate has been directly elected by citizens since the Seventeenth Amendment was ratified in 1913.

15. Pub. L. 117–107. Inskeep and Snell, "Congress Passes an Anti-Lynching Bill."

The Urgency of the Democratic Duties of Citizens

Supreme Court Justice Louis Brandeis said, "The most important office, and the one which all of us can and should fill, is that of private
citizen. The duties of the office of private citizen cannot under a republican form of government be neglected without serious injury to the
public."[16] Brandeis's quote invites us to ask: What are the duties of the
office of citizen? Why would it seriously injure the public to neglect
them?

It might be assumed that democratic duties for citizens are unneces-
sary, because institutions are sufficient to protect rights, without the
active participation of ordinary citizens. In Federalist 51, Madison wrote
that "the constant aim is to divide and arrange the several offices in such
a manner as that each may be a check on the other that the private interest of every individual may be a sentinel over the public rights."[17] The
ambition of officials from each branch staves off the amassing of power
by the other branches.

Later in his career, Madison came to see, under the impact of the
Sedition Act's stifling suppression of speech and the press, that institutions alone do not raise a sufficient barrier against abuses of power. The
vigilance of citizens is necessary to stand guard on the ramparts of institutions. Together with Jefferson, he founded a political party that
organized citizens to overturn the Sedition Act and bring its candidates
to power in the next election.[18] Madison realized the paramount role
of citizens:

> In bestowing the eulogies due to the partitions and internal checks
> of power, it ought not the less to be remembered, that they are
> neither the sole nor the chief palladium of constitutional liberty.
> The people who are the authors of this blessing, must also be its
> guardians.[19]

16. Mason, *Brandeis*, 122.
17. Madison, "Federalist No. 51," 252–53.
18. Sedition Act, 1 Stat. 596 (1798).
19. James Madison, "Government of the United States," for the *National Gazette*, February 4,
1792, in *Writings of James Madison*, 93. The word *palladium*, meaning "safeguard," is derived from
the statue of Pallas Athena said to watch over the city of Troy, and later Rome.

It is revealing that Madison came to herald citizens as the *chief* guardians of liberty. I regard the union of our democratic duties and institutions as the guarantor of our liberties. The democratic duties of citizens are indispensable because institutions are not self-executing machines. They are staffed by and respond to citizens. If those who operate institutions or influence them harbor a hostility to rights, their enmity will be translated into the blunt impact of institutions on the marginalized. Equal accountability combines institutions for democratic accountability and the democratic duties of citizens to secure our freedom as self-government. Whether we are faithful to our democratic duties will determine if we descend down the sinister road of Jim Crow or progress up the brighter path of the Civil Rights Movement.

I argue that the office of the citizen includes two types of responsibilities to participate in democratic accountability. The first is the *duty of oversight*, which calls on citizens to ensure their public servants use the power of government justly. This is a *principal-agent duty* that citizens should exercise over their public servants or agents.[20] An agent is a person who works for the principal. The Massachusetts Constitution refers to citizens as the principals who are in charge of their officials: "All power residing originally in the people, and being derived from them, the several magistrates and officers of government . . . are their substitutes and *agents*, and are at all times *accountable to them*."[21] The second responsibility of citizens is the *democratic duty of solidarity*. This is a *principal-principal duty* that citizens owe to each other.[22]

20. The prevailing interpretation of the principal-agent model of democratic accountability detaches principals from any democratic duties. I reformulate the principal-agent model as a *citizen–public servant model*. Citizens and public servants bear more demanding duties than ordinary principals and agents (such as clients and their accountants), because citizens and public servants wield the coercive power of government, which can injure or kill if misused. Citizens and public servants are therefore special types of principals and agents who occupy *offices* attached to democratic duties and limits on coercive power.

21. Massachusetts Constitution, part 1, article V (emphasis added).

22. In theorizing about principal-principal duties, I benefited greatly from Theodora Welch's work on principal-principal problems in corporate governance. Theodora Welch, "Effects of Privatization Transaction Strategy on Performance: An Examination of Large-Block Shareholding and Hybrid Governance Structures in Developing Economies" (PhD diss., Concordia University, 2002). The standard view of privatization prefers privatizing state-owned companies to a small number of large-shareholders or owners. A small number of owners would more easily

The distinction between these two types of responsibilities is that *principal-agent duties of oversight* focus on the vertical relation that flows downward from citizens to the public servants they employ. In this perspective, citizens should verify that their public servants are using the coercive power of government justly. *Principal-principal duties of solidarity* apply to the horizontal relation among citizens. We fulfill our duties of solidarity when we *recognize* the equal authority of all citizens. These duties are especially urgent in the case of marginalized citizens. For all citizens to be included in self-government, we must act in solidarity to end their marginalization.[23] Our public servants, in turn, owe us *agent-principal duties of fidelity*. This is the obligation to cooperate with democratic accountability and enact and enforce laws that respect, protect, and empower our equal authority.

The duties of democratic accountability often receive short shrift compared to democratic rights. But the tendency to shunt aside democratic duties neglects that the defining feature of rights is that they are entitlements imposing correlative duties. A right differs from a merely desirable benefit. For instance, it would be a windfall if you received a private airplane from the government. But you would have no right to it. The government does you no wrong if it abstains from providing you the gift of a private jet. But if officials deprive you of the right to free association or the vote as an adult, they would be negating one of your rights. They would be blameworthy for violating a duty they owe to you. A right imposes *correlative duties* on other people.[24] Rights and duties

coordinate together to monitor the company's management. The common assumption is that owners monitoring managers would solve the principal-agent problem that managers, the agents, might act against the interests of the owners, the principals. Against this view, Welch proposes and empirically confirms that privatizing to a greater number of owners is a superior strategy. The larger number of owners makes it more difficult for a few owners to collude in acting against the interests of the other principals, such as by diverting value from the firm to their own personal use.

23. Iris Marion Young defines marginalization as being excluded from a society's economy, especially the labor market: see *Justice and the Politics of Difference*, 53. Inspired by Young, I use the term *marginalization* to refer to exclusion, but I focus specifically on exclusion from democratic government.

24. On rights imposing duties, see Leif Wenar, "The Nature of Claim-Rights," *Ethics* 123, no. 2 (2013): 202–29; Henry Shue, *Basic Rights*, 2nd ed. (Princeton, NJ: Princeton University Press, 1996); and Wesley Hohfeld, *Fundamental Legal Conceptions*, ed. Walter Wheeler Cook (New

correlate because the "existence of one necessarily implies the existence of the other."[25] For there to be a right, there must be duties.

Three types of duties correlate with rights. First, the right imposes duties on both public servants and other citizens to *respect* or not to abuse it in their own actions. Second, the right correlates with duties for citizens and public servants to *protect* the entitlement from being violated by others. Third, the right imposes the correlative duty to *empower* the entitlement by providing the resources and conditions to exercise it. I combine these three correlative duties under the heading of the responsibility to *secure* rights. Substantive rights regard how we are treated by the government. Procedural rights pertain to whether we can participate democratically in our government. When our procedural democratic accountability rights and our substantive human rights are equally secure, we are *recognized* as equal authorities in the citizenry, and not marginalized as second-class citizens.

Citizens' Duties of Oversight

The principal-agent duties of oversight are grounded in how citizens collectively own the power of government and employ public servants to wield it on their behalf. The danger of government power is that it coerces by imposing or threatening force.[26] The government of a state is the institution that claims the sole right to enforce laws within its territory.[27] If people transgress the law, the government asserts that it alone has the right to arrest and punish them, and to impose the coercion of the police to compel compliance.

Haven, CT: Yale University Press, 1923), chaps. 1–2. A right secured by law is a legal or positive right. A right that ought to be guaranteed by law is a moral right. For instance, the right against being enslaved is a moral right. The right against slavery was guaranteed as a legal right when the United States ratified the Thirteenth Amendment to the Constitution in 1865.

25. Henry Black, *A Law Dictionary*, 2nd ed. (St. Paul, MN: West Publishing, 1910), 277.

26. Jane Mansbridge, "What Is Political Science For?" *Perspectives on Politics* 12, no. 1 (2014): 8–17. For a perspicuous discussion of coercion, see Alan Wertheimer, *Coercion* (Princeton, NJ: Princeton University Press, 1987). Wertheimer regards a threat as coercive when it violates rights, making the targets worse off than they should (217).

27. Max Weber, "Politics as a Vocation," in *From Max Weber: Essays in Sociology*, ed. H. H. Gerth and C. Wright Mills (New York: Routledge, 1998), 78.

There may be cases, all things considered, where it might be just to coerce someone. H.L.A. Hart and Immanuel Kant write that it could be just or morally legitimate in cases where it is necessary to stop an assault.[28] The "governance dilemma," as Robert Keohane puts it, is that government coercion is needed to protect our rights from being denied by others, but it is also a leading threat to those rights.[29] The same power that pulls over drunk drivers and prevents them from causing accidents can also threaten the lives and liberty of innocent Black drivers.[30] In his "Letter from a Birmingham Jail," Martin Luther King Jr. rebukes police chief Bull Connor for unleashing "dogs sinking their teeth into unarmed, nonviolent Negroes."[31]

We will see how we must reform and limit the state's police powers to guarantee equal accountability for all citizens. Democratic accountability is inhibited when we fear reprisals for protesting, associating, or voting. The understanding is beginning to emerge that we must redress the racially discriminatory injustices inflicted by the state's coercive powers. I offer *democratic* reasons for these reforms. The marginalized must be protected from discrimination to secure their standing as equal authorities in democracy. Citizens should hold their public servants democratically accountable for removing these obstacles to self-government.

To see how much is at stake in our democratic duties, consider that African American are 75 percent more likely to be charged with a crime

28. Immanuel Kant, *Metaphysics of Morals*, trans. Mary Gregor, ed. Lara Denis (Cambridge, UK: Cambridge University Press, 2017) 28 [6:231]; H.L.A. Hart, "Are There Any Natural Rights?" *Philosophical Review* 64 (1955): 175.

29. Rawls states the need for government coercion: "The supposed alternative to the government's so-called monopoly on power allows private violence for those with the will and the means to exercise it" (*Law of Peoples*, 26n22). On the governance dilemma, see Robert Keohane, "Governance in a Partially Globalized World," *American Political Science Review* 95, no. 1 (2001): 1–13.

30. The fear that this power induces, when applied with a racial bias, is recounted in harrowing terms by an African American physician in Christopher Thomas Veal, "At the Intersection of Fear, Grief, and Love," *Annals of Internal Medicine*, November 17, 2020, https://www.acpjournals.org/doi/10.7326/M20-4113.

31. King, "Letter from Birmingham Jail." Bull Connor, the Birmingham, Alabama, police chief, sent "dogs and fire hoses to break up civil rights demonstrations." See Associated Press, "Eugene 'Bull' Connor Dies at 75; Police Head Fought Integration," *New York Times*, March 11, 1976.

carrying a mandatory minimum sentence than a white defendant who commits the same offence.[32] Even when they are charged with the identical crime, African Americans are punished with longer prison terms. The United States Sentencing Commission reports that African Americans receive federal prison sentences that are 20 percent longer than those inflicted on white citizens, even when controlling for their prior criminal records.[33] W.E.B. Du Bois documented similar injustices in his time: "Daily the Negro is coming more and more to look upon law and justice, not as protecting safeguards, but as sources of humiliation and oppression. The laws are made by men who have little interest in him; they are executed by men who have absolutely no motive for treating the black people with courtesy or consideration."[34] Should citizens participate in democratic accountability to correct these outright injustices?

A tempting misconception is to assume that citizens are absolved of any role in injustice. In this view, citizens can wash their hands of unjust acts by their government, since the abuses are committed by officials, and not themselves. Such a stance recalls a passage from Marcel Proust's celebrated novel, *Remembrance of Things Past*. The narrator comments, "In my cowardice I became at once a man, and did what all we grown men do when face to face with suffering and injustice: I preferred not to see them."[35]

The excuse runs aground, however, because the coercive power of government is not inflicted by a distant third party with no connection with citizens. I argue that the collective ownership of government power confers on citizens the duty of oversight to hold their public servants democratically accountable for using that power justly.

32. Sonja Starr and M. Marit Rehavi, "Racial Disparity in Federal Criminal Sentences," *Journal of Political Economy* 122, no. 6 (2014): 1320–54.

33. United States Sentencing Commission, *Demographic Differences in Sentencing* (Washington, DC: United States Sentencing Commission, 2017), https://www.ussc.gov/sites/default/files/pdf/research-and-publications/research-publications/2017/20171114_Demographics.pdf.

34. W.E.B. Du Bois, *The Souls of Black Folk* (New York: Routledge, 2016), 94.

35. Marcel Proust, *Remembrance of Things Past*, vol. 1, trans. C. K. Scott Moncrieff (Hertfordshire, UK: Wordsworth Editions, 2006), 33.

How Citizens Should Hold Their Public Servants Democratically Accountable

How should citizens meet their duty of oversight? One way is through campaigning for candidates and voting in elections. Attorney General Merrick Garland announced renewed efforts by the Department of Justice Civil Rights Division to defend the right to vote. Garland declared that "the right to vote is the cornerstone of our democracy, the right from which all other rights ultimately flow."[36] I regard voting not only as a right, but as a duty. In elections, citizens should authorize public servants who will use power justly, and remove those who have imposed it unjustly.

Citizens should further fulfill their duty of oversight by holding their public servants democratically accountable *during office*. As President Barack Obama said, "For this democracy to endure, it requires our active citizenship and sustained focus on the issues—not just in an election season, but all the days in between. Our democracy needs all of us more than ever."[37] I maintain that between elections, citizens should hold their public servants democratically accountable through their freedom of speech, press, protest, petition, association, and other rights.

One of the purposes of protest is to rouse the conscience of fellow citizens, the media, and public servants around issues of injustice.[38] For example, freedom of protest and association permitted the NAACP, United Auto Workers union, National Urban League, and John Lewis's Student Nonviolent Coordinating Committee to organize the 1963

36. Merrick Garland, "Attorney General Merrick B. Garland Delivered a Policy Address Regarding Voting Rights," Department of Justice, Washington, DC, June 11, 2021, https://www
.justice.gov/opa/speech/attorney-general-merrick-b-garland-delivers-remarks-announcing
-lawsuit-against-state.

37. Quoted in Lynn Sweet, "Illinois Reacts to Joe Biden-Kamala Harris White House Win,"
Chicago Sun-Times, November 7, 2020, https://chicago.suntimes.com/elections/2020/11/7
/21554154/illinois-reacts-joe-biden-kamala-harris-white-house-win-president-trump.

38. Research by the political scientist Omar Wasow has found that minorities can leverage nonviolent protests "to capture the attention of the media and overcome political asymmetries." Peaceful protests, Wasow writes, "particularly when met with state or vigilante repression, drove media coverage, framing, congressional speech, and public opinion on civil rights." Omar Wasow, "Agenda Seeding: How 1960s Block Protests Moved Elites, Public Opinion and Voting,"
American Political Science Review 114, no. 3 (2020): 638.

March on Washington for Jobs and Freedom. It was the largest civil rights protest in the United States up to that date. A quarter million citizens demonstrated against racial segregation. The protest honored the hundredth anniversary of President Lincoln's Emancipation Proclamation, which had freed slaves in the South during the Civil War.[39] Speaking on the steps of the Lincoln Memorial, King embraced racial equality in his resonant "I Have a Dream" speech.[40]

Coverage of the march in the press and other media set off a groundswell of public support, convincing Congress to pass the watershed 1964 Civil Rights Act, which bans discrimination in public accommodations, public education, and federally assisted programs. It was followed up by the 1965 Voting Rights Act, which shields the vote from racial discrimination by both factions of other citizens and elected authoritarian officials.[41] Furthermore, the effort by vigilant and vocal citizens to secure the vote persuaded three-quarters of the states to ratify the Twenty-Fourth Amendment to the Constitution, which came into force in 1964. The amendment protects the right to vote from poll taxes, which had disempowered African Americans from voting for decades. As can be seen through this example, when citizens protest for racial equality, voting rights, and other issues of justice, they act on their democratic duty of oversight. Citizens evaluate whether their public servants are using power justly, and they sanction unjust officials. Citizens are also acting on their democratic duty of solidarity to safeguard their fellow citizens from marginalization.

39. Lucy G. Barber, *Marching on Washington: The Forging of an American Political Tradition* (Berkeley: University of California Press, 2002).

40. Martin Luther King Jr., "I Have a Dream," speech delivered in Washington, DC, August 28, 1963, available from NPR, https://www.npr.org/2010/01/18/122701268/i-have-a-dream-speech-in-its-entirety.

41. Civil Rights Act of 1964, Pub. L. 88-352 and Voting Rights Act of 1965, Pub. L. 89-110. U.S. Const. Amend. XV stipulates that the right to vote must not be denied on the basis of race, and U.S. Const. Amend. XIX provides that the right to vote must not be denied on the basis of sex. Section 2 of the Voting Rights Act protects the right to vote against state and local officials. Section 11 prohibits individuals from intimidating, threatening, or coercing voters. Kevin J. Coleman, *Voting Rights Act of 1965: Background and Overview* (Washington, DC: Congressional Research Service, 2015), 13, https://crsreports.congress.gov/product/pdf/R/R43626/15.

In meeting these duties, citizens should speak up through their freedom of speech and the press to hold their officials democratically accountable. Justice Brandeis laid great stress on how freedom of speech and the press are not only rights, but democratic duties. In *Whitney v. California*, Justice Brandeis wrote, "Those who won our independence believed that . . . in its government, the deliberative forces should prevail over the arbitrary, . . . that the greatest menace to freedom is an inert people; that public discussion is a political duty, and that this should be a fundamental principle of American government."[42] In equal accountability, the greatest menace to freedom is an inert people, because citizens who are silent will leave their officials unaccountable. Officials can then inflict injustices on the marginalized with impunity.

The Supreme Court later cited Justice Brandeis's opinion in its landmark decision on freedom of the press, *New York Times v. Sullivan*.[43] The *Times* had published an advertisement by the Committee to Defend Martin Luther King and the Struggle for Freedom in the South. The advertisement admonished the Montgomery police for its violent retribution against King and other civil rights protestors. The city's public safety commissioner sued the *Times* for defamation. The court ruled that newspapers are not liable for defamation against officials unless the statement was made with actual malice, or intent to harm by deception. Writing for a unanimous court, Justice William Brennan acclaimed the "citizen critic of the government."

It is as much his [the citizen's] duty to criticize as it is the official's duty to administer. As Madison said, "the censorial power is in the

42. Whitney v. California, 274 U.S. 357, 375 (1927) (Brandeis, J., concurring). The *Whitney* case concerned the punishment of Charlotte Anita Whitney for membership in the Communist Party. Whitney was convicted under the 1919 California Criminal Syndicalism Act, which had banned advocating the overthrow of the government. The court held that Whitney's free speech rights had not been violated by the Criminal Syndicalism Act. While Justice Brandeis wrote an opinion concurring on narrow grounds, he articulated more broadly one of the court's most resounding defenses of freedom of speech, which led to Whitney's pardon by the governor of California. On *Whitney*, see Geoffrey Stone, *Perilous Times* (New York: W. W. Norton, 2004), 237. The governor's pardon quoted from Justice Brandeis's opinion. See Haig A. Bosmajian, *Anita Whitney, Louis Brandeis, and the First Amendment* (Madison, NJ: Farleigh Dickinson University Press, 2010), 125.

43. New York Times v. Sullivan, 376 U.S. 254, 282 (1964).

people over the Government, and not in the Government over the people." It would give public servants an unjustified preference over the public they serve, if critics of official conduct did not have a fair equivalent of the immunity granted to the officials themselves.[44]

Justice Brandeis's and Justice Brennan's Supreme Court opinions are bedrocks of First Amendment jurisprudence. But they left open *why* citizens should deliberate about their government. Why is it "as much [the citizen's] duty to criticize as it is the official's duty to administer," as Brennan thought?

I answer that criticizing unjust officials is part of citizens' democratic duty of oversight. Citizens evaluate the justice of their public servants' actions by deliberating with one another through public discussion. After this evaluation uncovers injustices, citizens should voice their criticism to sanction the officials through freedom of speech and the press. The "censorial power" of citizens, as Madison calls it, brings unjust officials "into disrepute or contempt."[45] In addition to naming and shaming unjust officials, deliberation can make the more just public servants aware of the need for reforms. The duty of citizens to participate democratically includes the responsibility to contact their representatives. Studies find that representatives are more responsive to citizens who contact them more frequently.[46] Accordingly, citizens should petition their representatives to protect the marginalized against discrimination and violence.

44. *New York Times v. Sullivan* (internal quotation marks and citations omitted). The "immunity granted to the officials" protects public servants from being sued for libel when speaking in their official capacity. Brennan holds that citizens are entitled to a parallel immunity against being sued for libel when criticizing their public servants.

45. Quoted in New York Times v. Sullivan, 376 U.S. 254, 293. On Brennan's political thought, see Frank Michelman, *Brennan and Democracy* (Princeton, NJ: Princeton University Press, 1999).

46. The study implies that the contacts between representatives and their constituents should be made more equitable. Representatives systematically overestimate the extent their constituents hold conservative preferences, because conservatives are more likely to contact their representatives. David E. Broockman and Christopher Skovron, "Bias in Perceptions of Public Opinion among Political Elites," *American Political Science Review* 112, no. 3 (2018): 542–63. This finding has been replicated in an international dataset: Jean-Benoit Pilet et al., "Do Politicians Outside the United States Also Think Voters Are More Conservative Than They Really Are?" *American Political Science Review* 118, no. 2 (2024): 1037–45.

The Duties of Solidarity That Citizens Owe Each Other

The second type of democratic duty consists of the responsibilities that citizens owe one another. I call these *duties of solidarity*, or principal-principal duties. The principal-principal standpoint focuses on the horizontal relation among citizens as the principals or ultimate authorities in democracy. Do they *protect* one another from injustice by participating in democratic accountability? Do they *respect* each other's equal authority in their own actions? Do they *empower* the marginalized with the resources and civic education needed to exercise their democratic accountability rights? When citizens recognize one another's equal authority by respecting, protecting, and empowering it, they fulfill their duty of solidarity.

Solidarity secures freedom and equality for our fellow citizens. Even when we are not the ones directly oppressed, we should hold our government democratically accountable for its treatment of other citizens. King sounded a clarion call for citizens to act in solidarity:

> I cannot sit idly by in Atlanta and not be concerned about what happens in Birmingham. Injustice anywhere is a threat to justice everywhere. We are caught in an inescapable network of mutuality, tied in a single garment of destiny. Whatever affects one directly, affects all indirectly. . . . Anyone who lives inside the United States can never be considered an outsider anywhere within its bounds.[47]

King's "network of mutuality" is epitomized in the duty of solidarity, where we join the marginalized "as active partners in the struggle for freedom."[48]

Democratic Duties of Solidarity Protect Rights

The duties of solidarity are fundamental for three reasons. First, solidarity protects rights. The voices and votes of a broad coalition of citizens are necessary for reforms that secure the rights of the marginalized. For

47. King, "Letter from Birmingham Jail."
48. King, "Letter from Birmingham Jail."

example, citizens of every sexual orientation worked together in solidarity to legalize same-sex marriage and outlaw discrimination against LGBT citizens.[49]

To alleviate injustices, citizens should participate in democratic accountability, even when they are not the ones who are being unjustly coerced or neglected. If a broad set of citizens were apathetic and aloof bystanders, it would leave the marginalized isolated and abandoned.[50] Citizens should speak out against injustices, protest, petition their public servants, organize in associations, and vote in elections for change. The marginalized citizens who suffer injustices may comprise a numerical minority at the moment, but they can mobilize a politically effective majority when their fellow citizens join hands with them in solidarity.[51]

King appealed to his fellow citizens in his "I Have a Dream" speech at the March on Washington for Jobs and Freedom: "Many of our white brothers, as evidenced by their presence here today, have come to realize that their destiny is tied up with our destiny. And they have come to realize that their freedom is inextricably bound to our freedom. *We cannot walk alone.*"[52] King expressed the determination that we must not leave the marginalized stranded when they face injustice. The duty of

49. A powerful defense of same-sex marriage is Steven Macedo, *Just Married* (Princeton, NJ: Princeton University Press, 2015). The Supreme Court upheld the right of same-sex couples to marry in Obergefell v. Hodges, 576 U.S. 644 (2015), and it protected LBGT employees from discrimination in Bostock v. Clayton County, 590 U.S. 644 (2020). These efforts were strengthened by the advocacy of civil associations supporting LGBT citizens.

50. The idea that democracy includes a relationship between citizens has an antecedent in the "civic friendship" that Danielle Allen and John Rawls describe. Danielle Allen, *Talking to Strangers: Anxieties of Citizenship since Brown v. Board of Education* (Chicago: University of Chicago Press, 2004), 129. I thank Jackie Basu for discussion on this topic. On civic friendship, see Rawls, *Theory of Justice*, 90, 205; idem, *Justice as Fairness*, ed. Erin Kelly (Cambridge, MA: Harvard University Press, 2001), 126; idem, *Political Liberalism* (New York: Columbia University Press, 2005), 252, 465. Allen and Rawls view civic friendship as an equal sharing of the benefits and burdens of social cooperation. In my version, civic friendship is a relationship among citizens where they act in solidarity, participating democratically to protect each other from injustice.

51. On how citizens can protect each other's dignity, see Josiah Ober, "Democracy's Dignity," *American Political Science Review* 106, no. 4 (2012), 827–46. I would call the duty to protect one another's dignity a democratic duty of solidarity. I thank Jim Morone for discussion of the role of citizens in protecting the rights of the marginalized.

52. King, "I Have a Dream" (emphasis added).

solidarity marshals a coalition of citizens who stand shoulder to shoulder to fight for each other's freedom and equality.

To be clear, the idea of solidarity does not mean that other citizens can substitute for the participation of the marginalized.[53] The duty of solidarity requires us to protect and empower the ability of the marginalized themselves to participate democratically. My point is that marginalized citizens are more likely to vindicate their rights if their fellow citizens join them in solidarity, since winning elections requires assembling broad coalitions of voters and supporters.

Solidarity Constitutes a Freely Self-Governing Relationship among Citizens

The second reason for solidarity is that it creates a freely self-governing relationship among citizens. The Freedom Charter of Nelson Mandela's African National Congress sets forth how citizens must be included in government to be self-governing: "The People Shall Govern! Every man and woman shall have the right to vote for and to stand as a candidate for all bodies which make laws; All people shall be entitled to take part in the administration of the country; The rights of the people shall be the same, regardless of race, colour or sex."[54] Equal accountability agrees with the Freedom Charter that to be self-governing, citizens must possess both equal political rights and equal substantive rights. Otherwise, they are treated as second-class citizens who are marginalized in democracy. I argue that to create a free, self-governing relationship, citizens should act in solidarity. It is crucial that they hold their public servants democratically accountable for enacting and enforcing laws that recognize all citizens as equal authorities. This creates a relationship where all citizens are included in democracy as the ones in charge of their government.

53. I thank Eric Cheng for raising this question at the Western Political Science Association Conference.

54. United Nations Centre against Apartheid, *The Freedom Charter of South Africa* (New York: United Nations Centre against Apartheid, 1987), 3.

Solidarity Affirms the Self-Respect of Citizens in the Message It Expresses

The third reason for the duty of solidarity is the message it expresses. Solidarity publicly affirms the self-respect of citizens, or the sense of their own worth. In the absence of solidarity, other citizens would forsake us and turn away if we were struck down by injustice. They would behave as if our lives were beneath noticing or not worth helping, like the protagonist in Ralph Ellison's *Invisible Man*: "I am invisible, understand, simply because people refuse to see me."[55] Our self-respect would wither under this callous indifference toward our freedom and equality. Citizens who assist us in solidarity send the message that we are seen and matter, confirming and cultivating a lively sense of our self-worth.[56] The democratic duty of solidarity is intrinsically valuable in the message it sends and the freely self-governing relationship it constitutes.

The Duty to Respect: Avoiding Direct and Mediated Injustices

Citizens should meet their duty of solidarity by respecting, protecting, and empowering each other's equal authority.[57] Citizens *respect* one another when they refuse to commit either direct or mediated injustices.

55. Ralph Ellison, *Invisible Man* (New York: Vintage Books, 1995), 3.

56. This parallels Rawls's natural duty of mutual aid, which calls on others to rescue us when we are "in need or jeopardy" (*Theory of Justice*, 98). This duty expresses how our lives are important enough to be worth saving. If people closed their eyes when we were injured, it would communicate a contempt for our lives that would be destructive to our self-respect. As Rawls puts it, if "we try to picture the life of a society in which no one had the slightest desire to act on these duties, we see that it would express an indifference if not disdain for human beings that would make a sense of our own worth impossible" (*Theory of Justice*, 298). The duty of solidarity is distinctive in having a democratic basis, and in giving citizens the responsibility to participate in democratic accountability to protect each other from injustice.

57. On recognition, see Alan Patten, *Equal Recognition* (Princeton, NJ: Princeton University Press, 2014) and Seana Shiffrin, *Democratic Law* (New York: Oxford University Press, 2021). Shiffrin writes that the democratic purpose of law is to publicly affirm the status of all citizens as equal members. I argue that citizens and public officials bear democratic duties to recognize all citizens by respecting, protecting, and empowering each other's equal authority. These duties must be met for citizens to be freely self-governing.

Direct injustices are wrought by citizens in their own actions or by factions that "beget injustice and oppression of a part of the community."[58] Citizens are implicated in a *mediated injustice* when they employ public officials as the instruments of injustice. This support can run the gamut from voting for officials who enact discriminatory laws, to deeper forms of complicity, such as inciting officials into inflicting unjust policies.

After the Supreme Court ruled in *Brown v. Board of Education* that public schools must end racial segregation, factions of hostile citizens organized White Citizens' Councils. They conspired to mount a program of "Massive Resistance" to desegregation. The White Citizens' Councils sought to recruit public officials. When nine African American students enrolled in Little Rock Central High School, a hate-filled mob of over one thousand people descended upon the school.[59] The mob was guilty of a *direct* injustice when they surrounded the students and menaced their safety. The White Citizens' Councils perpetrated a *mediated injustice* as the instigators of racial segregation by their officials. Both direct and indirect injustices are blameworthy and contrary to the democratic duty of respect.

The Duty to Protect: Safeguarding against Factions and Elected Authoritarians

Citizens should hold their public servants democratically accountable for enacting and carrying out laws that *protect* the marginalized from factions and elected authoritarians. This is both a duty of solidarity they owe to the marginalized and a duty of oversight that citizens assume when they employ public servants in government. Public servants should fulfill their duty of fidelity and hold a firm line against the elected authoritarians and factions who prey upon the marginalized.

58. Hamilton, "Federalist No. 27," in *Federalist*, 125.

59. Ravi K. Perry and D. LaRouth Perry, *The Little Rock Crisis: What Desegregation Politics Says about Us* (New York: Palgrave Macmillan, 2015). Perry and Perry note that "the segregationists expected their legislators to achieve two things: (1) to identify, devise and enact legal schemas that would retain the status quo as their ideological beliefs defined it, and (2) to foment lobbying organizations that would bring pressure on influential people to join their ranks so as to keep the separatist viewpoint in the public eye" (107).

Factions are groups of citizens who target the rights of the marginalized. For example, factions were guilty of 6,603 violent hate incidents against Asian Americans in the United States from March 2020 to 2021.[60] The Williams Institute at UCLA Law School has found that that LGBT citizens are "nine times more likely than non-LGBT people to be victims of violent hate crimes."[61] The Anti-Defamation League recorded 3,697 antisemitic incidents in 2022, the highest level since the ADL started tracking in 1979.[62] According to the NAACP, hate crimes against Muslim Americans are "up 78 percent over the course of 2015," and in 2017, "two mosques in Texas and one in the state of Washington were destroyed by arson."[63]

Citizens should demand in solidarity that their public servants enact laws that give sanctuary to the marginalized from violence and discrimination. Public servants should act on their duty of fidelity and enact and enforce legislation and policies that protect the marginalized. For instance, the president and Congress passed the Matthew Shepard and James Byrd, Jr. Hate Crimes Prevention Act in 2009.[64] They did so in response to the heinous murders of Matthew Shepard for being gay and James Byrd for being African American. In 2023 President Joseph Biden set out the first ever National Strategy to Counter Antisemitism. Its objectives include "raising awareness, improving security, reversing normalization [of antisemitism], and building *solidarity*."[65] That same year, the administration announced the US National Strategy to Counter

60. Sprunt, "Here's What the New Hate Crimes Law Aims to Do."

61. Andrew Flores et al., "Hate Crimes against LGBT People: National Crime Victimization Survey, 2017–2019," *PLOS One* 17, no. 12 (2021): e0279363.

62. White House, *The U.S. National Strategy to Counter Antisemitism*, May 2023, https://www.whitehouse.gov/wp-content/uploads/2023/05/U.S.-National-Strategy-to-Counter-Antisemitism.pdf at 9.

63. NAACP, "Resolution: Hate Crimes against Muslims," 2017, https://naacp.org/resources/hate-crimes-against-muslims.

64. COVID-19 Hate Crimes Act, Public Law No: 117-13, https://www.congress.gov/bill/117th-congress/senate-bill/937/text; The Matthew Shepard and James Byrd, Jr., Hate Crimes Prevention Act of 2009, 18 U.S.C. § 249.

65. Rachel Treisman, "The First National Strategy for Fighting Antisemitism Is Finally Here. What's in It?" NPR, March 25, 2023, https://www.npr.org/2023/05/25/1178188513/biden-antisemitism-strategy (emphasis added).

Islamophobia and Related Forms of Bias and Discrimination, including hate against Arab, Sikh, and South Asian Americans.[66]

Earlier in the country's history, President Ulysses S. Grant and Congress honored their duty of fidelity when they created the Department of Justice in 1870. The founding mission of the department was to fight the Ku Klux Klan, an especially virulent faction.[67] Congress passed the Third Enforcement Act in April 1871 to prosecute the Klan.[68] The act sought to extend the equal protection of the law to African Americans under the Fourteenth Amendment and their right to vote under the Fifteenth Amendment.[69] Citizens who supported these laws and amendments acted on their duty of solidarity toward African Americans and their duty of oversight of public servants.

The Democratic Duty to Empower

The duty to *empower* secures self-government as a *substantive freedom*, with citizens possessing the material resources and education to apply their democratic accountability rights.[70] This guarantees our freedom as self-government from the threat of powerlessness. Martha Nussbaum and Amartya Sen distinguish between formal and substantive freedoms in their capability theory of freedom.[71] A capability is a substantive

---

66. White House, "Fact Sheet: Biden-Harris Administration Takes Action to Counter Islamophobia," June 16, 2024, https://www.whitehouse.gov/briefing-room/statements-releases/2024/06/16/fact-sheet-biden-%E2%81%A0harris-administration-takes-action-to-counter-islamophobia/.

67. Richard M. Valelly, "National Parties and Racial Disenfranchisement," in *Classifying by Race*, ed. Paul E. Peterson, (Princeton, NJ: Princeton University Press, 1995), 196.

68. An Act to Enforce the Provisions of the Fourteenth Amendment to the Constitution of the United States, and for Other Purposes, 17 Stat. 13 (1871).

69. U.S. Const. Amend. XIV and XV.

70. I am grateful to Alison McQueen, who asked astutely about the material resources needed to participate in democratic accountability during my talk at the Stanford faculty political theory workshop. To clarify, a *substantive freedom* is one where citizens have the resources to exercise that liberty. A *substantive right* regards how one is treated by the government.

71. Martha Nussbaum, *Frontiers of Justice* (Cambridge, MA: Harvard University Press, 2006); Amartya Sen, *The Idea of Justice* (Cambridge, MA: Harvard University Press, 2009); and idem, *Development as Freedom* (New York: Alfred A. Knopf, 1999).

freedom to act or to achieve a valuable condition.[72] A person who is impoverished may have the formal freedom or legal right to buy a loaf of bread, but she lacks the substantive freedom or resources to purchase it. Sen's research, which earned him the Nobel Prize in Economics, has shown that in famines, a sufficient food supply is often available, but a sharp rise in prices may leave food beyond the reach of many.[73] This was the case in the cataclysmic famine Sen witnessed as a child in India during British colonial rule. The 1943 Bengal Famine killed between two to three million people, but colonial administrators shut their eyes to the mass starvation, because food output had remained constant.[74] The colonial powers disregarded the need for substantive freedom: after prices rose, many South Asians could not afford to buy food. The store shelves were full but people's pockets and stomachs were empty.

Equal accountability specifies that we must have the resources to exercise our democratic accountability rights as substantive and not merely formal freedoms. The critics who assert that citizens are entitled only to formal freedoms on paper should ask themselves: Is it plausible to say that a homeless woman can hold her public servants democratically accountable? She may legally be entitled to the right to vote, but how can she afford transportation to a voting booth? How can she pay for a computer and printer to contact her representative and use her democratic accountability rights to free speech and the press? Even if she could make herself heard, she would be disparaged and ignored by other citizens. She cannot wield her democratic accountability rights, just as the indigent people in Bengal could not buy bread.

I argue for the democratic duty to *empower* marginalized citizens with the resources and civic education to make use of their democratic accountability rights as substantive freedoms. Empowerment is a duty of fidelity for public servants, a duty of solidarity that citizens owe the marginalized, and a duty of oversight that citizens should hold their

72. Sen, *Development as Freedom*, 18, 75.
73. Sen, *Development as Freedom*, 167.
74. Sen, *Development as Freedom*, 180, 209.

public servants democratically accountable for satisfying. I sketch the following guidelines as a starting point for deliberation about the measures to empower the marginalized. Additional policies may be needed, however.

The Rule of Law and Empowering Citizens with Legal Counsel

Among the rights central to democratic accountability are the rule of law and petition. When citizens suffer injustices, they should be able to correct those injustices and sanction the officials responsible by petitioning a court. Elizabeth Freeman invoked these rights in suing for her freedom. Citizens are excluded from the rule of law if they cannot afford a lawyer to thread the legal labyrinth. Freeman was fortunate to receive pro bono representation. But the Legal Services Corporation, founded by Congress, observes that "71 percent of low-income households had experienced at least one civil legal problem in the previous year, including conflicts around health care, housing conditions, disability access, veterans' benefits, and domestic violence."[75] In 86 percent of cases, the "civil legal problems reported by low-income Americans in 2017 received inadequate or no legal help."[76]

To empower the marginalized, citizens and their public servants should fund legal aid in both civil and criminal trials. In a civil trial, citizens have been injured, and they attempt to redeem their rights and remedy the harms they have suffered. In criminal trials, citizens are defendants accused of crimes and seek to prove their innocence or mitigate their sentence. Citizens would be vulnerable to having their rights invaded at will if they had no recourse to petition the courts in civil trials. Innocent citizens risk having their lives ruined and losing their liberty for decades if they lack an effective lawyer in criminal trials. Litigants without a lawyer are ill-equipped to defend themselves in the arcane arena of law, which requires years of study to master. John Levi, the chair of the board of the Legal Services Corporation, and David

---

75. John G. Levi and David M. Rubenstein, "Introduction," *Daedalus* 148, no. 1 (2019): 8.
76. Levi and Rubenstein, "Introduction," 8.

Rubenstein note that in "75 percent of civil cases in state courts, one or both parties go unrepresented. They largely forfeit meaningful access to justice since they are far less likely to prevail than represented litigants, particularly when opposed by parties with lawyers."[77] Equal accountability empowers marginalized citizens with legal representation to exercise their equal democratic accountability rights to the rule of law and petition.

Empowering Citizens with Resources to Participate in Deliberative Democracy

Citizens should be guaranteed at least the *social minimum,* or the resources necessary to meet their basic needs and to participate publicly in democratic deliberation without humiliation. In the *Wealth of Nations,* Adam Smith writes that there are goods necessary to participate in public life without being stamped with the stigma of shame.[78] These are the goods that "the custom of the country renders it indecent for creditable people, even of the lowest order, to be without."[79]

Martin Luther King Jr. espoused a social minimum for all Americans in the form of a guaranteed income. King wrote, "The solution to poverty is to abolish it directly by a now widely discussed measure: the guaranteed income."[80] President Nixon included a minimum income in his 1969 Family Assistance Plan, which was passed by the House, though it was stalled by the Senate.[81] Milton Friedman, the conservative Nobel laureate in economics, was a proponent of a guaranteed income,

77. Levi and Rubenstein, "Introduction," 8. I thank Alejandro Fernandez, who contributed discussion of legal access.

78. Quoted in Sen, *Development as Freedom,* 73. Elizabeth Anderson likewise concludes that democracy requires the conditions for citizens to appear in public without humiliation ("What Is the Point of Equality?" *Ethics* 109, no. 2 [1999]: 318).

79. Quoted in Sen, *Development as Freedom,* 73–74.

80. Martin Luther King, Jr., *Where Do We Go From Here: Chaos or Community?* (Boston: Beacon Press, 2010); Juliana Uhuru Bidadanure, "The Political Theory of Universal Basic Income," *Annual Review of Political Science* 22 (2019): 481–501.

81. Daniel Patrick Moynihan, *The Politics of a Guaranteed Income: The Nixon Administration and the Family Assistance Plan* (New York: Random House, 1973), 3.

which he called a "negative income tax."[82] The liberal political philosopher John Rawls advocated a "social minimum" that "covers at least the basic needs essential to a decent life."[83] Neo-republican theorists hold that a social minimum is needed to prevent the loss of freedom from domination. The social minimum, says Philip Pettit, is necessary for citizens to meet the "eyeball test" for freedom that they can look other citizens in the eye without fear or favor.[84] Citizens who are destitute are inevitably dominated. When their basic needs are insecure, citizens will be highly vulnerable to exploitation, as Debra Satz writes.[85] For the capability theorists like Sen and Nussbaum, assuaging poverty is a condition to "take part in the life of the community" without being socially humiliated.[86]

In equal accountability, a social minimum empowers citizens to exercise their democratic accountability rights. To take part in democratic deliberation as participants who are listened to and taken seriously, citizens must not be demeaned and disempowered because of their poverty. A hallmark of democratic accountability is the freedom of speech to address moral claims in deliberation with other citizens and public servants. However, if a homeless person did show up to her representative's office, it is unlikely that she would be accorded a respectful hearing. She may be treated as a pariah, rebuffed, and thrown outside, even if she has a pressing moral claim to petition her representative. This form of civic disempowerment impacts the 582,000 people who are homeless in the United States. African Americans comprise 12 percent of the population, but in 2022, 50 percent of families with children who are homeless are African American.[87] The resources of the homeless

82. Milton Friedman, *Capitalism and Freedom* (Chicago: University of Chicago Press, 2020), 230.

83. Rawls, *Justice as Fairness*, 130.

84. Pettit, *On the People's Terms*, 112.

85. Debra Satz, *Why Some Things Should Not Be for Sale: The Moral Limits of Markets* (New York: Oxford University Press, 2010), 97.

86. Sen, *Development as Freedom*, 73.

87. United States Office of Community Planning and Development, *The 2022 Annual Homeless Assessment Report (AHAR) to Congress* (Washington, DC: US Department of Housing and Urban Development, 2022), 2, https://www.huduser.gov/portal/sites/default/files/pdf/2022 -AHAR-Part-1.pdf.

are too meager to participate democratically, and their urgent needs are dismissed. We must not make the same mistake as the colonial administrators who presumed the people of Bengal could not perish from famine because they had the formal freedom to buy bread. Equal accountability's duty to empower gives citizens and public servants the responsibility to provide, through legislation, that all citizens have access to the resources to be included in democracy. For this purpose, we must be able to exercise our democratic accountability rights as *substantive freedoms*, without being ostracized due to poverty.

An additional reason we should relieve privation and illness is that citizens can hardly participate democratically if they are afflicted by destitution and sickness. The poverty rate of African Americans is three times higher than that of non-Hispanic whites.[88] Life expectancy for African American children born today "still lags nearly five years behind that of the average American child."[89] Black infant mortality is nearly twice the national average, and African Americans are "over twice as likely to die from diabetes, kidney disease, or infectious disease."[90] The gap in health and poverty has persisted since King's time.

The conventional view regards African American poverty and drastic disparities in health as matters of justice, and not of democracy. But someone confined in agony to a hospital bed cannot reach a voting booth or deliberate with other citizens. Although illness is part of a human lifespan, it is unfair and undemocratic that marginalized groups of citizens, such as racial minorities, are disproportionately disempowered by poor health. A meta-analysis from the University of Toronto Faculty of Medicine finds that "people with worse health tend to be less likely to engage in voting," as shown by data from the United States, Canada, and Europe.[91] Another study from the University of Michigan has uncovered that "from 1970–2004, there were 2.7 million excess black deaths due to racial inequality, which led to 1 million lost black votes in

88. Anderson, *Imperative of Integration*, 23.
89. Anderson, *Imperative of Integration*, 23.
90. Anderson, *Imperative of Integration*, 23.
91. Brown, Raza, and Pinto, "Voting, Health and Interventions in Healthcare Settings," 15.

the 2004 election."[92] African American excess deaths changed the results of elections. Researchers "estimate that between 1970 and 2004 the outcomes of 7 close senate elections and 11 close gubernatorial races could have been reversed" if African Americans had lived as long as whites.[93] The researchers stress that their work demonstrates how African American are excluded from democracy by high mortality and racial inequalities in health care: "Our findings highlight that black excess deaths are a challenge to democracy."[94]

One way that racial minorities can be blocked from voting is by officials or mobs that prevent them from casting a ballot. These are the obstacles to self-government from elected authoritarians and factions. But another barrier is if marginalized citizens are too ill to cast a ballot. This is the obstacle to freedom as self-government from powerlessness. Citizens and their public servants should fulfill their democratic duties to empower marginalized citizens through the provision of at least a social minimum, as health is a precondition for democratic participation.

Empowering Citizens with Greater Access to the Vote

Citizens should be empowered with more equal and easier access to voting. A precedent is the For the People Act, a proposed law that would have automatically registered voters who visited state or federal agencies. The act would have mandated same-day voter registration in all states, turned Election Day into a federal holiday, and prohibited purging voters from the electoral rolls if they had not voted in a recent election.[95] Along with *empowering* citizens by facilitating their voting, the For the People Act would have *protected* the democratic accountability right to vote by outlawing voter intimidation or interference. The House

---

92. Brown, Raza, and Pinto, 16, citing Rodriguez et al., "Black Lives Matter," (emphasis added).

93. Rodriguez et al., 197.

94. Rodriguez, et al., 198.

95. Michael Wines, "Here's How Democrats' Sweeping Voting Rights Law Would Work," *New York Times*, March 31, 2021; Nicholas Fandos, "Democrats Unite behind Voting Rights Bill as It Faces a Senate Roadblock," *New York Times*, June 21, 2021.

of Representatives passed the bill in 2021, and it commanded a majority of votes in the Senate. But it ran into resistance from a Senate filibuster, which allows a minority of forty-one senators to block legislation, even though the filibuster is never mentioned in the Constitution and was not devised until 1837. Several Republican legislators "privately acknowledge that the bill's broad aims are overwhelmingly popular, even among conservatives."[96]

Senator Mitch McConnell, the Senate minority leader, chided the effort to make Election Day a federal holiday, labeling it a "power grab."[97] But it should be asked who would be acquiring that power. It would be citizens, who would be more empowered to vote. According to a Census survey, 2.7 million people cannot cast their ballot because of work.[98] Many of these workers labor long hours and were declared essential during the pandemic, but they lack the free time to vote. Honoring Election Day as a holiday and easing voter registration are not illegitimate power grabs; rather, they restore power to citizens, who must be the ones in charge to be freely self-governing. Other democracies, including South Korea and Israel, have declared their Election Days holidays. Australia conducts its elections on Saturday, with turnout exceeding 90 percent of voters.[99]

Alexander Hamilton hailed the right to vote as "so fundamental a privilege" that it is "the characteristic right of freedom."[100] It imposes an intolerable burden on the right to vote, says Hamilton, when officials "[render] it impracticable to the citizens at large to partake in the choice."[101] Yet federal and state governments have obstructed the right

96. Wines, "Here's How Democrats." On the first filibuster, see Sarah A. Binder and Steven S. Smith, *Politics or Principle? Filibustering in the United States Senate* (Washington, DC: Brookings Institution Press, 1997), 2. I thank Tom Sullivan who asked about equal accountability and the filibuster in my research talk at the University of Vermont.

97. Matthew Haag, "McConnell Denounces Bill Making Elections a Holiday," *New York Times*, February 1, 2019.

98. Haag, "McConnell Denounces Bill."

99. Haag. Part of the reason Australia has high turnout is that it makes voting a mandatory duty, like jury service. An excellent discussion is Emilee Chapman, "The Distinctive Value of Elections and the Case for Compulsory Voting," *American Journal of Political Science* 63, no. 1 (2019): 101–12. On the importance of the right to vote, see Chapman, *Election Day*.

100. Hamilton, "Federalist No. 60," in *Federalist*, 291–92.

101. Hamilton, "Federalist No. 60," 291.

to vote of women and African Americans for decades. In an echo of Jim Crow, the "county with the state's largest Black population" in Kentucky was assigned "only one polling station" in the 2020 primary.[102]

In Georgia, 29 percent of residents of Lincoln County are African American, but officials sought to close six of seven polling stations, leaving only one site to vote. Reverend Christopher Johnson, a pastor who heads Greater Augusta's Interfaith Coalition, protested the cutbacks: "The poor and marginalized people won't be able to vote because, bottom line, they won't be able to get to the polls."[103] Their exclusion from democracy carries national repercussions. Georgia is a battleground state that can swing who controls the Senate, the House of Representatives, and the presidency. The Stanford political scientist Jonathan Rodden discovered that in Georgia polling places that were 90 percent white, the average evening wait time to vote on Election Day was a brisk six minutes. Wait times stretched nearly nine times longer, to fifty-one minutes, in polling places that were 90 percent African-American.[104] An especially egregious delay took place in Union City, an Atlanta suburb that is 88 percent African American. Voters languished in lines over five hours long to vote, due to the paucity of polling places.[105]

Citizens and public servants should empower the marginalized to exercise their right to vote. They should be empowered with accessible polling stations, easier voter registration, and the dedication of Election Day as a federal holiday. Reverend Johnson and his allies protested the plan to cull the voting stations: "After a plan to close all but one polling place drew local protests and got national attention, the proposal has

102. Seth Cohen, "Jim Crow 2.0? How Kentucky's Poll Closures Could Suppress Black Votes," *Forbes*, June 22, 2020, https://www.forbes.com/sites/sethcohen/2020/06/22/kentucky-and-jim-crow-2-dot-o/.

103. Fredreka Schouten, "Plans to Close All But One Polling Place in a Rural Georgia County Reverberate through a Battleground State," CNN, January 20, 2022, https://www.cnn.com/2022/01/19/politics/poll-closures-rural-lincoln-county-georgia/index.html.

104. Schouten, "Plans to Close."

105. Stephen Fowler, "Why Do Nonwhite Georgia Voters Have to Wait in Line for Hours? Too Few Polling Places," NPR, October 17, 2020, https://www.npr.org/2020/10/17/924527679/why-do-nonwhite-georgia-voters-have-to-wait-in-line-for-hours-too-few-polling-pl.

been voted down in Lincoln County."[106] Our democratic duties are the price we pay to be free.

Empowering Citizens with More Equitable Campaign Finance

Public servants must answer to all citizens as equal authorities. It impairs freedom as self-government to treat citizens as *unequal* authorities, or less in charge of government, because they are not rich.[107] Martin Gilens and Benjamin Page find that "economic elites and organized groups representing business interests have substantial independent impacts on U.S. government policy, while average citizens and mass-based interest groups have little or no independent influence."[108] Increasing the percentage of ordinary citizens who support a policy barely budges the likelihood of it being adopted. However, raising the percentage of economic elites who prefer a policy from 10 percent to near unanimity steeply increases the likelihood of passage from 0 percent to 60 percent.[109] Compared to average-income citizens, economic elites are less likely to support Social Security, Medicare, and food stamps[110]

While it would go beyond our scope to survey in detail campaign finance policies, I contend that monetary clout should be decoupled from campaign finance. Rawls suggests that the "reforms to that end are likely to involve such things as the public funding of elections and restrictions on campaign contributions," and "the assurance of a more

---

106. Clare Allen, "Lincoln County Leaders Opt against Plan to Close Voting Sites," *WRDW News*, March 11, 2022, https://www.wrdw.com/2022/03/11/lincoln-county-leaders-opt-against-plan-close-voting-sites/.

107. As Rawls states, our rights hinge on whether democracy hears our voices, and not just those of the wealthy: "What is fundamental is a political procedure which secures for all citizens a full and equally effective voice in a fair scheme of representation. Such a scheme is fundamental because the adequate protection of other basic rights depends on it. Formal equality is not enough" (*Political Liberalism*, 361). Michael Walzer writes, in his theory of complex equality, that the sphere of money should be separated from the sphere of politics. A "sphere" is an area of social life with rules governing the distribution of a set of goods. See Walzer, *Spheres of Justice* (New York: Basic Books, 1983).

108. Gilens and Page, "Testing Theories of American Politics," 564.

109. Gilens and Page, 573, figure 1.

110. Gilens and Page, 571, 576.

even access to public media."[111] These arrangements abound in many stable democracies, but they have been rolled back in the United States.[112] The Supreme Court in *Buckley v. Valeo* struck down limits on campaign expenditures. In *Citizens United*, the court in a narrow five-to-four decision overturned the Bipartisan Campaign Reform Act (BCRA).[113]

The court based its decisions in these cases on freedom of speech. Indeed, free speech is a democratic accountability right. But since rights can clash, they need to be adjusted to cohere in the system of liberty. It would weaken democratic accountability as a whole if public servants only answered to the wealthy. The conservative Justice Byron White in his dissent in *Buckley* balked at the effect of campaign donations. He was disquieted by how the overflowing current of campaign donations corrupts the integrity of officials: "The act of giving money to political candidates, however, may have illegal or other undesirable consequences: it may be used to secure the express or tacit understanding that the giver will enjoy political favor if the candidate is elected. Both Congress and this Court's cases have recognized this as a *mortal danger* against which effective preventive and curative steps must be taken."[114]

Citizens unite across the political spectrum on ridding democracy of the baleful influence of money. In a poll, a supermajority of 84 percent of Americans said that money holds too much sway over political campaigns. 85 percent believe that officials tilt their policies to favor their

---

111. Rawls, *Justice as Fairness*, 149. On the values of equal respect, free choice, and popular sovereignty that ought to guide campaign finance regulations, see Dennis F. Thompson, *Just Elections: Creating a Fair Electoral Process in the United States* (Chicago: University of Chicago Press, 2002).

112. Magnus Ohman, *Political Finance Regulations around the World: An Overview of the International IDEA Database* (Stockholm: International Institute for Democracy and Electoral Assistance, 2012), https://www.idea.int/sites/default/files/publications/political-finance-regulations-around-the-world.pdf.

113. Buckley v. Valeo, 424 U.S. 1 (1976); Citizens United v. FEC, 558 U.S. 310 (2010); The Bipartisan Campaign Reform Act of 2002, Pub. L. 107-155.

114. 424 U.S. 1, 259 (1976) (White, J., dissenting) (emphasis added). Although the Supreme Court majority upheld campaign donation limits, Justice White argued that preventing corruption also required caps on campaign spending. Justice White added presciently that without limits on campaign spending, elected officials would become increasingly distracted by incessant fundraising and cater to their wealthy donors.

campaign donors. The same percentage, 85 percent, expressed the conviction that either fundamental changes are needed, or "the system for funding political campaigns has so much wrong with it that we need to *completely rebuild it.*"[115] Reforms to campaign finance are imperative to render democracy equally accountable to all citizens. Aristotle tellingly contrasts democracy not with dictatorship but with oligarchy, or the rule of the rich.[116] I maintain that a democratic government must answer to all citizens, of every economic background, as equals.

Empowering Citizens with Civic Education

As citizens, we should be empowered with a strong civic education, which teaches students about the rights and duties of democratic citizenship.[117] It equips students with the skills and knowledge of government to participate democratically. It kindles a knowledge of the history of our democracy and imparts the ability to think critically about its contemporary challenges and future. Civic education cultivates the moral dispositions of mutual respect, compromise, and the willingness to listen openly to diverse other citizens. These virtues are foundational

115. New York Times CBS News Poll, "Americans' Views on Money in Politics," *New York Times,* June 2, 2015, https://www.nytimes.com/interactive/2015/06/02/us/politics/money-in -politics-poll.html (emphasis added).

116. Aristotle, *The Politics,* trans. T. A. Sinclair and Trevor J. Saunders (New York: Penguin, 1992), 296–99 [1301a–b]. I am planning in my next book to demonstrate that a democracy requires a strong middle class and protections against oligarchy, drawing on the political thought of the Progressive Era, Reconstruction, the American Framers, Aristotle, and the lessons of the Great Depression.

117. On the significance of civic education in democracy, see Stephen Macedo, *Diversity and Distrust: Civic Education in a Multicultural Democracy* (Cambridge, MA: Harvard University Press, 2000); Danielle Allen and Rob Reich, eds., *Education, Justice and Democracy* (Chicago: University of Chicago Press, 2013); Manville and Ober, *Civic Bargain*; Amy Gutmann, *Democratic Education,* rev. ed. (Princeton, NJ: Princeton University Press, 1999); Bob Pepperman Taylor, *Horace Mann's Troubling Legacy: The Education of American Citizens* (Lawrence: University Press of Kansas, 2010); Debra Satz, "Equality, Adequacy, and Education for Citizenship," *Ethics* 117 (2007): 623–48; Josiah Ober, *Demopolis* (Cambridge, UK: Cambridge University Press, 2017), 71–76; Debra Satz and Dan Edelstein, "By Abandoning Civics, Colleges Helped Create the Culture Wars," *New York Times,* September 7, 2023; and Sigal Ben-Porath, Amy Gutmann, and Dennis F. Thompson, "Teaching Competition and Cooperation in Civic Education," *Civic Education in Polarized Times, Nomos LXVI,* ed. Elizabeth Beaumont and Eric Beerbohm (New York: New York University Press, 2024), chap. 10.

for citizens to work together in their shared democracy, and to meet the duties of the office of the citizen.[118] Civic education prepares citizens for self-government.

If citizens looked away in indifference when aspiring autocrats attempt to seize power, or when marginalized citizens are excluded, the prospects for democracy would be bleak indeed. However, citizens would be more capable of meeting their democratic duties if they learned about the responsibilities and rights of democratic citizenship through a robust civic education.

Civic education is crucial to closing what Dennis Thompson, Amy Gutmann, and Sigal Ben-Porath aptly call the "civic empowerment gap."[119] Marginalized citizens can be disempowered, because they may not receive a civic education to learn about how to use their democratic accountability rights. Depriving the marginalized of a civic education would deepen their vulnerability and intensify their exclusion from self-government. They would be exposed to even greater risk of injustice compared to wealthier citizens who are well-acquainted with how to navigate and pull the levers of government. To close the civic empowerment gap, civic education must not be confined to the rich but should be guaranteed as a set of skills to all democratic citizens.

The Framers were acutely aware of the lifeline civic education provides to a republic, which is a representative democracy that secures rights by limiting the power of government. President Washington's first public message to Congress linked civic education with the health of democracy. "Knowledge is in every country the surest basis of public happiness," he declared, and this is especially true in a representative democracy, which depends on an educated citizenry.[120]

---

118. On the virtues needed for deliberative democracy, including mutual respect and open-mindedness, see Gutmann and Thompson, *Why Deliberative Democracy*, 79–90, Gutmann and Thompson, *Democracy and Disagreement*, 91, and Macedo, "Against Majoritarianism," 10. On compromise, see Amy Gutmann and Dennis F. Thompson, *The Spirit of Compromise* (Princeton, NJ: Princeton University Press, 2014) and Manville and Ober, *Civic Bargain*.

119. Ben-Porath, Gutmann, and Thompson, "Teaching Competition and Cooperation in Civic Education."

120. George Washington, "First Annual Address to Congress," January 8, 1790, American Presidency Project, www.presidency.ucsb.edu/documents/first-annual-address-congress-0.

We can glean from Washington's address three insights regarding how civic education safeguards our democratic freedom.[121] First, civic education fosters the ability of citizens to protect their freedom by teaching them about their rights. Civic education, says Washington, affords security for our freedom "by teaching the people themselves to know and to value their own rights."[122] This prepares citizens to wield their rights proficiently, with readiness "to discern and provide against invasions" of their liberty.[123] Citizens cannot secure their freedom if they are unfamiliar with their rights to hold their government democratically accountable.

Second, civic education teaches future government officials, and the citizens who hold them democratically accountable, about the duties of fidelity inherent in the office of public servant. Civic education promotes liberty, says President Washington, "by convincing those who are intrusted with the public administration, that every valuable end of Government is best answered by the enlightened confidence of the people."[124] The word "intrusted," I wrote in chapter 2, embodies the principle that government service is a trust. The power of government is collectively owned by citizens. In using that power, officials bear the duty of fidelity to comply with democratic accountability and recognize the equal authority of all citizens. Public servants are more likely to satisfy their duties of fidelity in office if they are taught these responsibilities through their civic education.

A third lesson from President Washington is that civic education prepares citizens to meet the democratic duties of the office of the citizen. To fulfill these duties of oversight and solidarity, citizens must distinguish liberty from mere license. Liberty is freedom that respects the rights of others, while license is action heedless of duty. As Washington said, civic education teaches citizens "to discriminate the spirit of Liberty from that of licentiousness, cherishing the first, avoiding the last."[125]

---

121. Washington, "First Annual Address to Congress."
122. Washington.
123. Washington.
124. Washington.
125. Washington.

Despite the importance of civic education, it has fallen to the wayside. Ten states do not require even a single rudimentary high school civics class to graduate.[126] We are now paying the toll. Less than half of citizens (47 percent) can name all three branches of government. A paltry 24 percent realize that freedom of religion is one of the rights protected in the First Amendment to the Constitution.[127] In a 2009 survey, 83 percent of participants failed a basic test of civic knowledge similar to the exam immigrants are expected to pass.[128] We are far from meeting President Washington's precept that the people must be equipped to "know and to value their own rights."

Other democracies have accorded far higher priority to civic education. Within the United Kingdom, England has adopted a Citizenship National Curriculum to educate students in civics for a full five years from ages eleven to sixteen. In close alignment with equal accountability, England's Citizenship National Curriculum teaches "the role of citizens and Parliament in holding those in power *to account.*" The curriculum aims to "prepare students to take their place in society as *responsible citizens.*"[129] The breadth of the five-year national civic education is impressive, instilling students with knowledge and appreciation of "the precious liberties enjoyed by the citizens of the United Kingdom."[130] Students shall achieve an understanding of "the different roles of the executive, legislature and judiciary and a free press," and the "need for mutual respect and understanding" among diverse citizens. They will

126. Sophia Craiutu and Jed Ngalande, "State Civics Requirements in 2024," Hoover Institution, December 17, 2024, https://www.hoover.org/research/state-civics-requirements-2024.

127. University of Pennsylvania Annenberg Public Policy Center, "Annenberg Civics Knowledge Survey," accessed March 14, 2025, www.annenbergpublicpolicycenter.org/political-communication/civics-knowledge-survey/.

128. Jonathan R. Cole, "Ignorance Does Not Lead to Election Bliss," *Atlantic*, November 8, 2016, www.theatlantic.com/education/archive/2016/11/ignorance-does-not-lead-to-election-bliss/506894/.

129. United Kingdom Department of Education, "Citizenship Programmes of Study: Key Stages 3 and 4: National Curriculum in England," 2013, https://assets.publishing.service.gov.uk/government/uploads/system/uploads/attachment_data/file/908347/SECONDARY_national_curriculum_-_Citizenship.pdf, pp. 2 (emphasis added). England, Wales, Scotland, and Northern Ireland include civic education in their curricula but adopt distinct approaches.

130. United Kingdom Department of Education, "Citizenship Programmes of Study," 2.

attain knowledge of "human rights law and international law," and even the sound management of the nation's public finances.[131] A civic education is an education in freedom. It nourishes the capacity for critical thinking and responsible participation in democracy: "Teaching should equip pupils with the skills and knowledge to explore political and social issues critically, to weigh evidence, debate and make reasoned arguments."[132]

It is particularly urgent to teach students critical thinking, given that we live in a time saturated with disinformation.[133] Finland has taken the lead in an education for media literacy, and its efforts have borne fruit to the point where Finland ranks first among all European countries in "resilience against misinformation."[134] The Finnish approach teaches media literacy as "part of the national core curriculum starting in preschool."[135] During class, students practice spotting attempted manipulation in videos and online. They learn to assess the credibility of the creators, critically examine their motivations, and scour the evidence. The Finns understand media literacy to be a national security imperative and know that their independence hinges on the resistance of their citizenry to propaganda from foreign actors and their domestic accomplices.

Former Supreme Court justice David Souter has drawn attention to the need for civic education. Since the 1970s, civic education has receded from the curriculum in US schools. The ensuing erosion of civic capabilities has blighted American democracy: "I don't believe there is any problem of American politics in American public life which is more significant today than the pervasive civic ignorance of the Constitution

131. United Kingdom Department of Education, 2–3.

132. United Kingdom Department of Education, 2–3.

133. On these challenges, see Russell Muirhead and Nancy Rosenblum, *A Lot of People Are Saying: The New Conspiracism and the Assault on Democracy* (Princeton, NJ: Princeton University Press, 2019), and Adam J. Berinsky, *Political Rumors: Why We Accept Misinformation and How to Fight It* (Princeton, NJ: Princeton University Press, 2023).

134. Jenny Gross, "How Finland Is Teaching a Generation to Spot Misinformation," *New York Times*, January 11, 2023, https://www.nytimes.com/2023/01/10/world/europe/finland-misinformation-classes.html.

135. Gross, "How Finland Is Teaching."

of the United States and the structure of government."[136] Justice Souter reminded his audience of the Roman Republic, which served as a main model for the Constitution. Although the Roman Republic stood for nearly five hundred years, it was unraveled not by military defeat, but by civic illiteracy. Alluding to Caesar and other demagogues, Justice Souter warned of the bane of civic ignorance, "What I worry about is, when problems are not addressed and the people do not know who is responsible . . . some one person will come forward and say, 'Give me total power and I will solve this problem.' . . . That is how the Roman Republic fell. That is the way democracy dies."[137]

To prevent the demise of democracy, citizens should be empowered with a civic education, preparing them with the skills to exercise their democratic accountability rights and to meet their democratic duties. At the K-12 level, Educating for American Democracy (EAD) is a new program in civic education headed by Danielle Allen, Paul Carrese, Peter Levine, and other scholars. The initiative is funded by the Department of Education and administered by iCivics, a nonprofit founded by former Supreme Court Justice Sandra Day O'Connor. In close cooperation with hundreds of state educators and university researchers, Educating for American Democracy seeks to prepare one million teachers to "teach civic knowledge, civic skills, and civic dispositions" to sixty million students. The EAD report states its mission eloquently: "We as a nation have failed to prepare young Americans for self-government, leaving the world's oldest constitutional democracy in grave danger. . . . Our civic strength requires excellent civic and history education to repair the foundations of our democratic republic."[138] Similarly, the Alliance for Civics in the Academy, led by Josiah Ober, Mary Clark, Peter Levine, and Jenna Storey, is

136. Ryan Lessard, "Former Justice Souter Warns about the State of Civics Education," New Hampshire Public Radio, September 14, 2012, https://www.nhpr.org/nh-news/2012-09-14/former-justice-souter-warns-about-the-state-of-civics-education.

137. Margaret Warner, "Justice Souter's Old Warning Finds New Life in Election," *PBS News Hour*, October 24, 2016, https://www.pbs.org/newshour/politics/justice-souters-old-warning-finds-new-life-election.

138. Educating for American Democracy, "Educating for American Democracy: Excellence in History and Civics for All Learners," *iCivics*, 2021, https://www.educatingforamerican democracy.org/wp-content/uploads/2021/02/Educating-for-American-Democracy-Report-Excellence-in-History-and-Civics-for-All-Learners.pdf at p. 6.

now seeking to expand civic education to colleges and university nation-wide, *empowering* citizens to participate in democratic accountability.

Conclusion

Many writers have looked only at rights to democracy. This chapter reflects anew about the *duties* of democracy. The duties are democratic in securing our rights to participate in democratic accountability and to govern ourselves freely. The injustices that exclude citizens from democracy do not correct themselves. Dr. Martin Luther King Jr. raised our sights to how the remedy is the "tireless efforts" of citizens: "We must use time creatively, in the knowledge that the time is always ripe to do right. Now is the time to make real the promise of democracy and transform our pending national elegy into a creative psalm of brotherhood."[139]

This chapter identified three essential democratic duties. First, citizens should fulfill their *democratic duty of oversight*, holding their public servants democratically accountable for using the power of government justly. The foundation of the duty of oversight is that citizens collectively own the coercive power of government and employ public servants to use that power on their behalf. They work for us, so we are responsible for holding them democratically accountable.

Second, citizens owe each other the *duty of solidarity*. We should *recognize* the equal authority of other citizens by respecting, protecting, and empowering it. These duties of solidarity are necessary to include all citizens in self-government. Citizens fell short in this duty for decades when they abandoned African Americans to racial segregation and the terror of lynching in the Jim Crow era. By contrast, citizens acted on this duty of solidarity in the Civil Rights Movement. They demanded that their public servants enact and enforce legislation to protect the marginalized from segregation, violence, and disenfranchisement.

Third, public servants should loyally fulfill their *duties of fidelity*. Citizens who work in the office of public servant should legislate and enforce laws that recognize our equal authority. Our public servants

139. King, "Letter from Birmingham Jail," 5.

should cooperate with democratic accountability by being transparent and justifying how they are using our power. In addition, the duty of fidelity commands public servants to meet their fiduciary duties of loyalty, care, and good faith, as I wrote in chapter 2.

A keystone of citizens' duties of solidarity and oversight, and public servants' duties of fidelity, is to *empower* the equal authority of all citizens in democracy. This chapter outlined five measures to empower citizens. We should provide all citizens a robust *civic education*, so that they learn about their democratic accountability rights and the duties of the offices of the citizen and public servant. We must improve *access to voting*, reversing the prevailing trend of closing polling sites in poor and minority neighborhoods. Citizens should be granted *legal aid*, so that income is no bar to the democratic accountability rights to the rule of law and to petition the courts. We should ensure a *social minimum* for citizens, to overcome the obstacles to democratic accountability from privation, debilitating illness, and homelessness, which exclude minorities disproportionately from participating democratically. Finally, citizens must be empowered with more *equitable campaign finance*, to make our public servants answer equally to all of us. Empowerment guarantees democratic accountability rights as real, substantive freedoms that citizens can effectively exercise.

Our participating democratically to protect and empower our fellow citizens expresses how they are seen and matter. It affirms their sense of self-worth when we show, by our actions, that we are honored to stand beside them in their hour of peril. Protecting our fellow citizens from exclusion also creates a freely self-governing relationship, where all citizens are included in democracy as the ones ultimately in charge of government. When we act in solidarity to end the marginalization of our fellow citizens, said Dr. King, we work together to "lift our national policy from the quicksand of racial injustice to the solid rock of human dignity."[140]

---

140. King, "Letter from Birmingham Jail," 5.

4

Defending the Duties of Democratic Accountability

A RECENT SUPREME COURT RULING had riven the country, bringing to a head the issue of slavery. Chief Justice Roger Taney cast the court on the side of the slave states. The 7–2 decision in *Dred Scott* deemed that any effort by Congress to ban slavery would offend the property rights of the slave-owners. Decades earlier, in 1783, the Massachusetts Supreme Judicial Court had prohibited slavery statewide. It condemned slavery as "totally repugnant" to the deep-seated conviction, articulated by the Declaration of Independence and Massachusetts Constitution, that "all men are born free and equal."[1] Justice Taney in his 1857 ruling came to the opposite conclusion for the federal Constitution. He insisted that African Americans could never be citizens of the United States.[2] In the shadow of the court's decision, two candidates faced each other in the 1858 Senate race for Illinois.[3]

---

1. Chief Justice William Cushing of the Massachusetts Supreme Judicial Court said in his instructions to the jury in *Commonwealth v. Jennison* (1783), "Our Constitution of Government, by which the people of this Commonwealth have solemnly bound themselves, sets out with declaring that all men are born free and equal . . . and in short is totally repugnant to the idea of being born slaves." See Albert P. Blaustein and Robert L. Zangrando, eds., *Civil Rights and African Americans: A Documentary History* (Evaston, IL: Northwestern University Press, 1991), 46.

2. Dred Scott v. Sandford, 60 U.S. 393, 404–5.

3. As discussed earlier in this book, at the time, senators were selected by state legislators. In their debates, Lincoln and Douglass were courting the votes of the state legislators both directly and indirectly through the legislators' constituents.

The debate between the two rivals turned on the meaning of freedom as self-government. Tens of thousands of spectators crowded into the fields surrounding the platform. Senator Stephen Douglas, the incumbent, tried to distance himself from the *Dred Scott* ruling. Senator Douglas asserted that self-government granted the majority of voters in each state the right to decide whether to permit slavery. In his opening speech at Alton, Illinois, Douglas said, "I look forward to a time when a State shall be allowed to do as it pleases. If it chooses to keep slavery forever, it is not my business, but its own; if it chooses to abolish slavery, it is its own business,—not mine. I care more for the great principle of self-government, the right of the people to rule, than I do for all the [Africans] in Christendom."[4] Douglas doubled down on his position in Galesburg, Illinois, "I hold to that great principle of self-government which asserts the right of every people to decide for themselves the nature and character of the domestic institutions and fundamental law under which they are to live."[5]

Douglas's opponent, a forty-nine-year-old frontiersman, took the stage, seeking to wrest the mantle of self-government from the senator. "No man believed more than I," said Abraham Lincoln, "in the principle of self-government; that it lies at the bottom of all my ideas of just government from beginning to end. I have denied that his [Douglas'] use of that term applies properly."[6] Self-government does not mean "that if any one man chooses to enslave another, no third man shall be allowed to object."[7] Freedom as self-government signifies the right of people to chart the course of their lives, consistent with the same freedom of others and protected by the equal rights of all: "Each individual is naturally entitled to do as he pleases with himself . . . so far as it in no wise interferes with any other man's rights."[8] In Peoria, Illinois, Lincoln said:

---

4. Stephen Douglas, "Douglas at Alton," in *The Lincoln Douglas Debates of 1858*, ed. Edwin Erle Sparks (Springfield: Illinois State Historical Library, 1908), 492–93.

5. Stephen Douglas, "Douglas at Galesburg," in Sparks, *Lincoln Douglas Debates*, 335.

6. Lincoln, "Speech of Hon. Abraham Lincoln at Springfield, June 17, 1858," 8.

7. Lincoln, "Speech of Hon. Abraham Lincoln at Springfield, June 17, 1858," 8.

8. Abraham Lincoln, "Speech of Hon. Abraham Lincoln, Delivered at Chicago, July 10, 1858," in Lincoln and Douglas, *Political Debates*, 28.

[I]f the negro *is* a man, is it not to that extent, a total destruction of self-government, to say that he too shall not govern *himself*? When the white man governs himself that is self-government; but when he governs himself, and also governs *another* man, that is *more* than self-government—that is despotism. . . . [N]o man is good enough to govern another man, *without that other's consent*. I say this is the leading principle—the sheet anchor of American republicanism. . . . Now the relation of masters and slaves is, pro tanto, a total violation of this principle. The master not only governs the slave without his consent; but he governs him by a set of rules altogether different from those which he prescribes for himself. Allow ALL the governed an equal voice in government, and that, and that only is self-government.[9]

Lincoln did not win the Senate race, but he had the better of the argument regarding self-government. Lincoln's speeches were read with acclaim, contributing to his successful run for the presidency in 1860.

I share two key commitments with Lincoln. First, self-government is not the right of one group of voters to exercise tyranny over others. Self-government means the *inclusion* of all the governed in government. I interpret inclusion to require that all citizens be equally empowered to participate in democratic accountability. Lincoln thought that citizens should be included by asking for their consent to be governed. Second, Lincoln and I agree that citizens bear democratic duties. We are entitled to freedom as self-government to do as we please, individually and collectively, compatible with the rights of others. We must meet our *duty* to respect each other's rights, so that *all* the governed are free.

By contrast, Senator Douglas assumed that citizens had no duties regarding the preferences they impose by force on others through the law. Senator Douglas laid down the challenge that we must answer: "Whenever you put a limitation upon the right of any people to decide what laws they want, you have destroyed the fundamental principle of

9. Abraham Lincoln, "Speech at Peoria, Illinois, October 16, 1854," in *The Collected Works of Abraham Lincoln*, vol. 2, ed. Roy P. Basler, Marion Dolores Pratt, and Lloyd A. Dunlap (New Brunswick, NJ: Rutgers University Press, 1953), 265 (emphasis in original).

self-government."[10] Douglas went so far as to claim that it would be democratic to carry out the preference to enact laws enforcing slavery. For Douglas, in short, citizens owe no duties of solidarity to respect or protect each other's freedom and equality.

This chapter defends democratic duties from five criticisms. First, I address the concern that, contrary to Lincoln's assertion, most citizens do not consent to their government. Aside from naturalized citizens, most people are born under the rule of a specific government and therefore are not asked to agree to the laws before being subject to them. Since consent does not explain why citizens are bound by laws, there is supposedly no duty of solidarity to make sure that self-government as consensual rule extends to all citizens.

While self-government is not grounded in consent, I suggest that it would be a mistake to discard the principle of self-government. We do not always agree with the laws. But I argue that we can be self-governing, or the ones in charge of our government, if we can hold our public servants democratically accountable and they secure our equal human rights. Slaves were denied their freedom as self-government, because they were subject to unaccountable government power, and their human rights were violated. Instead of being treated as citizens with equal authority over their public servants, slaves were excluded from the citizenry. Citizens bear the democratic duty of solidarity to recognize the equal authority of all the governed as fellow citizens.

Second, I allay the worry that democratic duties may limit our freedom. It is commonly believed that duties are burdens that restrict our bare liberty, or the ability to do whatever we want. I draw on John Stuart Mill to explain why democratic duties protect what we are entitled to: a rightful freedom compatible with the equal freedom of others. I introduce a schema from Mill of the ways that duties can be enforced to secure our freedom.

10. Stephen Douglas, "Douglas at Chicago, July 9, 1858," in *The Complete Lincoln-Douglass Debates of 1858*, ed. Paul M. Angle (Chicago: University of Chicago Press, 1991), 17.

Third, I reply to empirical objections to democratic accountability rights and duties.[11] If democratic duties are so essential, how can they promoted? I outline how these responsibilities may be fostered through deliberation, civic associations, and civic education. Writers such as Chris Achen and Larry Bartels raise the further concern that citizens exercise their democratic accountability rights arbitrarily.[12] If democratic accountability rights are used so capriciously, it might lead us to question the value of those rights and the duty to protect them.

To answer this skepticism, I present a *revealed preferences argument*: the behavior of elected authoritarians exposes their belief that democratic rights curb their autocratic power. Elected authoritarians have a strong incentive to preserve their rule and to perceive correctly the potential threat from democratic rights.[13] Their repressive actions reveal that they implicitly fear the power of democratic accountability. The protective effect of democracy is given credence by how African Americans wielded their democratic rights to gain access to public education and economic opportunity during Reconstruction, from 1865 to 1877. When they lost those rights afterward under Jim Crow, African Americans were harshly oppressed.

Fourth, the chapter refutes attempts to exempt citizens from the *democratic duty of oversight*. It might be thought that marginalized citizens bear no duty to hold their public servants democratically accountable. Because they are denied their equal authority, marginalized citizens are not among the people in charge of government, and they incur no responsibility for what officials do. I reply that we should fulfill our *duty of solidarity* to end the marginalization of our fellow citizens, so they can be self-governing and take responsibility for their government's actions.

Fifth, I challenge the popular will accountability approach's wholesale neglect of democratic duties. In this view, democratic accountability

11. I am grateful to reviewer 2, who asked how democratic duties can be promoted. Reviewer 2 also raised empirical concerns with democratic accountability rights based on the work of Achen and Bartels.

12. Achen and Bartels, *Democracy for Realists*.

13. I thank Jack Pitblado for discussion to clarify my revealed preferences argument.

consists of elections to induce officials to follow the will of the people. Popular will accountability is neutral about the preferences that citizens adopt. If they demand that their officials impose racial discrimination, then it would be democratic to discriminate, as Senator Douglas believed. I reply that the absence of democratic duties renders popular will accountability self-defeating. A majority can vote to deny democracy to other citizens.

It was, as Lincoln said, "a total destruction of self-government" to drive out African Americans from democratic government.[14] To protect the inclusion of all citizens in democracy, we should fulfill our *democratic duties* of solidarity and oversight, ensuring that our public servants abide by their duty of fidelity. This chapter vindicates the duties of democratic accountability vital to securing freedom as self-government for all citizens.

Defending the Democratic Duty of Solidarity from the Consent Objection

Lincoln invoked the Declaration of Independence to found self-government on the consent of the governed.[15] I am sympathetic to this approach, but I build self-government on the more solid foundation of equal accountability. I pursue this path due to the incisive criticisms leveled by Ronald Dworkin, Anna Stilz, David Estlund, and other scholars against the consent theory.[16] The citizens who voted in favor of a winning candidate in an election might have consented to her election, but other citizens did not agree.[17] They wanted someone else in office.

14. Lincoln, *Collected Works of Abraham Lincoln*, vol. 2, 265.

15. A proponent of the consent theory of political authority is Joseph Tussman, *Obligation and the Body Politic* (New York: Oxford University Press, 1960).

16. I thank Eric Cheng who asked about the relation between equal accountability and consent at the Western Political Science Association conference. Compelling critiques of the consent theory include Anna Stilz, "Review of Pauline Kleingeld," *Social Theory and Practice* 39, no. 3 (2013): 548–54; Ronald Dworkin, *Justice for Hedgehogs* (Cambridge, MA: Harvard University Press, 2013), chap. 14; and David Estlund, *Democratic Authority: A Philosophical Framework* (Princeton, NJ: Princeton University Press, 2008).

17. Scholars who make this argument include Kolodny, "Rule Over None I," 204–6, and Estlund, *Democratic Authority*, 109–10.

Even when we did vote for the candidate who won, she may pursue policies that clash with our own preferences. The philosopher Henry Sidgwick commented that even when we support the winning candidate and agree with her policies, she may be outvoted in the legislature.[18] How can consent to that law be imputed to us?

The common thread running through these criticisms is that consent is *individually decisive*. Your consent is necessary for an action to occur. If you do not consent to a marriage, it cannot take place. Your individual decision cannot be overridden by a majority vote. Yet a democracy routinely enacts laws that contradict your preferences. A frequent fallback is to respond that we may not consent to the laws, but we have consented to the constitution. Yet aside from naturalized citizens, most citizens are born subject to a government and never take an oath or sign on the dotted line.

Since many citizens have not granted their consent to the laws, it is tempting to believe that they are not morally obliged to obey those laws, as philosophical anarchists assert.[19] This position would hand individuals a veto over laws when they withhold their consent. But philosophical anarchism would imply implausibly that racists are not bound by anti-discrimination ordinances, because they object to them. Billionaires would not have to pay taxes, if they scoff at those laws. Philosophical anarchism also invites the charge that it is self-undermining. It fails to secure its basic moral commitment that our freedom should never be restricted without our consent. Laws that protect us from nonconsensual treatment would be ineffectual if some recalcitrant citizens, such as murderers, refused to agree to those laws.

James Madison observes that if the consent of all the governed were required for a law to take effect, the government would be powerless to protect our rights. He writes in an 1835 essay that the purpose of government is not simply to do anything the majority wants, no matter how

18. Henry Sidgwick, *The Method of Ethics*, 7th ed. (Indianapolis, IN: Hackett, 1981), 298–99.

19. Robert Paul Wolff, *In Defense of Anarchism* (Berkeley: University of California Press, 1970), and A. John Simmons and Christopher Heath Wellman, *Is There a Duty to Obey the Law? For and Against* (Cambridge, UK: Cambridge University Press, 2005).

unjust. The proper role of government (which Senator Stephen Douglas forgot) is that "the rights, the safety, and the interest of each may be under the safeguard of the whole."[20] The unanimity rule of consent would annul the measures needed to protect the rights of all: "The objects in view could not be attained, if every measure conducive to them, required the consent of every member of the Society."[21] In lieu of the consent of all, citizens should rely on majority voting to choose their legislators, who can enact laws on the citizens' behalf. Madison adds the crucial qualification that the legislature must act consistently with the rights of all, since securing these rights is the legitimating purpose that government must fulfill for its power to be just. It is just for the government to "do any thing that could be *rightfully* done, by the unanimous concurrence of the members; the reserved rights of individuals (of Conscience for example), in becoming parties to the original compact, being beyond the legitimate reach of Sovereignty."[22] For government power to be morally legitimate or permissible, it must secure our rights, which citizens continue to be entitled to after establishing their government.

If freedom as self-government is not founded on consent, where do we find its moral foundation? I argue that freedom as self-government should be grounded in equal *democratic accountability*. Unlike consent, democratic accountability does not condition citizens' obligation to obey the law on their agreement with it. But it mandates that we possess equal authority over our public servants, so they answer to us. Democratic

20. James Madison, "Essay on Sovereignty, December 1835," Founders Online, National Archives, https://founders.archives.gov/documents/Madison/99-02-02-3188.

21. Madison, "Essay on Sovereignty." John Locke takes a similar position against unanimity rule: if "nothing but the consent of every individual can make any thing to be the act of the whole" or a law, "such a consent is next to impossible ever to be had" (Locke, *Two Treatises of Government*, 332, §98). Consent is unlikely because of moral disagreement and the fact that not everyone can attend the legislature that makes the laws. The result of unanimity rule is that the government must dissolve.

22. Madison, "Essay on Sovereignty" (underscore in original). Madison importantly refers to "what *could be* rightfully done by the unanimous concurrence of its members." This implies a hypothetical consent standard. It is just, or morally legitimate, for the government to act with its coercive power in ways that could be agreed to by citizens consistent with their freedom and equality. Immanuel Kant endorses a similar hypothetical consent standard for the laws when he proposes an "idea of reason" that every legislator "frame his laws in such a way that they could have been produced by the united will of a whole nation." See Kant, "Theory and Practice," in *Political Writings*, 79.

accountability preserves the insight from the consent theory that we are self-governing when we are *included* in government. But democratic accountability interprets inclusion as our having the standing as equal authorities to hold our public servants democratically accountable. This avoids the defect Madison diagnosed with consent, namely that unreasonable citizens could veto the laws requisite to securing rights.

Two additional advantages accrue to grounding freedom as self-government on democratic accountability. First, doing so avoids a hidden hazard of the consent argument. The idea of consent can be distorted to impugn democratic opposition, especially if consent is conflated with unbounded majority rule. Consent is a type of moral power, which alters the rights and responsibilities of others. Your property right in your home gives you the right to exclude others from it. Other people are under a correlative duty, imposed by your property right, not to trespass. However, if you give your consent to others to enter your home, it changes their duty, granting them the permission to step onto your property. The trap here is to conclude that if you have consented to the laws of a democracy, then you have no basis for objecting if those laws treat you or anyone else unjustly. Just as your consent converts a prohibited trespass into a permitted entry, your democratic consent might be thought to turn a prohibited abuse of power into a permitted law that you have accepted. Thomas Hobbes voices a version of this view: "He that complaineth of injury from his Soveraigne, complaineth of that whereof he himselfe is Author; and therefore ought not to accuse any man but himselfe."[23] Hobbes allowed the possibility that the sovereign could be a democracy.[24] We are the author of everything the sovereign ruler does, says Hobbes, given that we have consented to the creation of the sovereign: "From this Institution of a Commonwealth are derived all the Rights . . . on whom the Soveraigne [*sic*] Power is conferred by the *consent* of the People assembled."[25] Hobbes surmises that we cannot object to anything that the government may

---

23. Hobbes, *Leviathan*, 124.
24. Hobbes, 129.
25. Hobbes, 121 (emphasis added).

do to us because we have consented to it: "Nothing done to a man, by his own consent can be injury."[26]

However, once we see that even a democratic government is not consensual, this opens space for us to protest the injustices that our government metes out to us and others. We never agreed to be treated or to treat others this way. The nonconsensual nature of government power, and the fact that it is coercive, make it essential that we possess rights to hold our public servants democratically accountable.[27] Otherwise our liberty would be vulnerable to a nonconsensual and coercive force that is unaccountable to us.

The second advantage of founding freedom as self-government on democratic accountability is that it highlights the importance of rights. If government power is imposed on us nonconsensually, and if it threatens us with injury, what could possibly make that just? It must be the overriding importance of what that power secures. The purpose of government cannot simply be to do what a group of citizens subjectively prefer, even if it is to enslave, as Senator Douglas thought. That goal is insufficiently important to place us under a duty to submit to a power we disagree with, that we do not consent to, and that threatens us with imprisonment. The only end that could be so urgent as to override consent in cases of coercion is *justice*. As Madison says in Federalist 51, "Justice is the end of government. It is the end of civil society."[28] Madison expands on this point in his 1835 essay. Requiring unanimous consent for laws would interfere with the just role of government, which is that

---

26. Hobbes, 104.

27. Rawls acknowledges that the coercive power of government is nonconsensual: "While social cooperation can be willing and harmonious, and in this sense voluntary, it is not voluntary in the sense that our joining or belonging to associations and groups within society is voluntary. There is no alternative to social cooperation except unwilling and resentful compliance, or resistance and civil war" (*Political Liberalism*, 301). Rawls believes that the nonconsensual, coercive aspect of government can be morally legitimate if it meets principles of justice that could be accepted by the governed. This is a standard of hypothetical consent (68). By contrast, I argue that the coercive power of government, to be morally legitimate, must also be *democratically accountable* to the governed, so that they are *freely self-governing*. This requires not actual consent but actual democratic accountability.

28. Madison, "Federalist No. 51," 254.

"the rights, the safety, and the interest of each may be under the safe-guard of the whole."[29]

I show in chapter 5 that justice contains both substantive require-ments in how the government treats us, and procedural requirements entitling us to participate in government. The substantive aspect of jus-tice is that the government should secure our equal human rights. The procedural aspect is that we be equally empowered to participate in democratic accountability. Both requirements must be satisfied to make government power just, and to recognize citizens as equal authorities. When citizens are recognized as equal authorities, they freely govern themselves as the ones in charge of their government.

I argue that once we realize that government power is coercive and nonconsensual, we can gain a greater appreciation for why the standards of democratic accountability that our public servants must heed are not merely subjective and do not depend on whatever the plurality of voters happen to want. The standards of democratic accountability that we have the duty of oversight to hold our public servants for fulfilling are defined by the rights and responsibilities of justice.

The Democratic Duty of Solidarity Secures Our Freedom

A potential worry is that the duty of solidarity might seem to clash with citizens' rights.[30] For instance, should citizens be imprisoned if they speak or write in favor of racist or sexist laws that would marginalize others? How can democratic duties be consistent with the rights of free speech and the press? I hold that these freedoms should be protected. Free speech and the press are both democratic accountability rights and human rights, as we will show in chapter 6. At the same time, rights dif-fer from merely desirable benefits, because rights impose correlative duties that must be enforced.

29. Madison, "Essay on Sovereignty."
30. I thank Natasha Patel, who asked this question in her astute comments on this book at the Stanford Political Theory Workshop. I appreciate Dongxian Jiang's thoughtful suggestion to distinguish between duties enforceable by law and from those enforceable by moral blame.

We should match the type of enforcement with the severity of the breach of duty. Citizens who violently assault the rights of others, like the Klan, should be stopped by the force of legal penalties. Citizens who seek to impose racial segregation but are nonviolent deserve the social sanctions of moral criticism for their attempts to discriminate against vulnerable minorities. Other citizens may incur moral blame for neglecting their duty to protect the marginalized from injustice, but they should be reasoned with and persuaded to fulfill their responsibility.[31]

I adopt a typology from John Stuart Mill of the three ways to uphold duties: persuasion and education, the social sanctions of moral criticism, and legal enforcement. Mill was the leading proponent of free speech and action, but he understood that a right to speak is not a right against criticism. The right to act freely is not a right to act violently.

The first mode to uphold duties is coercive, through government enforced laws. There are certain democratic duties that the government can duly enforce as legal responsibilities, including the duty not to violate rights. If militias assault marginalized citizens casting their ballots, it would be just for the government to defend the right to vote. As we read in chapter 3, President Grant and Congress founded the Department of Justice in 1870 to combat the violence of the Ku Klux Klan. In doing so they acted on their *democratic duty of fidelity* to protect the equal authority of citizens and their rights.[32] Citizens met their *democratic duty of solidarity* when they participated democratically to support laws safeguarding African Americans. These citizens also acted on their *duty of oversight* to ensure that their public servants exercise power justly.

The second way of upholding democratic duties is through persuasion and education. Although citizens bear a duty of oversight to criticize the injustices of their public servants, it would interfere with freedom of speech to coercively enforce that duty. We should respect

31. If the failure to protect the marginalized is sufficiently egregious and persistent, it may deserve social sanctions.

32. Richard M. Valelly, "National Parties and Racial Disenfranchisement," in *Classifying by Race*, ed. Paul E. Peterson, (Princeton, NJ: Princeton University Press, 1995), 196.

the human dignity of citizens, as persons capable of reason and conscience, by recognizing their rights to free speech and the press.[33] Citizens should be encouraged to meet their duties of oversight and solidarity through persuasion, deliberation, and civic education. These forms of communication respect citizens' capacity for reason by engaging with and cultivating that capacity. When citizens deliberate together, they can testify about the impact of injustices on their own lives, advance moral claims, and convince one another to take each other's rights seriously.[34]

A third mode of upholding duties is through the social sanctions of moral criticism. For instance, recall from our earlier discussion that members of Congress failed more than two hundred times to pass anti-lynching laws. They deserved reproach for having forsaken their duty of fidelity to guarantee the rights of African Americans. Perhaps it might be thought that moral criticism should be applied only toward officials who are remiss in their duties, but not to citizens. Mill gives voice to the well-known reservation about the "tyranny of the prevailing thought and feeling" against ordinary citizens.[35] But this forms only part of the picture he draws.

Mill proposes a standard in "On Liberty" to determine when it is proper to morally criticize the injustices committed by citizens. Specifically, he maintains that when our rights are safeguarded by society, we owe duties in return to guarantee those rights: "Every one who receives the protection of society owes a return for the benefit, and the fact of living in society renders it indispensable that each should be bound to observe a certain line of conduct towards the rest."[36] People could not be free if others insolently attacked their freedom, and if no one had a duty to aid the victims.

33. On the two moral powers justifying the basic liberties of citizens, see Rawls, *Political Liberalism*, chap. 8.

34. On democratic persuasion by officials, encouraging citizens to respect each other's rights, see Corey Brettschneider, *When the State Speaks, What Should It Say?* (Princeton, NJ: Princeton University Press, 2012).

35. Mill, "On Liberty," 220.

36. Mill, "On Liberty," 276. I thank Rob Reich, who suggested the requirements of justice include the three values of security, freedom, and equality.

Mill expounds the meaning of a moral right in *Utilitarianism*: "To have a right, then, is ... to have something which society ought to *defend me* in the possession of."[37] He defines rights as entitlements to interests that are so paramount they impose correlative duties on others. The prime interest that rights defend is "security, to every one's feelings the most vital of all interests."[38] The security to enjoy our freedom is the precondition to pursuing any life worth living: "Security no human being can possibly do without; on it we depend for all our immunity from evil, and for the whole value of all and every good."[39] For our rights to endure, citizens and public servants must protect those rights: "Now this most indispensable of all necessaries, after physical nutriment, cannot be had, unless the machinery for providing it is kept unintermittedly in active play."[40] Rights possess an urgent status and priority, which is why they impose correlative duties.

Mill distinguishes three types of duties, each with a proper mode of enforcement. First, citizens bear a duty to respect each other's rights. The conduct to be enforced consists "in not injuring the interests of one another ... which, either by express legal provision or by tacit understanding, ought to be considered as rights."[41] For instance, citizens are entitled to the right to vote. The duty to respect that right can be enforced by government through laws that prohibit interference with voters.

While rights impose weighty correlative duties, it is possible for rights to come into conflict with each other. Our entitlement to each right should be adjusted to cohere with the other rights in a larger system of liberty.[42] Freedom of speech is the right of citizens to express their views. But freedom of speech must be consonant with other rights, such as privacy. No one has the free speech right to share other people's confidential health-care information.

37. John Stuart Mill, "Utilitarianism," in John Stuart Mill, *Essays on Ethics, Religion and Society*, ed. J. M. Robson (Toronto, ON: University of Toronto Press, 1969), 250 (emphasis added).
38. Mill, "Utilitarianism," 251.
39. Mill, "Utilitarianism," 251.
40. Mill, "Utilitarianism," 251.
41. Mill, "On Liberty," 276.
42. Rawls, *Political Liberalism*, 295; idem, *Justice as Fairness*, 111.

In addition to the duty to respect rights, the second type of duty is the responsibility to contribute to the maintenance of government. This duty entails "each person's bearing his share . . . of the labors and sacrifices incurred for defending the society or its members from injury."[43] Mill has in mind the payment of taxes, giving evidence to courts, and the public service of national defense.[44] This type of duty can be coercively enforced to sustain the government institutions that protect and empower rights.

The third type of duty is not to injure or neglect. If the harm does not rise to the level of violating rights, the duty can be enforced by social sanctions or moral criticism, though not by legal coercion. Mill remarks, "The acts of an individual may be hurtful to others, or wanting in due consideration for their welfare, without going the length of violating any of their constituted rights. The offender may then be punished by opinion, though not by law."[45] He gives as examples "falsehood or duplicity in dealing with them; unfair or ungenerous use of advantages over them; even selfish abstinence from defending them against injury—these are fit objects of moral reprobation and, in grave cases, of moral retribution and punishment."[46]

Consider the White Citizens' Councils, which resisted the desegregation of public schools. Suppose that some members advocated racial segregation but refrained from using violence. The right to free speech would rule out coercively censoring their expression. However, the White Citizens' Council members, by pushing for discriminatory laws against the marginalized, were "making unfair or ungenerous use of advantages over them," in Mill's phrase.[47] They scorned the equal standing

---

43. Mill, "On Liberty," 276. I thank Josh Ober, who insightfully asked me, during a Stanford faculty research seminar, whether citizens have a duty to contribute to the protection of their society and government. I consider this part of the duty to protect the rights of others, which is a principal-principal democratic duty of solidarity. Payment of taxes to fund national defense and public safety is integral to the duty to empower the rights of others, which is also a duty of solidarity.

44. Mill, "On Liberty," 225.

45. Mill, "On Liberty," 276.

46. Mill, "On Liberty," 276.

47. Mill, "On Liberty," 276.

of African Americans and violated their democratic duty of solidarity, and so deserved moral criticism.

The right to free speech is not an immunity from blame. A person has a right to free speech to lash out and insult a couple as they walk down the aisle to get married. The right to free speech protects that expression from legal interference by the state. But it misses the mark to claim that the profane outburst should be free from any moral censure. Likewise, citizens may voice their support for discriminatory laws, in breach of their duties of solidarity. They should not be arrested for their expression, out of respect for their capacity for reason and conscience that makes people free and equal. But other people also possess a right to free speech to argue against and rebuke the instigators of discrimination and segregation for seeking to marginalize other citizens. We should be steadfast in "interposing to protect the defenceless against ill-usage," as Mill said.[48] Our democratic duties are not only compatible with our rights, but rights impose correlative duties. The significance of rights is that they call on "our fellow-creatures to join in making safe for us the very groundwork of our existence," in Mill's words.[49] The phrase "join in making safe for us" exemplifies what I call the duty of solidarity, where we participate democratically to secure each other's rights.[50]

Addressing Empirical Concerns about Democratic Rights and Duties

Chris Achen and Larry Bartels find empirical evidence to be skeptical of democratic accountability in their influential book, *Democracy for Realists*.[51] In one form of democratic accountability, which they call retrospective accountability, voters look back at how their lives fared

48. Mill, "On Liberty," 225.
49. Mill, "Utilitarianism," 251.
50. Mill, "Utilitarianism," 251.
51. Achen and Bartels, *Democracy for Realists*.

under the incumbent.[52] Did they enjoy peace and prosperity, as they did during President Dwight Eisenhower's first term in office? If so, voters will reelect the incumbent. Did the voters suffer an economic collapse and an unemployment rate that rose precipitously from 3.2 percent to 24.9 percent, as they did under President Herbert Hoover?[53] In that case, they will vote to remove the incumbent. Despite the plausibility of this mechanism, Achen and Bartels cast doubts about retrospective accountability. In their most widely discussed finding, they claim that New Jersey voters blamed the incumbent, Woodrow Wilson, for shark attacks, cutting into his share of the 1916 presidential vote.[54] Achen and Bartels believe that this finding is representative of voters and not an aberration. They conclude that voters are irrational in punishing incumbents for events outside their control: "Blind retrospection . . . seems to us to provide a significant challenge to the conventional understanding of political accountability in modern democracies."[55] While Achen and Bartels support democracy as the least objectionable form of government, their results might lead us to wonder: Why should we act in solidarity to guarantee the vote to citizens when they will use it so senselessly?

Other scholars, including Anthony Fowler from the University of Chicago and Andrew Hall from Stanford, have questioned the shark attack finding. Fowler and Hall looked at "data on every fatal shark attack in US history and county-level returns from every presidential election from 1872 to 2012." They discovered "no systematic evidence that shark attacks affect elections."[56]

52. Achen and Bartels, 90–115. A classic defense of retrospective voting is Morris Fiorina, *Retrospective Voting in American Elections* (New Haven, CT: Yale University Press, 1981).

53. UPI, "Unemployment under Presidencies since Depression," *New York Times*, October 9, 1982.

54. Achen and Bartels, *Democracy for Realists*, 116–45. Anthony Fowler and Andrew B. Hall call this finding the "centerpiece" of Achen and Bartels's book, in "Do Shark Attacks Influence Presidential Elections? Reassessing a Prominent Finding on Voter Competence," *Journal of Politics* 80, no. 4 (2018): 1423.

55. Achen and Bartels, *Democracy for Realists*, 142.

56. Fowler and Hall, "Do Shark Attacks Influence Presidential Elections," 1423.

I offer a novel *revealed preferences argument* to defend democratic accountability rights.[57] In attacking democratic accountability rights, elected authoritarians reveal their belief that those very rights impede tyranny and protect citizens.[58] For example, the 1933 Reichstag Fire Decree in Germany outlawed democratic accountability rights in terms that could have been written in apartheid South Africa: "Thus restrictions on personal liberty, on the right of free expression of opinion, including freedom of the press, on the right of assembly and association . . . are permissible beyond the legal limits otherwise prescribed."[59] Apartheid officials targeted the very same democratic accountability rights in their declarations of emergency.[60]

In 1860 the abolitionist Frederick Douglass delivered a revelatory address about the power of freedom of speech. Douglass said, "Liberty is meaningless where the right to utter one's thoughts and opinions has ceased to exist. That, of all rights, is the dread of tyrants. It is the right which they first of all strike down. They know its power."[61] What Douglass praised in freedom of speech holds true of our democratic accountability rights more broadly: they are dreaded by tyrants. My revealed preference argument points out that if democratic accountability rights were not so formidable a deterrent to despotism, dictators would not be so bent on abolishing them. The unease of authoritarians

57. In economics, the revealed preference theory holds that consumers' preferences are best shown by their behavior. Paul A. Samuelsohn, "A Note on the Pure Theory of Consumers' Behavior," *Economica* 5, no. 17 (1938): 61–71. I adopt the notion of revealed preferences to suggest that we should infer the views of elected authoritarians from their behavior. It is implied by their suppressing democratic accountability rights that those rights threaten their despotic rule. Elected authoritarians have every incentive to discern correctly the threat to their rule from democratic accountability, given their desire to stay in power.

58. Achen and Bartels agree that "an independent judiciary, freedom of speech and assembly, and other features of democratic institutions and culture are undoubtedly important" (*Democracy for Realists*, 309). My revealed preference argument posits that citizens do not vote in an arbitrary way, but they can use their democratic accountability rights to defend themselves, as elected authoritarians themselves realize.

59. Quoted in Richard J. Evans, *The Third Reich in Power* (New York: Penguin, 2006), 333.

60. Apartheid officials cited state of emergency laws to detain "a major proportion of the most effective leadership of the ANC" [African National Congress]. See Tom Lodge, *Sharpeville: An Apartheid Massacre and its Consequences* (New York: Oxford University Press, 2011), 167.

61. Frederick Douglass, "Plea for Freedom of Speech in Boston," speech in Boston, December 3, 1860, in *Free Speech*, ed. Corey Brettschneider (New York: Penguin 2021), 87.

when they behold democratic accountability is the ultimate tribute to how it secures us from tyranny.

The revealed preference argument gains credibility from a prominent historical example. Many African American slaves were prohibited by law from attending school or even learning how to read. If uneducated voters made poor use of retrospective accountability, then the newly liberated African American slaves would not have voted for their own interests after the Civil War. Endowing them with the vote would have made little difference in their lives, as they would have cast their ballots based on the vagaries of shark attacks or other random events.[62]

Contrary to this expectation, the newly enfranchised African Americans voted against racial discrimination and in favor of educational opportunities for their families. Daniel Ziblatt and Steven Levitsky note that more than two thousand African Americans were elected to public office in the 1870s, "including fourteen congressmen and two U.S. senators."[63] In the Louisiana and South Carolina, during Reconstruction over 40 percent of the representatives elected in the lower house of the state legislature were African Americans.[64] With the right to vote came legislation creating a public education system in the South that was open to African Americans and laws guarding against forced labor and servitude.[65]

Democracy was pivotal for protecting African Americans. The former states of the Confederacy responded by enacting new constitutions between 1895 and 1908 to obstruct African Americans from voting.[66]

---

62. This may be the expectation of "epistocrats," who criticize ordinary citizens for being uneducated. Epistocrats propose to replace democracy with the rule of an unaccountable elite who claim to be experts. See Brennan, *Against Democracy*; Caplan, *Myth of the Rational Voter*; Lee and Zakaria, "Culture Is Destiny"; and Bell, *China Model*.

63. Levitsky and Ziblatt, *How Democracies Die*, 89–90.

64. Levitsky and Ziblatt, 90.

65. Eric Foner, *Freedom's Lawmakers: A Directory of Black Officeholders during Reconstruction* (Baton Rouge: Louisiana State University Press, 1996).

66. Levitsky and Ziblatt, *How Democracies Die*, 90. Achen and Bartels might respond to my argument by maintaining that some voters in Germany and the United States voted for the Nazis and white supremacist parties. While that is the case, the Nazis never won a majority, topping out at 37 percent of the vote in the 1932 parliamentary elections. Their seizure of power was abetted by wealthy elites, Junkers, and industrialists, such as the Prussian nobleman Franz von Papen and Chancellor Paul von Hindenburg, who wanted to wield Hitler to suppress

Under the specter of violence, voter turnout in South Carolina plunged from 96 percent of African American adults in 1876 to 11 percent in 1898.[67] After being deprived of the right to vote, African Americans were subjected to Jim Crow laws that enforced racial segregation in employment, schools, hotels, and transportation.

To be clear, citizens do not always use their democratic accountability rights wisely. Achen and Bartels raise valid concerns about whether voters are sufficiently informed. They are correct that democracy is distorted by the preponderant power of the rich.[68] To mitigate these problems, I argue that we should *empower* citizens to participate in democracy. As I charted in chapter 3, citizens should be empowered with a robust civic education to understand their democratic rights and duties, and to be more informed. Citizens also need to be empowered with access to the vote, legal aid, campaign finance reform, and a social minimum, so they have the resources to use their democratic accountability rights. The revealed preferences argument and the example of Reconstruction suggest that the difficulties with democratic accountability are to be surmounted by strengthening and empowering those rights.

Another source of skepticism turns to democratic duties. If these duties are so vital, how are they to be instilled? This book focuses on answering the normative question of what rights and duties should constitute democratic accountability. While space does not permit a full empirical study, we can sketch a set of paths to promoting democratic duties. Drawing on the literature on norm diffusion, I outline how deliberation, civic associations, activist networks, social sanctions, civic education, and social emulation can instill these responsibilities.

---

democratic demands for workers' rights. Elites put an end to democracy. I am not suggesting that voters always use their vote in an informed or just way. Rather, citizens need democratic accountability rights to protect their substantive rights and to respect their freedom as self-government. According to my revealed preferences argument, elected authoritarians are well aware that citizens are capable of voting to curb autocracy. On the Nazis never winning a majority, see Robert O. Paxton, *The Anatomy of Fascism* (New York: Vintage Books, 2005), 67.

67. Levitsky and Ziblatt, *How Democracies Die*, 91.

68. Achen and Bartels, *Democracy for Realists*, 320, and Larry M. Bartels, *Unequal Democracy: The Political Economy of the New Gilded Age*, 2nd ed. (Princeton, NJ: Princeton University Press, 2016).

A democratic duty is a type of *norm* that applies to the responsibilities of citizens or public servants. A norm is a "shared standard of appropriate behavior."[69] For example, one of the norms in the duty of solidarity is that citizens should respect each other's rights. Political scientists who study norm diffusion explain that norms are social in nature and can be promoted or altered based on shared deliberation. People can then "change the norms that are seen to apply to a particular situation, or even develop new norms, through contestation and argument; that is, through *discursive politics*."[70]

Leigh Raymond, S. Laurel Weldon, and their coauthors set out two mechanisms for how deliberation can revise norms. First, activists can engage in "normative reframing."[71] They can foreground a problematic norm and argue that another, existing norm would better fit a given context. For example, Raymond and Weldon write about the case of environmental activists opposed to global warming, who have challenged the prevailing norm of granting rights to resources based on beneficial prior use.[72] This norm allowed polluters to emit greenhouse gases for free. Environmental activists retorted that the emission of greenhouse gases was not beneficial, but harmful. This made it more suitable to apply another norm, which laid down the principle that compensation should be paid for damages. Overcoming resistance from industry, activists convinced Connecticut, Delaware, Maine, Maryland, Massachusetts, New Hampshire, New Jersey, New York, Rhode Island, Vermont, and Virginia to join the Regional Greenhouse Gas Initiative (RGGI), the first legally mandated cap-and-trade program in the United States.[73]

69. Leigh Raymond et al., "Making Change: Norm-Based Strategies for Institutional Change to Address Intractable Problems," *Political Research Quarterly* 67, no. 1 (2014): 197 (emphasis in original).

70. Raymond et al. 2014, "Making Change," 199.

71. Raymond et al., 200–201.

72. Raymond et al., "Making Change," 205, and Leigh Raymond, *Private Rights in Public Resources: Equity and Property Allocation in Market-Based Environmental Policy* (Washington, DC: Resources for the Future Press, 2003).

73. Raymond, *Private Rights in Public Resources*, 2003.

Furthermore, deliberation can change norms through "normative innovation."[74] Here, deliberation reveals how an existing norm is problematic and then creates a new norm to take its place. S. Laurel Weldon describes how activists engaged in normative innovation to contest the norm that violence against women is a private matter. They replaced it with a new norm that classified the security of women against violence as an urgent human rights issue. This new norm in turn drove the ratification of the landmark 1993 United Nations Declaration on the Elimination of Violence against Women (DEVAW).[75]

When citizens deliberate, they inform each other of injustices and the need to remedy them. As Rawls writes, "in everyday life the exchange of opinion with others checks our partiality and widens our perspective; we are made to see things from their standpoint and the limits of our vision are brought home to us."[76] Deliberation can make us more aware of other people's experiences and the perspectives of those who have suffered injustice. This form of deliberation among citizens has steadily increased public support in the United States for same-sex marriage, which has risen from 27 percent in 1996 to 70 percent in 2021, according to Gallup.[77] Personal contact with same-sex couples and deliberation with LGBT citizens influenced public opinion. A Pew poll found that 32 percent person of people who changed their minds to endorse same-sex marriage did because they knew someone who is LGBT, and 25 percent became more supportive from reflection and thinking about the subject.[78] Deliberation led citizens to be more likely to meet their duty of solidarity to respect the rights of LGBT citizens.

74. Raymond et al., "Making Change," 206–7.
75. Raymond et al., 206; S. Laurel Weldon, "Inclusion, Solidarity and Social Movements: The Global Movement on Gender Violence," *Perspectives on Politics* 4, no. 1 (2006): 55–74; UN General Assembly, Declaration on the Elimination of Violence against Women, A/RES/48/104, UN General Assembly, December 20, 1993.
76. See Rawls, *Theory of Justice*, 315, and Ly, "Human Right to Deliberative Justification." Amy Gutmann and Dennis Thompson write that a "purpose of deliberation is to encourage public-spirited perspectives on public issues" (*Why Deliberative Democracy*, 10).
77. Tori B. Powell, "Same-Sex Marriage Sees Record-High Support in U.S., Poll Finds," *CBS News*, June 8, 2021, https://www.cbsnews.com/news/same-sex-gay-marriage-record-support/.
78. Pew Research Center, "Growing Support for Gay Marriage: Changed Minds and Changing Demographics," March 20, 2013, https://www.pewresearch.org/politics/2013/03/20/growing-support-for-gay-marriage-changed-minds-and-changing-demographics/. Robert

Through normative reframing, innovation, and testimony about injustices, citizens can promote democratic duties.[79] Consider how Susan B. Anthony cited the Declaration of Independence to advocate the right to vote for women. After she was arrested for voting as a woman, she gave a widely circulated speech in 1873. Anthony normatively reframed the vote for women as required by the existing norm of self-government. Like Lincoln, Anthony invoked the Declaration of Independence: "And here, in the very first paragraph of the Declaration, is the assertion of the natural right of all to the ballot, for how can 'the consent of the governed' be given, if the right to vote be denied."[80] In the wake of deliberation related to her arguments, states began recognizing the right to vote for women, starting with Wyoming in 1890 and Colorado in 1893.

Citizens can work through civic associations to support the duty of solidarity. Raymond and Weldon observe that "it was strong, autonomous women's movements that first articulated the issue of violence against women."[81] These civic associations held deliberation where "women *collectively* developed analysis of social problems, devising new social practices, models and ways of living."[82] Women took the ideas generated in this internal deliberation and sought to persuade their fellow citizens in external deliberation with the larger public. Women's associations spoke out, published books, circulated petitions, and launched protests.[83] Fittingly, Alexis de Tocqueville extolled the organizational power of associations, writing in *Democracy in America*,

---

Goodin elucidates how citizens need to engage in "deliberation within," or internal reflection about justice, in addition to interpersonal deliberation in "Democratic Deliberation Within," *Philosophy and Public Affairs* 29, no. 1 (2000): 81–109.

79. I classify this as a democratic duty of solidarity, which citizens owe each other.

80. Susan B. Anthony, "Is It a Crime to Vote?" in *History of Woman's Suffrage*, vol. 2, ed. Elizabeth Cady Stanton, Susan B. Anthony, and Matilda Joslyn Gage (New York: Fowler & Wells, 1882), 631. Wyoming granted the right to vote to women as a U.S. territory in 1869, and it recognized the right to vote for women when it became a U.S. state in 1890.

81. Raymond et al., "Making Change," 206.

82. Raymond et al., 206–7 (emphasis in original).

83. Raymond et al., 207.

"The association gathers the efforts of divergent minds in a cluster and drives them vigorously toward a single goal clearly indicated by it."[84]

Civic associations can be even more effective when they coordinate their efforts in what Margaret Keck and Kathryn Sikkink call "activist networks."[85] These networks enable multiple civic associations to pool information, funds, personnel, and services in pursuit of a common goal. On March 3, 1913, the day before President Woodrow Wilson's inauguration, a network of women associations assembled a massive Woman Suffrage Procession in Washington, DC. An audience of more than 250,000 spectators gathered to witness the march. The procession featured delegations from every US state, and women representatives of professions, ranging from teachers to lawyers, businesswomen, nurses, doctors, and librarians. Their shared banner proclaimed, "We demand an amendment to the Constitution of the United States enfranchising the women of this country."[86] The suffragettes formed an activist network, which fostered the duty of solidarity to recognize the rights of women.

In the first stage of norm diffusion, citizens accept a norm after being persuaded by deliberation, which is amplified by the activism of civic associations. The democratic accountability rights to free speech, the

---

84. Tocqueville, *Democracy in America*, 181. Putnam sheds light on the importance to democracy of civic associations, which build social capital and trust among citizens and provide schools where citizens learn how to practice democracy. Within this context, citizens learn to engage in civil dialogue, conduct meetings, make collective decisions, and cooperate together in a self-governing group. See Robert D. Putnam with Robert Leonardi and Raffaella Y. Nanetti, *Making Democracy Work: Civic Traditions in Modern Italy* (Princeton, NJ: Princeton University Press, 1993), and Robert D. Putnam, *Bowling Alone: Revised and Updated* (New York: Simon & Schuster, 2020). To see how associations can teach democratic norms, consider how the core values of the YMCA include responsibility, or being "accountable for your promises and actions"; respect, or treating "each other as we'd all like to be treated"; and caring, or "showing a sincere concern for others." These values align with equal accountability and its democratic duty of solidarity. YMCA, "Our Culture and Values," 2024, https://www.ymca.org/get-involved /careers/culture.

85. Margaret Keck and Kathryn Sikkink, *Activists beyond Borders: Advocacy Networks in International Politics* (Ithaca, NY: Cornell University Press, 1998). Keck and Sikkink write on transnational advocacy networks, but their points also pertain to the domestic context.

86. Belinda A. Stillion Southard, *Militant Citizenship: Rhetorical Strategies of the National Woman's Party, 1913–1920* (College Station: Texas A&M University Press, 2011), 76 and 73.

press, protest, petition, and association, which we set out in chapter 2, are crucial to this process of norm diffusion.

To speed up the uptake of the new norm, citizens can turn to social sanctions, legal enforcement, and civic education. These measures map onto Mill's schema of the ways to enforce duties from earlier in this chapter. Mill recommends social sanctions for harms that do not rise to the level of violating rights, and legal enforcement for acts that are in breach of rights. In a similar vein, Raymond and Weldon emphasize how social sanctions can propel norm diffusion: "Informal sanctions for norm violation, such as shaming, negative gossip, or extra-legal punishments, are a powerful form of enforcing and maintaining social norms."[87] Social sanctions are potent because persons depend on their reputation to secure the trust and cooperation of others.[88] Legal enforcement can augment these social sanctions. Laws deter norm violation and send the message that society values the norm.[89]

The norm can be fostered further, at a formative age, through civic education. As we saw in chapter 3, England has instituted a five-year Citizenship National Curriculum for all students aged eleven to sixteen. It teaches "the role of citizens and Parliament in holding those in power *to account*" and aims to "prepare students to take their place in society as *responsible citizens*."[90] Studies have found that "citizenship education [has] had a significant impact on three key factors of civic engagement, namely, efficacy, participation, and knowledge."[91]

Once a critical mass of citizens accepts a reframed or innovative norm, there is a second stage of norm diffusion. A tipping point is reached where more citizens sign onto the norm out of a desire to *emulate* others, or what Kathryn Sikkink refers to as the "justice cascade."[92] Emulation occurs when people learn norms by observing

87. Raymond et al., "Making Change," 203.
88. Ostrom, "Behavioral Approach to the Rational Choice."
89. Raymond et al., "Making Change," 203.
90. United Kingdom Department of Education, "Citizenship Programmes of Study," 2 (emphasis added).
91. Paul Whiteley, "Does Citizenship Education Work? Evidence from a Decade of Citizenship Education in Secondary Schools in England," *Parliamentary Affairs* 67 (2014): 530.
92. Raymond et al., "Making Change," 203; Kathryn Sikkink, *The Justice Cascade: How Human Rights Prosecutions Are Changing World Politics* (New York: W. W. Norton, 2011).

the behavior of other people.[93] For instance, once the right to vote for women took hold in states in the American West, it spread to other parts of the United States. Kansas recognized the right to vote for women in 1912, New York in 1917, and Michigan in 1918. The efforts of the suffragettes culminated in the nationwide passage of the Nineteenth Amendment to the US Constitution, protecting citizens from being denied the right to vote based on their sex.[94] It was widely called the Susan B. Anthony Amendment, in honor of its leading advocate.

This brief sketch suggests that it is viable to inculcate democratic duties, as seen in the suffragette and LGBT movements. The static view that democratic duties cannot be promoted would find it difficult to grapple with how these transformative changes were accomplished. That is not to say that the spread of these duties is automatic or should be taken for granted. Citizens can organize for the civil rights of African Americans, but they can also associate in groups like the Klan.[95] The choices of citizens will make a decisive difference, which is why the duties that apply to those choices matter. Crucially, the importance of citizens fulfilling their duties can be driven home in deliberation by normative reframing, normative innovation, and testimony. We can magnify the power of deliberation through civic associations, activist networks, social sanctions, legal enforcement, civic education, and social emulation.

Defending the Duty of Oversight from Exemptions

It might be objected that not all citizens are equally implicated in the injustices of their public servants. An alibi for inaction is that some citizens bear less of a duty of oversight to participate in democratic accountability to correct injustices, since they are less complicit. Scrupulous citizens may have opposed unjust officials by voting against them. Marginalized citizens may be less blameworthy because they are

93. Taylor Davis, Erin Hennes, and Leigh Raymond, "Cultural Evolution of Normative Motivations for Sustainable Behavior," *Nature Sustainability* 1 (2018): 220.

94. U.S. Const. Amend. XIX.

95. Sheri Berman, "Civil Society and the Collapse of the Weimar Republic," *World Politics* 49, no. 3 (1997): 401–29.

disempowered. The marginalized are not responsible for the injustices committed by officials they cannot hold democratically accountable.[96]

I agree that marginalization and active opposition to injustice are exonerating factors for the complicity of citizens in the injustices that their public servants commit. But I want to offer three responses. First, we should end the marginalization of our fellow citizens. We must empower all citizens with the rights, resources, and civic education to participate in democratic accountability. The goal should be to restore the equal authority of citizens, so that they would be in a position to take responsibility for the conduct of their public servants.

Second, until that happens, it would be prudent for the marginalized to participate democratically, for the sake of safeguarding themselves from injustice. When citizens have contributed to an injustice, they deepen their duty to correct it. They broke it, so they should fix it. Yet if we are among the marginalized, we may still want to participate democratically, even when we did not cause the injustices. We would want to avoid the perverse incentive that the oppressors who are most responsible for injustices would be the ones with the greatest political participation. That would skew politics to ignore the marginalized even more. If we are members of the marginalized, it would be prudent for us to participate in democratic accountability, as African Americans did in the Civil Rights Movement, instead of leaving the field to the most blameworthy citizens.

Third, I contest the premise that the only reason to participate in democratic accountability is one's blameworthiness in causing particular injustices. I argue that citizens bear a *baseline* or fundamental level of democratic responsibility on two grounds. The first is our *collective ownership* of the coercive power of government, which I laid out in chapter 3.

As citizens, we should fulfill the *democratic duty of oversight* to ensure that our public servants exercise our power justly. They work for us, so we should hold them democratically accountable. We also assume a baseline responsibility to participate in democratic accountability because of our *duty of solidarity* that we owe to the marginalized. Even

---

96. I thank Kevin Elliott, who raised this question at one of my talks at an APSA conference.

when we did not impose an injustice ourselves, we should stand ready to assist our fellow citizens when their rights are imperiled. While the previous chapter gave arguments in support of this duty of solidarity, here I offer an analogy to illustrate the baseline duty to participate democratically. Suppose that our neighbors' house catches on fire because other people are playing recklessly with fireworks. Do we have a duty to help our neighbors? Should we call the fire department? It would be implausible to say that we are exempt from any duty to alert them to the danger, since we did not ignite the inferno ourselves. We are in a position to help, and our assistance would make it more likely that our neighbors would be saved from injury. Our act of solidarity would also express the importance of their lives and create a relationship of solidarity. If we fiddled while their house burned, it would communicate a callous disregard for their lives that would insult their self-respect and corrode our relationship with our neighbors.

Drawing the analogy closer to democracy, our duty to help would be compounded if we owned the fireworks and employed the workers using them. Even if we did not intend the pyrotechnics to ignite the neighbors' house, it would be negligent if we just handed over the dangerous incendiaries to our employees and abdicated our duty of oversight. The baseline of responsibility springs from our ownership of the fireworks and our employment of the workers. Similarly, our collective ownership of the coercive power of government and our employment of public servants ground a fundamental level of responsibility to hold them democratically accountable. This duty of oversight is a pressing priority, given that government power is necessary to secure rights, but it is also capable of injuring and killing if abused, like the fireworks, though on a larger and more terrifying scale. The responsibility to participate democratically to remedy injustices may increase for citizens who did more to aid and abet injustices, but this only adds to the baseline. If citizens voted against officials who later commit injustices, that opposition is admirable.[97] But the citizens should continue to hold

97. I am grateful to Lucas Swaine, who asked me, during my presentation at Dartmouth College, why citizens who have voted against unjust officials still have a duty to hold them democratically accountable during office.

them democratically accountable *during office* by speaking, writing, protesting, organizing associations, petitioning representatives, and campaigning for candidates who will act justly.

Perhaps it might be thought that the duties of oversight and solidarity
are too onerous for many citizens. They are short on time to work and
care for their families. How can they be expected to participate politically? To this, I propose three responses. First, this objection under-
scores the importance of *empowering* citizens with the resources, including
the free time, to participate democratically.[98] Second, ordinary citizens
are capable of participating in democratic accountability, as shown in the
work of the suffragettes and the Civil Rights Movement. Third, the
political scientist Eitan Hersh has found that a third of Americans spend
two hours or more a day on politics.[99] But they largely dedicate that time
passively to "political hobbyism." Their political engagement consists of
scrolling the internet for political news and watching television, which
the average American spends 2.5 hours a day viewing on weekdays.[100]
Hersh indicates that existing political time could be spend more
effectively if it were directed at the "real political work" of contacting
representatives, listening to other citizens, organizing politically, and
campaigning for candidates. This form of engagement would involve
citizens participating in democratic accountability.

Answering Popular Will Accountability's Challenge
to Democratic Duties

The most sophisticated argument against democratic duties comes from
popular will accountability. Jeremy Waldron depicts democratic accountability as using elections to induce officials to follow the
preferences of a majority of voters: "In a democracy, we say that it is
important for the government as a whole to be controlled *by the*

---

98. See Julie Rose, *Free Time* (Princeton, NJ: Princeton University Press, 2016).

99. Eitan Hersh, *Politics Is for Power: How to Move beyond Political Hobbyism, Take Action,
and Make Real Change* (New York: Scribner, 2020), 3. I thank Alex Zakaras for helpful discussion
of Hersh on political participation.

100. Hersh, *Politics Is for Power*, 135.

people . . . as a matter of affirmative response to the people's will."[101]
John Ferejohn agrees that "responsiveness is a measure of how much
accountability an institutional structure permits."[102] The measures that
compel officials to be responsive are either thin or thick. "Thin" popular
will accountability relies mainly on the mechanism of elections, which
perform two functions. First, they prospectively select officials who citizens think will follow their preferences in the future.[103] Elections also
hold officials retrospectively accountable by removing them if their past
actions have run afoul of the people's will.[104] "Thick" popular will accountability expands its mechanisms to freedom of speech, the press,
and other liberties for citizens to form and express their preferences.[105]
While thick popular will accountability provides more procedures for
citizens to declare what they want, it still restricts the aim of democracy
to responding to and carrying out citizens' preferences.

In popular will accountability, the standards that officials are held accountable for meeting are *subjective*, or dictated solely by the preferences
of a plurality of voters.[106] There is no way for voters to be mistaken about

101. Jeremy Waldron, "Constitutionalism: A Skeptical View," in *Political Political Theory*, 31
(emphasis in original); idem, "Accountability: Fundamental to Democracy"; and idem, *Law
and Disagreement* (New York: Oxford University Press, 1999).

102. Ferejohn, "Accountability and Authority," 131.

103. Manin, Przeworski, and Stokes refer to this as the "mandate" view that "elections serve
to select good policies or policy-bearing politicians" (*Democracy, Accountability, and Representation*, 29).

104. This is called the "accountability" view by Manin, Przeworski, and Stokes: "elections
serve to hold governments responsible for the results of their past actions" (*Democracy, Accountability, and Representation*, 29).

105. A democratic theory that includes liberties to form and express preferences is Robert
Dahl, *Democracy and Its Critics* (New Haven, CT: Yale University Press, 1989). Joshua Cohen,
in a trenchant review, points out that Dahl develops a form of aggregative democracy that seeks
to combine and express the preferences of citizens. Cohen contrasts aggregative democracy
with deliberative democracy, where citizens justify democratic decisions on the basis of reasons
that they can mutually accept, because those reasons respect the freedom and equality of each
citizen. Joshua Cohen, "Democratic Ideals and Substantive Values: Dahl on Democracy," *Journal of Politics* 53, no. 1 (1991): 221–25. I thank Bob Keohane who asked insightfully about the
difference between my view and Dahl's.

106. This point recalls Scanlon's distinction between subjective and objective theories of
well-being. For Scanlon, subjective theories, like utilitarianism, define well-being according to
people's preferences. Objective theories characterize well-being using a preference-independent
standard, such as the attainment of primary goods for Rawls or capabilities for Nussbaum and
Sen. I distinguish between subjective and objective (or duty-based) standards of democratic

subjective standards, because it is up to them to select the standards based on what they want.[107] Popular will accountability is *neutral* about preferences: there is no democratic duty for citizens to adopt any preferences when they vote on how to impose the coercive power of government on others.[108] Ferejohn characterizes popular will accountability as involving neutral responsiveness: "Political accountability is fundamentally arbitrary in the sense that it is up to the 'principal' as to whether to base its decisions on reasons, or not to offer any reasons at all."[109] What is democratic in popular will accountability is the enactment of preferences, and not the content of those preferences.

I advance three arguments against popular will accountability and its dearth of democratic duties. First, this approach is self-defeating in failing to guarantee responsiveness to all citizens. Pluralities of voters can strip either minorities or majorities of other citizens of their rights to participate in democracy. Second, popular will accountability lacks a nonideal theory to explain how we should defend the democratic inclusion of citizens. It is missing the duties needed to protect citizens from the threats of elected authoritarians, factions, and powerlessness that threaten self-government. Third, popular will accountability assumes that citizens are principals or bosses entitled to have any of their preferences carried out by their agents, the officials. However, it overlooks how officials differ starkly from other

---

accountability. See T. M. Scanlon, "Preference and Urgency," *Journal of Philosophy* 72, no. 19 (1975): 655–69.

107. Gutmann and Thompson cogently criticize the preference neutrality of popular will theories, which "take the expressed preferences as the privileged or primary material for democratic decision-making. Preferences as such do not need to be justified, and aggregative conceptions pay little or no attention to the reasons that citizens or their representatives give or fail to give" (*Why Deliberative Democracy*, 15).

108. Preference neutrality is a trait that popular will accountability shares with utilitarianism. Preference neutrality attempts to treat citizens fairly and equally, but it relies on a truncated conception of fairness and equality. On neutrality toward preferences, see Kenneth May, "A Set of Independent Necessary and Sufficient Conditions for Simple Majority Decisions," *Econometrica* 20, no. 4 (1952): 680–84. Waldron invokes May in defending neutrality in *Political Political Theory*, 359n91. Will Kymlicka argues that utilitarianism's view of fairness and equality is incomplete, in *Contemporary Political Philosophy*, 2nd ed. (New York: Oxford University Press, 2002), 37.

109. John Ferejohn, "Accountability in a Global Context," International Law and Justice Working Paper 2007/5, New York University School of Law Global Administrative Law Series, abstract.

agents who work for us as fiduciaries, such as accountants or real estate agents. Officials impose government coercion, which can injure or kill. Citizens and their public servants bear duties to ensure that this power is used in accordance with justice, instead of inflicting brute force. I recast the principal-agent relation as a *citizen–public servant model*, where citizens and public servants hold offices that are attached to democratic duties stemming from how they exercise the coercive power of government.

Popular Will Accountability Is Self-Defeating

Popular will accountability cannot deliver freedom as self-government, even on its own terms that conflate self-government with responsiveness to preferences. If the majority's preference is to deny the democratic accountability rights of the minority, then the minority is not self-governing. It cannot make its preferences heard and hold its officials accountable.

Even more surprisingly, popular will accountability can fail to make *majorities* self-governing. This flaw flows from how popular will accountability's neutrality about preferences. This neutrality seems desirable, because if citizens disagree, it seems fair that the procedure should not prejudge the outcome toward any particular preference. As Jeremy Waldron notes, "better than any other rule, MD [majority decision] is neutral between the contested outcomes."[110] Kenneth May similarly views democracy as a majoritarian decision procedure that is *neutral* between options, positively responsive to preferences, decisive, and anonymous (changing the identity of the voters does not alter the outcome if we hold constant the number of votes each side receives).[111] Neutrality treats no preference as undemocratic in its content.

But if it is democratic to enforce any preference, then it would be democratic for citizens to vote to disenfranchise their fellow citizens. This would yield the undemocratic rule of a handful of elites over a mass of subjects. Consider a case that Josiah Ober offers in his book *Demopolis*.

110. Waldron, *Political Political Theory*, 227.
111. May, "Set of Independent Necessary and Sufficient Conditions."

Suppose that 51 percent of all adult citizens vote to remove the right to vote for the other 49 percent. The process recurs, with 51 percent of the remaining voters disenfranchising the other 49 percent. After just two rounds, only 26 percent of citizens retain the right to vote.[112] Following three rounds, merely 13.3 percent are left. If this process repeats itself, the citizens allowed to vote could whittle down to two people, who would reign over millions of subjects. Repeated rounds of disenfranchisement would shrink the electorate to a sliver of the citizenry, which is the very antithesis of majority rule. *Majorities* are no longer self-governing. Popular will accountability does not confer on citizens any democratic duties of solidarity to respect or protect each other's democratic accountability rights. It can thus produce a *tyranny of the minority* when the plurality can enact any preference, even the wish to blot out the standing of other citizens as principals.

It is a misnomer to call popular will accountability "majoritarian." Rather, it involves the rule by pluralities, or the largest group of participants in a procedure, who may fall considerably short of a majority or 50 percent plus one of citizens.[113] Even if all citizens have the right to vote, the level of voter turnout can produce plurality rule.[114] Consider the common case where half of citizens participate in an election. 52 percent of these vote for the winning candidate. But since only half of citizens turned out to vote, this amounts to only 26 percent of all citizens of voting age. If the plurality in the election selects a candidate who promises to disenfranchise the rest of the citizenry, 26 percent of adult citizens can revoke the right to vote for the remaining 74 percent. The popular will theory, instead of delivering majority rule, would impose the rule of 26 percent or less of citizens over the rest.

112. Ober, *Demopolis*.
113. On elections being won by candidates without majority support, see Macedo, "Against Majoritarianism," and Robert Dahl, *How Democratic Is the American Constitution?* 2nd ed. (New Haven, CT: Yale University Press, 2003).
114. For example, in the United States, many citizens are disenfranchised due to voter suppression and the disenfranchisement of current or former felons. Alec Ewald, "'Civic Death': The Ideological Paradox of Criminal Disenfranchisement Law in the United States," *Wisconsin Law Review* (2002): 1045–137; Alec Ewald and Brandon Rottinghaus, eds., *Criminal Disenfranchisement in an International Perspective* (Cambridge, UK: Cambridge University Press, 2009).

Popular Will Accountability Lacks a Nonideal Theory to Respond to Injustice

Waldron's main argument in favor of majority (or more accurately, plurality) voting is that it is the fairest way of settling disagreements among citizens regarding the standards of democratic accountability. The majority vote purports to be fair since it weighs the preferences of voters equally.[115] However, he concedes that a majority decision is fair only when citizens respect each other's rights and do not impose racial discrimination or other forms of majoritarian tyranny.[116]

The question that Waldron leaves unresolved is what to do when uniform respect for rights is lacking. The besetting problem of popular will accountability is that it leaves unexplained what to do when some officials or citizens violate the rights of the marginalized. Popular will accountability is missing a *nonideal theory* to guide how citizens should respond to the injustices of factions, elected authoritarians, and powerlessness.

I propose that we must integrate duties into democratic accountability to preserve freedom as self-government for all citizens. Waldron frames these duties as requirements of justice that are external to democracy. In contrast, I maintain that these duties are *democratic* because they secure the inclusion of all citizens in democracy, and they require the exercise of our democratic accountability rights.

My conception of equal accountability offers both an ideal and nonideal theory.[117] John Rawls describes nonideal theory as providing "the principles that govern how we are to deal with injustice."[118] In equal accountability, the nonideal theory identifies the democratic duties that citizens and public servants should fulfill when citizens are marginalized and officials are using power unjustly.[119] When a portion of citizens or their officials

115. Waldron, "Accountability," 7, 22; Waldron, *Political Political Theory*, 227. I thank Emilee Chapman and Brian Coyne for helpful discussion of the fairness argument for majority rule.

116. Waldron, *Political Political Theory*, 205, 207.

117. I thank Alison McQueen, who asked perceptively whether equal accountability is an ideal or nonideal theory.

118. Rawls, *Theory of Justice*, 8.

119. If injustices become more drastic, other measures may be required to establish greater political autonomy for the marginalized. Anna Stilz, Alan Patten, Arendt Lijphart, and other

abuse their power as factions or elected authoritarians, rights-respecting citizens should participate in democratic accountability to fend off these threats, with the aid of the more faithful public servants.[120]

The *ideal theory* contributes a "social ideal," or "a vision of the way in which the aims and purposes of social cooperation are to be understood."[121] In equal accountability, the social ideal is a fully democratic government, where all citizens freely govern themselves and the power of government is used justly by their public servants. The ideal theory works in tandem with the nonideal theory. The ideal element of equal accountability sets the goal: full inclusion for all the governed as equal authorities in democracy. The nonideal element informs the democratic duties to close the gap between the ideal of democracy and the current exclusion of marginalized citizens. We should act on our democratic duties of solidarity to include the marginalized in democracy, guarantee their freedom as self-government, and enable them to hold their public servants democratically accountable. Fulfilling our duty of solidarity staves off injustices, an essential protective element missing from popular will accountability.

---

scholars describe these institutions. They range from "confederal institutions, internal autonomy, special representation rights, or devolution," to the power-sharing of consociationalism in multiethnic societies. See Anna Stilz, "On Self-Determination," in *Political Philosophy Here and Now: Essays in Honour of David Miller*, ed. Daniel Butt, Sarah Fine, and Zofia Stemplowska (New York: Oxford University Press, 2022), 8–29. I thank Annie Stilz, who asked what institutions may be required when the marginalized face severe and persistent injustices. See also Anna Stilz, *Territorial Sovereignty: A Philosophical Exploration* (New York: Oxford University Press, 2019); Patten, *Equal Recognition*; and Arendt Lijphart, *Patterns of Democracy, Government Forms and Performance in Thirty-Six Countries* (New Haven, CT: Yale University Press, 1999).

120. There is a parallel here to Rawls's and David Hume's concept of the *circumstances of justice* (*Theory of Justice*, 110). The value of justice applies to cases of social cooperation involving "moderate scarcity." Conditions are not so abundant that rules of justice to determine the benefits and burdens of social cooperation would be superfluous. At the same time, conditions are not so harsh that cooperation would invariably break down. Similarly, the duty to hold the government democratically accountable is especially urgent when injustices must be corrected, but the injustices are not so extreme that democratic accountability would be unavailing and resort to revolution would be needed. I thank Desmond Jagmohan for his question about whether to pursue revolution or democratic accountability when citizens are marginalized. On revolution, see Locke, *Two Treatises of Government*, §§222–25.

121. Rawls, *Theory of Justice*, 9. Although Rawls is often seen as only providing an ideal theory, his conception of civil disobedience is a noted contribution to nonideal theory.

Popular Will Accountability Distorts the
Principal-Agent Relation

To defend our democratic duties, it is instructive to examine the potential appeal of purely subjective standards in popular will accountability. This approach might seem attractive if we think of citizens as the principals, and officials as their agents.[122] As discussed earlier, an agent is someone who acts on the behalf of another person, the principal. The principal authorizes the agent to work for her and has the power to remove the agent. The Framers saw officials as agents who work for citizens, who are the principals.[123]

One pitfall of popular will accountability is that it takes the compelling picture of citizens being the principals and combines it with a subjective standard of democratic accountability shorn of democratic duties. Waldron refers to popular will accountability as "agent-accountability." Here, "the principals are entitled to choose their own criteria for assessing the work of their agents."[124] In other words, the principals can select and replace their agents using any standard they prefer. Since the standards are up to the principals, their agents are only responsible for securing rights if the plurality of voters prefer that standard. Waldron's own preference is to respect rights.[125] But if the plurality chooses the opposite preference, then the subjective standard of democratic accountability would give officials the duty to negate those rights, as we saw with Senator Douglas's argument about slavery.

Popular will accountability trades heavily on an analogy with ordinary principal-agent relations. As Waldron writes,

122. On agential theories of democracy, see James Fearon, "Electoral Accountability and the Control of Politicians: Selecting Good Types versus Sanctioning Poor Performance," in Manin, Przeworski, and Stokes, *Democracy, Accountability, and Representation*, 55–97; Beerbohm, *In Our Name*; Waldron, *Political Political Theory*, chap. 8; and Ferejohn, "Accountability and Authority."

123. Madison, "Federalist No. 46," 228.

124. Waldron, "Accountability: Fundamental to Democracy," 19.

125. Jeremy Waldron, *Liberal Rights* (Cambridge, UK: Cambridge University Press, 1993), and idem, *Dignity, Rank and Rights*, with Wai Chee Dimock, Don Herzog, and Michael Rosen, ed. Meir Dan-Cohen (New York: Oxford University Press, 2012).

When my wife and I hire a realtor, we may disagree sometimes about what we want him to do, about what standards we should use to assess what he has been doing, and about the application of those standards. . . . This, as we will see, is one of the reasons democracies need elections; elections are not just ways of holding rulers accountable, they are ways of resolving disagreements about holding rulers accountable.[126]

However, as suggested earlier, the analogy to ordinary agents is misplaced. Merely subjective standards of democratic accountability are inadequate, because officials exercise the coercive force of government, unlike more prosaic agents, such as financial advisers and accountants.[127] Coercion imposes or threatens force to compel compliance with the law. This coercion is nonconsensual, because the laws apply to citizens, even when they disagree with those laws.

Coercion raises a vexing moral problem, in that it can potentially violate our right against being restrained, injured, or killed. There may be cases where it might be morally legitimate to coerce someone, such as to stop an assault. But acting for a principal as an agent cannot, by itself, make coercion morally permissible. Otherwise, it would follow that coercion would be morally permissible so long as one were committing an assault, kidnapping, or murder as an agent on a principal's behalf, like a capo for a mafia don. Nor does a vote held by the principals make coercion morally legitimate. A mafioso would not acquire a right to kidnap and murder if the principals he works for took a vote to resolve their disagreements about who he should target. Coercing at someone else's behest can, in fact, justify punishing the coercive act more severely. The law of conspiracy punishes more harshly crimes that are committed cooperatively or in an agential relationship. The reason is that cooperative crimes inflict greater harm and are harder to deter than

---

126. Waldron, "Accountability: Fundamental to Democracy," 6–7.

127. This is not to say that officials are the only persons who coerce. Officials are distinct in wielding the coercive power of *government*. Space does not permit addressing whether democratic accountability applies to the corporation for employees to be self-governing, but I am friendly to that view. See Theodora Welch and Minh Ly, "Rawls on the Justice of Corporate Governance," *Business Ethics Journal Review* 5, no. 2 (2017): 7–14.

crimes committed by individuals.[128] Popular will accountability is confounded by the question of why agents have any right to coerce.

The Citizen–Public Servant Model
and Its Democratic Duties

My *citizen–public servant model* reframes the principal-agent relation. In ordinary principal-agent relations, such as a client who employs a real estate agent, the principal has few or no duties. The role of the principal is only to select preferences, such as whether to buy a house. The agent's duties are limited to carrying out the principal's preferences, and perhaps to keep the principal informed about what the agent is doing.[129]

The citizen–public servant model is a special type of principal-agent relation with more demanding duties for both parties. Like the standard principal-agent relation, citizens are the bosses, and public servants work as their agents. But we should mark two important differences. The first is that the citizen–public servant relation involves the use of the coercive power to deploy the police, imprisonment, and the military. This power can injure, incarcerate the innocent, and kill on a massive scale if misdirected. Citizens and public servants carry more stringent duties to see to it that government power is used justly.

The second feature that distinguishes the citizen–public servant model from ordinary principal-agent relations is the sheer number of citizens or principals. In ordinary principal-agent relations, there is usually only one or a few principals. For instance, one homeowner acts as a principal to employ a real estate agent. I argue that in a democracy, the number of principals grounds crucial *principal-principal duties* among citizens.[130] I refer to these horizontal, citizen-to-citizen responsibilities

128. Neal K. Katyal, "Conspiracy Theory," *Yale Law Journal* 112 (2003): 1307–98. See Callanan v. United States, 364 U.S. 587, 593–94 (1961), upholding the constitutionality of charging conspiracy as a crime in addition to the substantive crime committed, quoted in Katyal, 1315.

129. Waldron analogizes democracy to ordinary principal-agent relations in "Accountability: Fundamental to Democracy."

130. A valuable and pioneering discussion of the principal-principal problem in the corporate governance context is Welch, "Effects of Privatization Transaction Strategy on Performance." In a principal-principal problem, the owners of a firm can take resources from each other. In the

as *duties of solidarity*. These duties are urgent, because to be freely self-governing, citizens must possess the standing of being equal authorities. But citizens face the threat that the coercive power of government or factions of other citizens can purge them of their standing. As Madison writes in Federalist 51, "It is of great importance in a republic not only to guard the society against the oppression of its rulers, but to guard one part of the society against the injustice of the other part."[131] The "oppression of its rulers" is the threat to self-government inflicted by elected authoritarians or rights-violating officials. The need to "guard one part of the society against the injustice of the other part" arises because of the threat to self-government from rights-violating factions.

To ensure that all citizens are freely self-governing, citizens must meet their duties of solidarity and protect each other from elected authoritarians and factions. These principal-principal duties of solidarity are absent from ordinary principal-agent relations, where there is only one principal. But the duties of solidarity are at the core of my citizen–public servant model, where there are millions of citizens and their standing as equal authorities hangs in the balance.

---

more traditionally recognized principal-agent problem, the managers employed by the owners can take resources away from the owners. The principal-agent framework arose in economics to explain how the interests of corporate management as agents can diverge from the interests of their principals, the owners of the corporation. For example, managers may divert value from the firm to their own excessive compensation, instead of investing it in the growth and profits of the firm. This potential conflict is the "principal-agent problem," or the "agency dilemma." The principal-agent problem between owners and managers becomes more acute when there is an asymmetry of information. If the agent possesses more information than the principals about her performance, it may impair the principals from monitoring their agent. For instance, the shareholders who own a publicly traded company may be kept in the dark about how their agents, the managers, are spending the firm's resources. The expense of the agent deviating from the principals' interests is the "agency cost." See Kathleen M. Eisenhardt, "Agency Theory: An Assessment and Review," *Academy of Management Review* 14 (1989): 57–74; Michael C. Jensen and William H. Meckling, "Theory of the Firm: Managerial Behavior, Agency Costs, and Ownership Structure," *Journal of Financial Economics* 3 (1976): 305–60; Barry M. Mitnick, "Origin of the Theory of Agency," https://ssrn.com/abstract=1020378; and Stephen A. Ross, "The Economic Theory of Agency: The Principal's Problem," *American Economic Review* 62 (1973): 134–39. Political scientists have taken up the principal-agent theory and applied it to the relation between citizens as the principals and officials as their agents (Fearon, "Electoral Accountability and the Control of Politicians"; Gailmard, "Accountability and Principal-Agent Theory").

131. Madison, "Federalist No. 51," 254.

I attach democratic duties to the offices of citizen and public servant due to their exercising the coercive power of government, as I set out in chapter 3. The office of the public servant directly uses coercion by legislating, enforcing, or applying the law. The office of the citizen indirectly wields coercion through its collective ownership of government, and its employing public servants to use that power as a democratically accountable trust. An office limits the power of government and embeds it in democratic duties to channel it to just purposes. The limits of office prevent the abuse of power and preserve freedom as self-government for all citizens. The responsibility of the office of the citizen is to hold public servants democratically accountable for using government power consistently with justice.

My citizen–public servant model includes standards of democratic accountability that are *duty-based* or preference-independent. These are standards that citizens are duty-bound to apply when they hold their public servants democratically accountable. For instance, citizens should ensure their public servants do not perpetuate slavery or racial discrimination. Citizens owe this as a duty of oversight in their role as the ones in charge of their government, and they owe this as a duty of solidarity toward their fellow citizens. These duties cannot be erased by citizens choosing the malicious preference of wanting to impose slavery. This is not to say that all standards of democratic accountability are duty-based. Citizens in one city may have the preference to spend public funds on a library. Citizens in another city may opt to build an art museum. They may vote for their public servants in elections, and evaluate them during office, according to this subjective standard of democratic accountability.

My contention is that the subjective standards should respect the duty-based standards of democratic accountability. The idea that our subjective preferences are bound by our duties is familiar from everyday life. You can choose to move your body as you wish, but not to pummel another person. As Lincoln said, "Each individual is naturally entitled to do as he pleases with himself . . . so far as it in no wise interferes with any other man's rights."[132] Lincoln applied this principle not just to

132. Lincoln, "Speech of Hon. Abraham Lincoln, Delivered at Chicago, July 10, 1858," 28.

individuals, but to governments.[133] We can chart the course of our own lives, and govern ourselves collectively, following our wishes, provided we respect the rights of others. These rights guarantee freedom for all.

Conclusion

I have defended in this chapter the democratic duties that I introduced in chapter 3. I grounded these duties in my *citizen–public servant model*, which recasts the principal-agent relationship. Citizens are the bosses or principals, and public servants work as their agents. But unlike ordinary principals and agents, the citizen–public servant relation deploys coercive government power, which can injure or kill. The danger of coercion increases the urgency that citizens meet their duty of oversight, and public servants their duty of fidelity, to ensure that government power is just. The citizen–public servant model differs further from ordinary principal-agent relations in that there are multiple principals. Our capacity to remain freely self-governing hinges on whether other citizens recognize our rights. In the office of the citizen, we bear principal-principal duties of solidarity to respect, protect, and empower each other's standing as equal authorities.

I sided with President Lincoln against Senator Douglas on the meaning of freedom as self-government. Like Lincoln, I argue that self-government requires the inclusion of all the governed in government. However, I ground self-government not in consent, but on democratic accountability. Laws are nonconsensual, as they bind us even when we disagree with them. But to be morally legitimate, and not impositions of brute force, the laws must be made by our public servants, who are democratically accountable to us, and must secure our equal human rights.

---

133. As Lincoln said, "Each community, as a State, has a right to do exactly as it pleases with all the concerns within that State that interfere with the rights of no other State, and that the general government, upon principle, has no right to interfere with anything other than that general class of things that does concern the whole" ("Speech of Hon. Abraham Lincoln, Delivered at Chicago, July 10, 1858," 28).

Citizens should hold their public servants democratically account-able for using government power justly. It might be thought that some citizens are exempt from this duty of oversight, because they voted against the officials who committed the injustices. But I showed that all citizens owe a *baseline of democratic duties.* My citizen–public servant model roots this baseline of responsibility in the collective ownership of government power by citizens, and their employing public servants to wield it on their behalf. Citizens should continue to hold their public servants democratically accountable during office, speaking out against injustices, organizing opposition, protesting, and campaigning to re-place unjust officials in the next election. I drew an analogy to a case where our neighbors' house is set on fire by fireworks ignited by our employees. We should hold accountable our employees, who are handling the hazardous incendiaries that we own.

Democratic duties need to be enforced for our democratic account-ability rights to be secure. Rights entitle us to goods that are so impor-tant they impose correlative duties on others to respect, protect, and empower those rights. I offered a Millian typology of duties to enforce rights, ranging from persuasion to moral criticism to legal sanctions. When citizens violate the duty to respect each other's rights, such as in acts of violence, they should be stopped by the force of law. If citizens advocate injustices but are nonviolent, they should be morally criti-cized. If citizens fall short in their duty to protect each other's rights, they should be persuaded to step up and protect the marginalized.

I drew on the norm diffusion literature to sketch how democratic duties can be promoted in deliberation by normative reframing, norma-tive innovation, and testimony. We can further cultivate duties by work-ing together in civic associations and activist networks, as we saw in the women's rights movement. Citizens can be encouraged to fulfill their duties through social sanctions, legal enforcement, civic education, and social emulation.

The dominant view of democratic accountability, popular will ac-countability, appears attractive for making citizens freely self-governing. It seeks to induce the government to respond to the preferences of a plurality of voters. But theorists of popular will accountability concede that it is fair only when citizens are committed to respecting each other's rights. Popular will accountability is missing a *nonideal theory* to explain what citizens ought to do when elected authoritarians or factions efface rights. By contrast, equal accountability contributes both a nonideal and ideal theory. The *ideal theory* in equal accountability offers a standard to guide our democratic duties. The goal is that all the governed should be included as equal authorities in democracy, and our public servants should answer to us and wield our power justly. The nonideal theory gives citizens duties to participate in democratic accountability to remedy injustices. As citizens, we should act on our democratic duties of oversight to ensure that our public servants use the power we own justly. It is essential that we fulfill our duties of solidarity to respect, protect, and empower the equal authority of our fellow citizens, so that all of us are liberated to govern ourselves.

5

Justice as the Standard of Democratic Accountability

THE EQUAL ACCOUNTABILITY PRINCIPLE, EQUAL HUMAN RIGHTS PRINCIPLE, AND INCLUSION PRINCIPLE

Justice is the end of government. It is the end of civil society.

—JAMES MADISON[1]

IF YOU VISIT MANCHESTER, you may be surprised to discover a bronze statue of President Abraham Lincoln. Why is this monument to an American president standing in an English city? Before the American Civil War, England imported nearly 80 percent of its cotton from the United States, produced by the toil of African American slaves.[2] The dependence on Southern cotton bred the confident expectation that England would take the South's side in any conflict with the North over slavery. South Carolina Senator James Henry Hammond, a cotton plantation owner, boasted, "Would any sane nation make war on cotton?" If Southern cotton were cut off, "England would topple headlong and

---

1. Madison, "Federalist No. 51," 254. By "end," Madison means that justice is the proper purpose of government.
2. Sven Beckert, *Empire of Cotton: A Global History* (New York: Vintage Books, 2015), 243.

carry the whole civilized world with her. . . . Cotton is king."[3] With the outbreak of the war, the surge of cotton imports slowed to a trickle. Once booming English factories shuttered. In the county of Lancashire, where Manchester is located, a "quarter of the inhabitants . . . were out of work, receiving some form of public or private assistance."[4] Hunger grew rife among the workers during the Lancashire Cotton Famine. Chancellor of the Exchequer and future Prime Minister William Glad-stone clamored to recognize the Confederacy and resume the cotton trade. Other members of the British Cabinet intimated that the Royal Navy should break the Union blockade of the South.[5]

As the crisis roiled Manchester, six thousand workers convened with Mayor Abel Haywood on New Year's Eve, 1862, in Free Trade Hall. Al-though expediency would have suggested that they should side with the Confederacy, their convictions of justice led them to embrace the eman-cipation of the slaves. In an epistle to President Lincoln, the workers paid tribute to the Declaration of Independence:

> We joyfully honor you, as the President, and the Congress with you, for many decisive steps toward practically exemplifying your belief in the words of your great founders: "All men are created free and equal." You have procured the liberation of the slaves in the district around Washington, and thereby made the centre of your Federation visibly free. . . . You have nobly decided to receive ambassadors from the negro republics of Hayti [sic] and Liberia, thus forever renounc-ing that unworthy prejudice which refuses the rights of humanity to men and women on account of their color.[6]

President Lincoln wrote to the workers of Manchester with gratitude, dispatching ships laden with provisions to relieve the famine. He hailed the workers' missive as "an energetic and reinspiring assurance of the

---

3. Christopher J. Olsen, *The American Civil War* (New York: Hill and Wang, 2006), 121; Drew Gilpin Faust, *James Henry Hammond and the Old South: A Design for Mastery* (Baton Rouge: Louisiana State University Press, 1982), 120 and 360.

4. Beckert, *Empire of Cotton*, 247.

5. Beckert, 250 and 261.

6. Linus Pierpont Brockett, *The Life and Times of Abraham Lincoln* (Philadelphia: Bradley, 1865), 424–25.

inherent power of truth and of the ultimate and universal triumph of justice, humanity, and freedom."[7] Lincoln pledged that the government of the Union "was built upon the foundation of *human rights,*" unlike that of the Confederacy, which rested "exclusively on the basis of human slavery."[8] W.E.B. Du Bois said that the mass meetings in Manchester, as well as London, sent a potent message to the British government. The workers "stirred the nation, and gave notice to [Prime Minister] Palmerston that he could not yet take the chance of recognizing the South."[9] Du Bois quoted John Stuart Mill, then serving in Parliament: "Higher political and social freedom has been established in the United States."[10] A passage from Lincoln's letter is engraved on the pedestal of his statue, close to the center of Manchester.

Lincoln resolved that the government must honor human rights and the values of "justice, humanity, and freedom."[11] This chapter asks: What standards of justice should guide the duties of democratic accountability for citizens and public servants? I define *justice* as the requirements the government must fulfill for its coercive power to be morally legitimate. Power is morally legitimate when it is morally permissible to exercise and not morally blameworthy. Government power that is just contrasts with brute force, which no one has the right to impose.

I argue that justice calls for the government to recognize the equal authority of all citizens and secure their human rights, while respecting the human rights of noncitizens. This is a *benchmark* standard of justice that government power must fulfill at minimum. We can enlarge justice

7. Abraham Lincoln, "To the Workingmen of Manchester, England," January 19, 1863, in *The Collected Works of Abraham Lincoln,* vol. 6, ed. Roy P. Basler, Marion Dolores Pratt, and Lloyd A. Dunlap (New Brunswick, NJ: Rutgers University Press, 1953), 64.

8. Lincoln, "To the Workingmen of Manchester" (emphasis added).

9. W.E.B. Du Bois, *Black Reconstruction* (New York: Routledge, 2017), 81.

10. Du Bois, *Black Reconstruction,* 81. On Mill's parliamentary career, see Dennis F. Thompson, "Mill in Parliament: When Should a Philosopher Compromise?" in *J. S. Mill's Political Thought: A Bicentennial Reassessment,* ed. Nadia Urbinati and Alex Zakaras (New York: Cambridge University Press, 2007).

11. Lincoln, "To the Workingmen of Manchester," 64. British laborers lacked the right to vote until the British Reform Act of 1867 (30 & 31 Vict. c. 102). But they asserted their democratic accountability rights to free association, protest, speech, and the press.

to other requirements once we have laid that groundwork.[12] The benchmark standard is crucial because the government is necessary to guarantee human rights, which protect urgent human interests. No other institution can mobilize the resources and the monopoly on coercion to secure human rights in its territory.

The importance of justice as the legitimating standard of democratic accountability faces the following challenge. Theorists of popular will accountability claim that citizens disagree about the meaning of rights, and the fairest way of settling that disagreement is through a majority vote.[13] This view limits our rights to the legal rights chosen by the popular will. Its advocates admit that a majority decision is only fair when it does not generate tyranny of the majority. They overlook, however, that the concept of tyranny of the majority presumes there are moral rights independent of the voting procedure. A *moral right* is a right that the government *should* recognize. As Mill defines it, "to have a right, then, is . . . to have something which society *ought* to defend me in the possession of."[14] If there were no moral rights, we could never diagnose cases of majoritarian tyranny. The majority could vote to abolish the legal right, and there would be no more rights for it to violate tyrannically.

I turn to the Declaration of Independence to locate two sources of moral rights and requirements of justice: "That to secure these rights, Governments are instituted among Men, deriving their just powers from the consent of the governed."[15] The first standard of justice is *procedural*, regarding how decisions are made and governments are formed. The declaration's procedural standard is that the government's powers, to be just, must originate from the consent of the governed. The previous chapter recast the procedural standard as more accurately

12. I thank reviewer 1 for instructively recommending that the standards are what justice requires, at minimum. A full theory of justice would consider the important questions of what justice calls for in the treatment of animals, the environment, and future generations. I focus on the benchmark standards, since they are manageable to argue for within one book. Once we have established the benchmark standards, we can expand the requirements of justice.

13. Waldron, "Accountability: Fundamental to Democracy," 22.

14. Mill, "Utilitarianism," 250 (emphasis added).

15. Declaration of Independence.

requiring equal democratic accountability. Here I contribute the *Equal Accountability Principle* to evaluate whether our democratic accountability rights are secured.[16] It states that public servants must ensure that citizens have the equal capacity to use their democratic accountability rights to correct injustices. The Equal Accountability Principle seeks to redress the denial of democracy to the poor, racial minorities, and other marginalized citizens. The marginalized are the people most exposed to injustices, yet the least able to correct them. The heavier the millstone of discrimination that weighs them down, the less their power to remove it. For the marginalized to have the capability to overcome injustices, they need more than formal rights on paper. The Equal Accountability Principle demands that we empower citizens with the resources and civic education to end their marginalization and enable them to participate in democracy as equals.

The second standard of justice consists of human rights, which are owed as moral rights that the government ought to defend. The Declaration of Independence proposes that the just purpose of government is "to secure these rights."[17] Human rights constitute a *substantive* standard of justice, regarding the output of decisions or the effect of government power. President Washington proclaimed in his address to Congress that "this Government" ought to be the "safeguard of human rights."[18] I explain that the primacy of human rights is rooted in how they protect the urgent interests of human beings from powerlessness and oppression by the state and factions. An especially urgent interest is securing respect for our human dignity, which contains two vital aspects. First, we should be regarded as members of the human family, and never dehumanized. Second, we must be respected as free and equal moral agents with reason and conscience. As moral agents, we can voice moral claims in deliberation with other human beings and can lead meaningful lives of our own. To be treated as a moral agent means that we are

16. I thank Natasha Patel and other participants in my talk at the Stanford Political Theory Workshop, who asked me how we can determine whether democracy as equal accountability is fulfilled.

17. Declaration of Independence.

18. George Washington, "Sixth Annual Message of George Washington," November 19, 1794, Yale Law School Avalon Project, https://avalon.law.yale.edu/18th_century/washs06.asp.

not ruled as passive pawns or subjects whose moral claims can be silenced and ignored. This aspect of moral agency entitles us to participate in democratic accountability. As moral agents, we also have our own lives to pursue and must not be treated as mere tools for others like slaves. This facet of moral agency entitles us to what the Declaration of Independence calls the "pursuit of happiness," or the freedom to set the course of our own lives. Human rights protect our dignity or profound value as members of the human family and moral agents.

I put forward the *Equal Human Rights Principle* to evaluate whether our public servants are satisfying the substantive standard of human rights. It specifies that our public servants should secure the equal human rights of all citizens, while respecting the human rights of noncitizens. I develop the *Delegation Principle* to show why respect for the human rights of noncitizens counts as a standard of democratic accountability. Citizens can only delegate powers they legitimately own to their public servants. But no one legitimately owns the power to abuse human rights and other human beings. The Manchester workers were correct that British citizens had a democratic duty of oversight to ensure their officials respected the human rights of African Americans and renounced war on the side of slavery.

Since states should secure the human rights of their citizens, while respecting the human rights of noncitizens, we must discover a moral criterion to determine who should be entitled to citizenship. I provide that criterion in my *Inclusion Principle*: the fact that a person is governed as a resident under a state's jurisdiction is a strong reason to grant that person citizenship in that state.[19] The Inclusion Principle stands in opposition to the *Dred Scott* decision, which blocked African Americans from ever becoming citizens.[20] That exclusion was anathema to the Declaration of Independence, cited by Lincoln and the Manchester workers. The Declaration envisages that a just government must protect

19. I thank reviewer 1, who asked about how the Inclusion Principle applies to tourists and other visitors. Since tourists and diplomats are traveling temporarily and expect to return, reside, and pay taxes in their home state, they are entitled to citizenship there. This differs from people who were born abroad but have lived for years in our state—harvesting our produce, cooking our food, and cleaning our schools. These residents should be recognized as citizens.

20. Dred Scott v. Sandford, 60 U.S. 393, 405 (1857).

human rights and answer to the *governed*. Citizenship must not be confined arbitrarily to one race or gender but extended to all persons subject to the jurisdiction of a government. Freedom as self-government means that we, the governed, are equal citizens who are in charge of our government. To govern ourselves freely, we must be equally empowered to hold our public servants democratically accountable, and our equal human rights must be secure.

Refuting the Fairness Argument That Defines Rights Solely by a Majority Vote

What rights should we hold our public servants democratically accountable for satisfying?[21] Popular will accountability might concede that rights are among the standards of democratic accountability. But since citizens disagree about the meaning of rights and justice, the fairest way to settle the dispute is by holding a vote where each citizen's preference counts equally. The vote resolves disagreement about the standards of democratic accountability. The equal weighing of citizens' votes in the *input* of the electoral procedure is presumed to translate into the fairness of the output.

The fairness argument for popular will accountability has attracted prominent proponents.[22] However, it shares similar shortcomings with preference-based utilitarianism. Utilitarianism posits that the morally right action maximizes the satisfaction of preferences, counting each person's preference equally. This corresponds to how in popular will accountability, the standards of democratic accountability are determined by weighing each participating voter's preferences equally. This resemblance is more than coincidental, since popular will accountability is the intellectual offspring of utilitarianism.[23]

21. I am grateful to my reviewers who asked which rights should be included as standards of democratic accountability.

22. Waldron, "Accountability: Fundamental to Democracy," 22; Tuck, *Active and Passive Citizens*.

23. On preference satisfaction utilitarianism, see R. M. Hare, *Moral Thinking* (New York: Oxford University Press, 1981). Popular will accountability originates from economists and

Both popular will accountability and utilitarianism limit the values of fairness and equality to a procedure's inputs. This approach ignores how fairness also applies to the procedure's *outputs*, or results. Consider the following example:

The Island Vote: Three crewmembers from a shipwreck land on a lush, deserted island that can sustain the lives of all three shipmates. Despite this, they disagree about how to live together. They hold a vote with each person's preference counting equally. Two of them vote to lash the third to a raft and cast her adrift in the sea to drown. The two claim that the decision is fair, because they disagreed about what to do, and the fairest way to settle the disagreement was by a vote counting each person's preference equally.

The preferences of other people, such as their families, would count on the utilitarian scale. But if the shipmates were the only survivors of a global calamity, what would utilitarianism dictate? Utilitarianism seeks to maximize the satisfaction of all preferences, even ones that discriminate or deny others liberty.[24] It is neutral about the preferences it fulfills.[25] Preference fulfillment utilitarianism would deem the third person's demise as moral in cases where it maximizes happiness as measured by preference satisfaction. Popular will accountability would likewise claim that the outcome is fair, as long as each voter's preference is counted equally.

The Island Vote case illustrates how popular will accountability paints too faint a picture of fairness, for three reasons. First, our considered convictions about fairness apply not only to a procedure's inputs

---

political scientists who adopted a preference satisfaction utilitarian framework (Downs, *Economic Theory of Democracy*).

24. Some utilitarians, like John Harsayni, might try to place a filter on preferences. But Rawls replies that utilitarians do not explain the moral basis of that filter or how it could cohere with utilitarianism (*Justice as Fairness*, 100).

25. Rawls describes utilitarianism's preference neutrality: "Thus if men take a certain pleasure in discriminating against one another, in subjecting others to a lesser liberty ... then the satisfaction of these desires must be weighed ... along with other desires" (*Theory of Justice*, 27). By contrast, "the principles of right, and so of justice, put limits on which satisfactions have value. ... The priority of justice is accounted for, in part, by holding that the interests requiring the violation of justice have no value" (*Theory of Justice*, 27–28).

but also to its substantive outputs. If an innocent person is sentenced to death, that substantive result impugns the fairness of the procedure. One component of fairness, which utilitarianism and popular will accountability miss, is the output of securing her equal rights. *Substantive rights*, like the right to personal integrity against injury and murder, place requirements on the outcomes of procedures.

Second, equal input to a procedure is insufficient for fairness because it is self-defeating.[26] If popular will accountability and utilitarianism neutrally allow any preferences to be enacted, the procedure will act on preferences to remove the equal input of other people.[27] The shipmates could vote to disenfranchise the third crewmember.

Popular will accountability's and utilitarianism's neutrality about preferences excludes *procedural rights*, which bear on how decisions are made and governments are formed. These rights protect our access over time to decision-making procedures. For instance, the right to vote mandates that the outcome of a vote must not restrict the continuing ability of citizens to cast their ballots. Procedural rights sustain equal inputs not only in the present but robustly into the future. Access to a procedure is *robust* when it is guaranteed across a range of circumstances, including variation in other voters' preferences.[28]

Popular will theorists might respond that the right to vote is a condition for popular will accountability to exist. Only then can each person be treated fairly by tallying her vote equally. But this move is closed off because the standards of popular will accountability are subjective or entirely up to the plurality to decide based on their preferences. The "principals are entitled to choose their own criteria for assessing the work of their agents," as Waldron says.[29] Popular will accountability is "neutral between the contested outcomes," since it counts as democratic

<hr />

26. On popular will accountability being self-defeating, see chap. 4.

27. Kymlicka characterizes this neutrality toward preferences: "Utilitarians assume that every source of happiness, or every kind of preference, should be given the same weight, if it yields equal utility" (*Contemporary Political Philosophy*, 37).

28. On robustness as requirements that persist across variations in circumstances, see Philip Pettit, *The Robust Demands of the Good* (New York: Oxford University Press, 2015).

29. Waldron, "Accountability: Fundamental to Democracy," 18–19.

the enactment of any preference regardless of its content.[30] Citizens as the principals can thus select the standard that their agents must disenfranchise a minority.

Even if popular will accountability were modified, ad hoc, to include the right to vote, it would entail that the standards of democratic accountability can no longer be entirely preference-based or neutral. There is at least one duty-based standard, which is protecting the right to vote. The popular will theorist might contend that the duty-based standards of democratic accountability are limited to this lone procedural right, but that is not viable. The right to vote could not be credibly exercised if people lacked the substantive right to the rule of law. Otherwise, citizens would be vulnerable to violence or imprisonment before they can even reach the polls. Once the case for duty-based standards of democratic accountability is granted, it would be unsound to restrict democratic duties only to securing procedural rights, which are precarious when detached from any substantive rights.

The third reason against the fairness argument for popular will accountability is that there is a fairer way to settle disagreements among citizens. Namely, it would be fairer if the government listened to citizens while guaranteeing their equal standing. This position follows from my earlier *bounded grounds argument* in chapter 1. To draw an analogy, friends should be responsive to each other when deciding what to do together. But the standing of being a friend is the bounded ground for responsiveness to preferences, as it regulates when it would be appropriate to carry out those preferences. The desire to enslave a friend has no weight, even if it is held by a majority, because it is repugnant to the standing of being a friend. The fairest way for friends to settle their disagreements is not by giving the majority unconstrained repressive power. Instead, fairness mandates listening to each friend's preferences while securing the equal standing of all friends. Similarly, when citizens vote to settle their disagreements, preferences to abuse each other should be assigned no weight. The fairest way to resolve disagreements among citizens is to listen to their views, expressed by their democratic

30. Waldron, "Accountability: Fundamental to Democracy," 227.

accountability rights in deliberation and voting, while protecting every citizen's continuing inclusion in democracy as an equal authority. This standing or status as a citizen is particularly vital to secure for the marginalized. Disagreement that is *respectful* acknowledges the standing of each citizen.[31] Respectful disagreement maintains our robust input into democratic procedures over time, and it bounds the substantive output to ensure our enduring standing as equal authorities.

Waldron concedes that a majority decision is a fair method to resolve disagreements provided that citizens take each other's rights seriously: "I assume that there is a strong commitment on the part of most members of the society we are contemplating to the idea of individual and minority rights."[32] The fairness argument is invalidated when the majority acts tyrannically, such as by imposing racial discrimination.[33]

This defense of popular will accountability is silent, however, about what to do when rights are not regularly respected. Popular will accountability lacks a *nonideal theory* to guide what to do in response to injustice. Due to its preference neutrality, popular will accountability is missing democratic duties for citizens and public servants to remedy injustices.

A further deficiency is that popular will accountability cannot identify cases of majoritarian tyranny. Tyranny of the majority is only a coherent concept if there are moral rights that persist, and can still be violated, when legal rights are repealed. If there were no moral rights, then the majority could simply vote to negate the legal right, and then there would be no remaining right for the majority to transgress. But popular will accountability is reticent about what our moral rights are. It reduces our rights to the legal rights that are given by the outcome of a majority vote. But if we are not entitled to any moral rights independent of the majority vote, then we cannot say that we can ever suffer tyranny of the majority. The voting procedure would provide the final word about our rights, leading majoritarian tyranny to drop out of sight.

31. I thank Brian Coyne for discussion of respectful disagreement at my research presentation in the Stanford Political Theory Workshop.

32. Waldron, *Political Political Theory*, 207.

33. Waldron, *Political Political Theory*, 236.

The Equal Accountability Principle

Despite its flaws, popular will accountability poses a genuine challenge. How can we discover duty-based standards of democratic accountability in conditions of moral disagreement? A duty-based standard is one that citizens bear a responsibility to apply to their public servants when holding them democratically accountable. How can we define the meaning of rights and justice as standards of democratic accountability apart from the outcome of any vote? I propose that inclusive deliberation can guide our understanding of justice. To the extent that popular will accountability lacks a deliberative perspective that is independent of the majority vote, it is missing a vantage point to diagnose cases of majority tyranny.

Justice is not merely something desirable. "Justice," says John Stuart Mill, "implies something which it is not only right to do, and wrong not to do, but which some individual person can claim from us as his *moral right*."[34] A moral right is an entitlement that *ought* to be protected, and that it would be morally blameworthy to violate. For example, we are owed a moral right against slavery. Laws would wrong us if they enslaved us or failed to protect us from servitude. Mill expresses how we need the concept of moral rights to criticize unjust laws:

> Among these diversities of opinion, it seems to be universally admitted that there may be unjust laws, and that law, consequently, is not the ultimate criterion of justice. . . . When, however, a law is thought to be unjust, it seems always to be regarded as being so in the same way in which a breach of law is unjust, namely, by infringing somebody's right; which, as it cannot in this case be a legal right, receives a different appellation, and is called a moral right. We may say, therefore, that a second case of injustice consists in taking or withholding from any person that to which he has a *moral right*.[35]

---

34. Mill, "Utilitarianism," 247 (emphasis added).

35. Mill, "Utilitarianism," 242 (emphasis in original). The first case of injustice is the deprivation of legal rights.

The Fugitive Slave Act deemed it a crime to harbor an escaped slave and directed officials to assist in the capture of slaves to return them to their human traffickers.[36] The law was unjust and an affront to the moral right against slavery. It is incumbent on our public servants to secure our moral rights by enshrining them as legal rights. The House of Representatives, Senate, and state legislators took this step when they ratified the Thirteenth Amendment prohibiting slavery.[37] They protected the moral right against slavery as a legal right backed by the coercive force of government. But how can we ascertain what our moral rights are?

I propose two sources of moral rights as standards of democratic accountability, one procedural and the other substantive. The first source is democratic accountability itself, and the second is human rights. The precedent for this strategy is the Declaration of Independence. The Declaration has been a beacon for reformers seeking the democratic inclusion of women and racial minorities in the United States and has served as an exemplar for supporters of democracy globally.[38] The document lays out two guiding principles to distinguish a government with "just powers."[39] It states: "That to secure these rights, Governments are instituted among Men, deriving their just powers from the consent of the governed." The substantive standard of justice is that government must secure our rights, and the procedural standard of justice is that government must be founded on the consent of the governed.

I interpret the procedural standard of justice to require that the government be equally democratically accountable to the governed. I adopt this procedural standard to defend the Declaration of Independence from concerns that the government's rule is nonconsensual.[40] We can be bound by laws, even when we do not agree to them. Aside from

36. Fugitive Slave Act of 1850, Pub. L. 31-60.
37. U.S. Const. Amend. XIII.
38. On the global influence of the Declaration of Independence as a model for democracy, see David Armitage, *The Declaration of Independence: A Global History* (Cambridge, MA: Harvard University Press, 2008). On how the Declaration combines the values of equality and freedom, see Danielle Allen, *Our Declaration: A Reading of the Declaration of Independence in Defense of Equality* (New York: W. W. Norton, 2014). I am grateful to my colleagues and students in the "Citizenship in the 21st Century" course at Stanford for discussion of the Declaration.
39. Declaration of Independence.
40. Kolodny, "Rule Over None I," 204–6 and Estlund, *Democratic Authority*, 109–10.

naturalized citizens, most citizens are born into a state and do not swear an oath consenting to its constitution. Rawls remarks on the nonconsensual rule of government, "Political society is not, and cannot be, an association. We do not enter it voluntarily. . . . In what sense, then, can citizens of a democracy be free?"[41]

I answer that citizens can be free when they can hold their public servants democratically accountable, and their human rights are secure. I propose the *Equal Accountability Principle* to evaluate whether our public servants have satisfied the procedural standard of democratic accountability. It assesses whether our public servants have recognized the equal authority of all citizens, including racial minorities and other marginalized groups.[42]

The Equal Accountability Principle: Public servants should secure the equal capability of all citizens to use their democratic accountability rights to correct injustices. The equal capability to exercise democratic accountability must not be hindered by membership in a marginalized group.

41. Rawls, *Justice as Fairness*, 4, 91–92.

42. It might be objected that I am unilaterally proposing a theory of justice. This view is similar to Habermas's criticism that Rawls offers a "monological" theory of justice, based on the author's own reasoning, and not justified by deliberation. The criticism does not attend to how Rawls and I both regard our conceptions of justice as contributions to deliberation. Our conceptions of justice are justified to the degree they can approach, over time, "general reflective equilibrium" in this public discussion. General reflective equilibrium occurs when citizens come to an agreement that is "intersubjective: that is, each citizen has taken into account the reasoning and arguments of every other citizen" (Rawls, *Political Liberalism*, 385n16). General reflective equilibrium resembles Habermas's ideal speech situation. Norms are justified in the ideal speech situation to the extent that they are endorsed in inclusive deliberation where the "forceless force" of the better argument prevails. This process leads us to an improved understanding, but one that is "provisional" or open to challenge by further deliberation that is freer, more inclusive of diverse human beings, and more carefully weighs considerations that might have been previously overlooked. The tenets that human reason is fallible, but that deliberation with other human beings can yield better answers, are central concepts in pragmatism. The pragmatist Charles Sanders Peirce, who influenced Habermas, held that we should have greater confidence in beliefs that can command a consensus among a community of inquirers. Charles S. Peirce, *The Essential Peirce*, vol. 1, ed. Nathan Houser and Christian Kloesel (Bloomington: Indiana University Press, 1992), 29. On provisionality, see Gutmann and Thompson, *Why Deliberative Democracy*, 97. On the monological and dialogical distinction, see Jürgen Habermas, *The Inclusion of the Other*, ed. Ciaran Cornin and Pablo De Greiff (Cambridge, MA: MIT Press, 2001), chap. 2. Rawls's response to Habermas is in *Political Liberalism*, lecture 9.

A capability is a freedom to act or to achieve a valuable condition.[43] The capacity to exercise democratic accountability rights is instrumentally valuable for protecting our substantive human rights from abuse.[44] Democratic accountability is also intrinsically valuable for creating a political relationship where we are freely self-governing. To wield our democratic accountability rights, we must be empowered with the resources and education to leverage those rights. It would violate the Equal Accountability Principle if our membership in a marginalized group disempowered us from holding our public servants democratically accountable.

One worry about the Equal Accountability Principle is that it might demand equal wealth and income for all citizens. The thought is that the ability of citizens to correct injustices will vary according to their material resources. The only way to equally empower citizens to exercise their democratic accountability rights would be to equalize their wealth and income.

However, this objection does not notice an alternative way to equally empower citizens. We can separate the influence of money from politics and empower citizens with a social minimum, the provision of legal aid, voting access, a strong civic education, and other resources, as I wrote in chapter 3. This would follow Michael Walzer's recommendation to separate the sphere of political power from the sphere of money.[45] For example, campaign finance might be reformed to prevent the wealthy from buying elections and bribing politicians. This approach differs from the current system of closely enmeshing money and political

---

43. Sen, *Development as Freedom*, 18, 75; Nussbaum, *Frontiers of Justice*.

44. John Dewey argued for democracy on the protective grounds that the citizens who live under a government are best placed to tell from experience whether they are governed well: "The man who wears the shoe knows best that it pinches and where it pinches, even if the expert shoemaker is the best judge of how the trouble is to be remedied." John Dewey, "The Public and Its Problems," in *Political Writings*, ed. Debra Morris and Ian Shapiro (Indianapolis: Hackett, 1993), 187. A precedent for Dewey's argument is Aristotle's *Politics*, in which the ancient Greek philosopher discusses the question of whether "the masses should not be put in control over either the election of magistrates or their audit." He answers that citizens have a claim to elect their officials, since the citizens are better judges of rule than the rulers themselves, the way "the diner judges a banquet better than the cook." Aristotle, *Politics*, trans. H. Rackham (Cambridge, MA: Harvard University Press, 1959), 227.

45. Walzer, *Spheres of Justice*.

power, allowing what Republican President Theodore Roosevelt criticized as the "swollen fortunes for the few."[46] Roosevelt drove the point home that "if our political institutions were perfect, they would absolutely prevent the political domination of money in any part of our affairs. We need to make our political institutions more quickly and sensitively responsive to the people whose servants they are."[47] To the extent that wealth is tightly entangled in political power, this fact would support reducing economic inequality.[48] President Roosevelt concluded that there should be "a graduated income tax on big fortunes, and . . . another tax which is far more easily collected and far more effective—a graduated inheritance tax on big fortunes."[49] The objectionable combination is drastic economic inequality linked closely with the control of a wealthy clique over the government, devolving democracy into an oligarchy.

A potential worry is that the Equal Accountability Principle is too demanding in requiring that membership in a marginalized group not hinder the ability to correct injustices. But what is truly demanding is the burden of discrimination placed on the marginalized. The marginalized suffer grave injustices but have the least resources to correct them. The plight to be avoided is that substantive and procedural injustices can descend into a vicious cycle. The deeper the pit of injustice the marginalized are thrown into, the steeper their climb and more remote their chances of escape. This bleak condition of receding hope cannot possibly be acceptable to the marginalized.

What racial minorities, the poor, and other marginalized citizens are urgently owed is the end of their vulnerability. This is the aim of the Equal Accountability Principle: our public servants must guarantee the equal capability of all citizens to correct injustices by exercising their

46. Theodore Roosevelt, *The New Nationalism* (New York: Outlook, 1910), 29. The passage is from Roosevelt's speech at Osawatomie, Kansas on August 31, 1910.

47. Roosevelt, *New Nationalism,* 29.

48. Scanlon argues that economic inequality leads to unacceptable inequalities of political power. T. M. Scanlon, "The Diversity of Objections to Inequality: The Lindley Lecture," (Lawrence: University of Kansas Press, 1996), 3.

49. Roosevelt, *New Nationalism,* 18. Rawls suggests that a main mode of enacting his principles of justice is through progressive income and inheritance taxation to "prevent excessive concentrations of private power" (*Justice as Fairness,* 51).

democratic accountability rights. The burden of proof falls on the critics of the Equal Accountability Principle to explain why it could ever be morally justified to saddle the most vulnerable citizens with the *lesser* capacity to correct injustices. As citizens, we should hold our public servants democratically accountable for fulfilling the Equal Accountability Principle, so that the power of our government is just.

The Equal Human Rights Principle

The second source of moral rights is human rights. This substantive standard of moral legitimacy is anticipated by the Declaration of Independence, which affirms that a just government must "secure these rights" to "Life, Liberty and the pursuit of Happiness."[50] Lincoln likewise subscribed to the principle that the government of the Union "was built upon the foundation of human rights," unlike that of the Confederacy, which rested "exclusively on the basis of human slavery."[51] In the Declaration, the rights that it seeks to secure are natural rights, which human beings are "endowed by their Creator."[52] Both human rights and natural rights are inalienable moral rights for human beings. The advantage of human rights is that they are not premised on any one religion, unlike natural rights.[53] Since human rights are compatible with diverse faiths, they can serve as moral rights that are suitable for conditions of pluralism.[54]

Another benefit of human rights is that they are supported by the *actual deliberation test*, which I elaborate in chapter 6. The Declaration frames natural rights as truths that are "self-evident" to reason.[55] However,

---

50. Declaration of Independence.

51. Lincoln, "To the Workingmen of Manchester, England," 64.

52. Declaration of Independence.

53. Beitz, *Idea of Human Rights*, 8. On how an overlapping consensus among diverse religions and other conceptions of the good can converge on human rights, see Amy Gutmann, "Introduction," in Michael Ignatieff, *Human Rights as Politics and Idolatry*, ed. Amy Gutmann (Princeton, NJ: Princeton University Press, 2001) and Rawls, *Law of Peoples*. On human rights in conditions of cultural diversity, see William Talbott, *Which Rights Should Be Universal?* (New York: Oxford University Press, 2005).

54. Gutmann, "Introduction"; Rawls, *Political Liberalism*.

55. Declaration of Independence.

the reasoning of different people, or what they consider self-evident, can diverge. This moral disagreement leads Waldron to resort to the majority decision procedure as the final word to define rights. But this left Waldron unable to recognize cases of majoritarian tyranny. I ground human rights instead in the actual deliberation test. The criterion to identify human rights is not merely the popular will in one election. The validity of a human right must be examined in public discussion. The outcome of this discussion is provisional and can be revised following more thorough and inclusive deliberation, as Amy Gutmann and Dennis Thompson write.[56] The more inclusive the deliberation, the greater the confidence we can vest in the validity of the human right. As Amartya Sen notes, human rights are morally justified when they can "survive open critical scrutiny in public reasoning."[57] Human rights have passed the actual deliberation test in many of the world's countries. The United Nations observes that all "member States have ratified at least one of the nine core international human rights treaties, and 80 percent have ratified four or more, giving concrete expression to the universality of the UDHR [Universal Declaration of Human Rights] and international human rights."[58] The validity of human rights is grounded in the inclusive deliberation that occurred when a vast array of diverse countries drafted, ratified, and appealed to the core international human rights treaties. For instance, the US judiciary recognizes human rights as a keystone of the democratic rule of law. It defines the rule of law as "the principle under which all persons, institutions, or entities are accountable to laws that are: publicly promulgated, equally enforced, independently adjudicated, and consistent with international human rights principles."[59]

56. Gutmann and Thompson, *Why Deliberative Democracy*, 97.
57. Amartya Sen, "Elements of a Theory of Human Rights," *Philosophy and Public Affairs* 32 (2004): 315–56.
58. United Nations, "The Foundation of International Human Rights Law," accessed March 15, 2025, https://www.un.org/en/about-us/udhr/foundation-of-international-human-rights-law.
59. United States Courts, "Overview—Rule of Law," accessed March 15, 2025, https://www.uscourts.gov/educational-resources/educational-activities/overview-rule-law#:~:text=Rule%20of%20law%20is%20a,with%20international%20human%20rights%20principles.

Human rights serve as standards to evaluate whether the coercive power of government is morally legitimate, and not an imposition of morally prohibited brute force. Charles Beitz puts the point clearly: "The central idea of international human rights is that states are responsible for satisfying certain conditions in their treatment of their own people."[60] As the Universal Declaration sets forth, human rights stand as "a common standard of achievement for all people and for all nations."[61] Public servants and citizens should meet their duty "to secure [the] universal and effective recognition and observance" of human rights.[62]

I argue that we should hold our public servants democratically accountable for satisfying the Equal Human Rights Principle as a substantive standard of justice. Namely,

> *The Equal Human Rights Principle*: Public servants should secure the equal human rights of all citizens, while respecting the human rights of noncitizens.

Public servants work for citizens and can prioritize dedicating the resources to protecting and empowering their human rights. The legitimating purpose of the government's monopoly on coercive power is to secure human rights in its territorial jurisdiction, where it enacts and enforces laws. At the same time, public servants must respect, or not abuse, the human rights of noncitizens. For example, British officials had a duty not to go to war to perpetuate slavery against African Americans. The Equal Human Rights Principle is a substantive standard that must be met for the coercive power of government to be morally legitimate.

---

60. Beitz, *Idea of Human Rights*, 13.

61. "Universal Declaration of Human Rights (UDHR)," December 10, 1948, United Nations General Assembly Res., 217 A (III), Preamble http://daccess-dds-ny.un.org/doc/RESOLUTION /GEN/NR0/043/88/IMG/NR004388.pdf?OpenElement.

62. "Universal Declaration of Human Rights."

The Meaning and Importance of Human Rights

I define a human right as a moral right that is morally owed to human beings and protects urgent human interests against threats. Human rights protect urgent human interests by imposing correlative duties on human beings and institutions.[63] The first property of human rights is that they are *moral rights*, which ought to be secured in the positive law or legal system.[64] The positive law is less legitimate if it violates human rights. The law should then be reformed to respect human rights. For example, it would be wrong for an apartheid state to claim that it has no moral duty to treat Blacks equally, since its legal system dispenses with the human right to nondiscrimination. The apartheid state is wrong, because the human right to nondiscrimination imposes a moral duty on the state to legally recognize the right. This moral duty is not cancelled simply by flouting it. The human right to nondiscrimination morally prescribes that states abolish apartheid and enact laws against discrimination.[65]

The second property of human rights is that they are morally owed to all human beings.[66] The Universal Declaration proclaims the universality of human rights in its first article: "All human beings are born free and equal in dignity and rights."[67] The Universal Declaration was adopted by the UN General Assembly with no dissenting votes in 1948. It is the most influential modern statement of human rights.[68] In language that recalls the Declaration of Independence's requirement to

63. Rights protect interests by imposing correlative duties. See Joseph Raz, *The Morality of Freedom* (New York: Oxford University Press, 1986), 165.

64. On human rights being moral rights, see John Tasioulas, "Human Dignity and the Foundation of Human Rights," in *Understanding Human Dignity*, ed. Christopher McCrudden (New York: Oxford University Press, 2013), chap. 16, and James Nickel, *Making Sense of Human Rights*, 2nd ed. (Malden, MA: Blackwell, 2007), chaps. 2–3.

65. Human rights generate duties for states and international actors to enact these rights in domestic and international law. See Thomas Christiano, "An Instrumental Argument for a Human Right to Democracy," *Philosophy and Public Affairs* 39 (2011): 144.

66. Nickel, *Making Sense of Human Rights*, chap. 2.

67. "Universal Declaration of Human Rights."

68. Mary Ann Glendon, *A World Made New: Eleanor Roosevelt and the Universal Declaration of Human Rights* (New York: Random House, 2001).

secure rights, the Universal Declaration puts forward the principle that human rights are the "equal and inalienable rights of all members of the human family."[69]

A third property of human rights is that they protect urgent human interests against threats.[70] The threats are defined by the experience, shared across countries, with the perils of political oppression, discrimination, arbitrary imprisonment, and other dangers to urgent human interests. We should "regard the practice of human rights as valuable," says Beitz, because "its norms seek to protect important human interests against threats of state-sponsored neglect or oppression which we know from historical experience are real and can be devastating when realized."[71] Among the most formidable of these risks, which Judith Shklar stresses, is the coercive power of the state: "The governments of this world with their overwhelming power to kill, maim, indoctrinate, and make war are not to be trusted unconditionally."[72]

The impetus for the Universal Declaration was the cataclysm of World War II and the Holocaust.[73] Human rights shield us against the oppression of state coercion and neglect. This is not to say that the state is always adverse to human rights. In anarchy, there would be no government to guard us from rampant private violence or external invasion. But I argue that given the force, scale, and violence of the state's coercive apparatus, it should be held democratically accountable for abiding by human rights.

69. "Universal Declaration of Human Rights," preamble.

70. On human rights protecting urgent human interests against standard threats, see Beitz, *Idea of Human Rights*, 109–11 and 139; Shue, *Basic Rights*, 29; Allen Buchanan, *Human Rights, Legitimacy, and the Use of Force* (New York: Oxford University Press, 2010), 5. On the interest theory of rights, see Raz, *Morality of Freedom*.

71. Beitz, *Idea of Human Rights*, 11.

72. Shklar, "Liberalism of Fear," 12. On Shklar's escape from the Nazis and Soviets, see Judith Shklar, "A Life of Learning," in *Liberalism without Illusions: Essays on Liberal Theory and the Political Vision of Judith N. Shklar*, ed. Bernard Yack (Chicago: University of Chicago Press, 1996), 263–79.

73. Johannes Morsink, *The Universal Declaration of Human Rights: Origins, Drafting, and Intent* (Philadelphia: University of Pennsylvania Press, 2000), 329.

Human Rights Duties

The United Nations and international law correlate human rights with three types of duties.[74] The first is the *duty to respect*, which prohibits violating a right in one's own actions. The second is the *duty to protect*, which calls on states to defend human rights from violators.[75] The third category is the *duty to fulfill* human rights by dedicating the resources and institutions to empower their exercise.[76] Each of these three duties is essential to defending urgent human interests. The duty to respect restricts people and institutions from abusing human rights. The duty to protect stops third parties who attack human rights. The duty to fulfill demands that resources be allotted and institutions created to enable the use of human rights.

I adopt a two-level theory of human rights duties. The first level regards the duties of the state, and the second, remedial level applies when the state fails in its duties.[77] In this model, the duty to respect applies most broadly. All people and institutions must refrain from abusing human rights. At the first level, the more demanding duties to protect and fulfill human rights are borne primarily by states. A state in international law is an entity with a permanent population, defined territory, and government that enacts and enforces laws in its territory. A state has the capacity to enter into relations with other states.[78] Since states are responsible for enacting and enforcing laws on their territory, they are obligated in their laws to protect and fulfill the human rights of the persons they govern. I refer to the combined duties to respect, protect, and fulfill human rights as the responsibility to *secure* those rights. The International Covenant on Civil and Political Rights (ICCPR), a legally

74. On the duties to respect, protect, and promote human rights, see Shue, *Basic Rights*.

75. Jonathan Wolff, *The Human Right to Health* (New York: W. W. Norton, 2012), 31.

76. The UN High Commissioner for Human Rights construes human rights duties as falling on both states and international organizations. See UN Habitat, "The Right to Adequate Housing," OHCHR Fact Sheet No. 21, Rev. 1 (November 2009): 34–36, http://www.ohchr.org /Documents/Publications/FS21_rev_1_Housing_en.pdf.

77. Beitz, *Idea of Human Rights*, 108–9; Shue, *Basic Rights*; and Nickel, *Making Sense of Human Rights*.

78. Frederick Tse-shyang Chen, "The Meaning of 'States' in the Membership Provisions of the United Nations Charter," *Indiana International and Comparative Law Review* 12, no. 1 (2001): 25–26.

binding treaty, stipulates that states should secure human rights in their territory without discrimination:

> Each State Party to the present Covenant undertakes to respect and to ensure to all individuals within its territory and subject to its jurisdiction the rights recognized in the present Covenant, without distinction of any kind, such as race, colour, sex, language, religion, political or other opinion, national or social origin, property, birth or other status.[79]

Combining the properties, I define human rights as entitlements that are morally owed to all human beings, that protect urgent human interests from threats, and that impose correlative duties. Human rights are moral rights that should be secured as legal rights in state and international law. To establish a human right, it should be shown that the proposed right secures an urgent human interest against threats.

In the two-level model, the purpose of a state's jurisdiction is to secure human rights within its territory using the coercive power to enact and enforce laws. There are three reasons for states bearing this responsibility. First, giving each state an internationally recognized territory guards against invasion. Article 2 of the UN Charter prohibits the use of force to cross borders into another state's territory.[80] Second, a state's jurisdiction designates a specific government with the duty to protect and empower human rights in its territory. This mitigates the problem of the diffusion of responsibility, which occurs when it is ambiguous who should be securing rights.[81] To avoid diffusion of responsibility, a specific actor, the state's government, bears the chief duty to secure human rights within its territory. Third, the territorial jurisdiction of a state enables the state to raise revenue and create the institutions to empower human rights. For instance, a state can levy taxes on

---

79. UN General Assembly, *International Covenant on Civil and Political Rights*, December 16, 1966, United Nations, Treaty Series, vol. 999, article 9, 173, https://www.refworld.org/docid/3ae6b3aao.html.

80. United Nations Charter, 1945, Art. 2(4); Michael Walzer, *Just and Unjust Wars*, 5th ed. (New York: Basic Books, 2015), part 2.

81. Rawls, *Law of Peoples*, 38–39.

its residents to fund a judicial system and the legal aid needed to secure the human right to the rule of law.

Equal accountability adopts this two-level model of human rights duties. At the first level, citizens bear the duty of oversight to hold their public servants democratically accountable for securing the human rights of their fellow citizens, while respecting the human rights of noncitizens. This is the substantive, duty-based standard of democratic accountability expressed by my Equal Human Rights Principle. At the second level, the question of remedial human rights duties is more complicated and can only be briefly sketched. A remedial duty is one that people have when the primary duty-bearer does not fulfill its responsibility. The second level provides that when a state fails to secure the human rights of its citizens, other states and international organizations bear remedial duties to aid that state.[82] Detailing the responsibilities of citizens to noncitizens from burdened societies is a question beyond the scope of this book.[83] A helpful heuristic is that citizens should engage in deliberation when contemplating their remedial duties. For instance, if the United Nations and the burdened state are calling for relief during a natural disaster, this should inform citizens when they seek to understand the requirements of justice toward noncitizens.

At minimum, citizens should hold their public servants democratically accountable for respecting the human rights of noncitizens. Once we have met that benchmark, we should build on it and consider whether the standards of democratic accountability should be expanded to additional requirements of justice. These requirements may be more demanding for wealthier states. Our first priority toward noncitizens, however, is to make sure our public servants do no harm. Citizens should stop their public servants from waging unjust wars, imposing colonialism, committing atrocities, inflicting torture, spreading slavery, exacerbating the mortal threat of climate change, and arming authoritarians against their subjects. The Manchester workers acted on

82. Rawls defends the "duty to assist burdened societies" that are unable to secure the human rights of their residents (*Law of Peoples*, 106).

83. A valuable book on the requirements of justice to noncitizens is Lucia Rafanelli, *Promoting Justice across Borders* (New York: Oxford University Press, 2021).

the democratic duties of the Equal Human Rights Principle when they demanded that their government respect the human rights of African Americans.

Human Rights Protect Our Human Dignity

What urgent human interests are defended by human rights?[84] The essential interest that the International Bill of Rights invokes is human dignity. The Universal Declaration articulates in its first article, "All human beings are born free and equal in dignity and rights. They are endowed with reason and conscience and should act toward one another in a spirit of brotherhood."[85] The International Covenant on Civil and Political Rights affirms that "these rights derive from the inherent dignity of the human person."[86]

The word dignity conveys how we have, as human beings, a profound worth that should be respected and never violated. I identify two elements of human dignity from the Universal Declaration and ICCPR. The first is our being included as members of the human family who deserve respect for their human dignity. As the Universal Declaration states, the "recognition of the inherent dignity and of the equal and inalienable rights of all members of the *human family* is the foundation of freedom, justice and peace in the world."[87] When we regard each other as fellow members of the human family, we "act toward one another in a spirit of brotherhood."[88] We should see each other as brothers and sisters. There are no strangers in the family of humanity.

---

84. On human dignity underpinning human rights, see Jürgen Habermas, "The Concept of Human Dignity and the Realistic Utopia of Human Rights," *Metaphilosophy* 41, no. 4 (2010): 464–80; George Kateb, *Human Dignity* (Cambridge, MA: Harvard University Press, 2011); Michael Rosen, *Dignity: Its History and Meaning* (Cambridge, MA: Harvard University Press, 2018); and Waldron, *Dignity, Rank and Rights*. Human rights may also protect other urgent interests in addition to human dignity, as noted by Beitz, *Idea of Human Rights*, 128.

85. "Universal Declaration of Human Rights," art. 1.

86. UN General Assembly, *International Covenant on Civil and Political Rights*, 173.

87. "Universal Declaration of Human Rights," preamble (emphasis added).

88. "Universal Declaration of Human Rights," art. 1.

Acknowledging each other as fellow members of the human family means that we should never view one another as subhuman enemies.[89] To disdain others as enemies is to aim at their ruin, and perversely to revel in their distress and anguish as part of one's own flourishing. This enmity is often rationalized by the heinous prejudice that they are less than human. The Nazis maligned Jews, gays and lesbians, Eastern Europeans, the disabled, and other groups with language that denigrated their humanity. American slaveholders malevolently slandered their slaves as "livestock."[90] After World War II, Allied authorities uncovered in the files of Auschwitz a sinister record of the concentration camp selling 150 women to IG Farben for chemical testing and torture. The German company wrote to Auschwitz, "We received your response but consider the price of 200 marks a woman too high. We propose to pay no more than 170 marks a head." The company coldly disclosed the results afterward: "The experiments were performed. All subjects died. We shall contact you shortly on the subject of a new load."[91] This is what a world without human dignity and human rights looks like. The language of dehumanization ends in genocide.

The Universal Declaration of Human Rights is suffused with the lesson from the Holocaust and World War II that "disregard and contempt for human rights have resulted in barbarous acts which have outraged the conscience of mankind."[92] The first meaning of human dignity is to embrace other human beings as fellow members of the human family, as brothers and sisters whose human rights we must respect. To honor human dignity is to resist, in all its forms, any attempt to dehumanize another human being. We must remember this as marginalized groups bear the brunt of dehumanization from elected authoritarians today.

89. Kateb contrasts human dignity with treating someone as "subhuman or as animals or lumps of matter" (*Human Dignity*, 19). My approach connects human dignity with both membership in the human family and the capacity for reason and conscience.

90. David Livingstone Smith, *Less than Human: Why We Demean, Enslave, and Exterminate Others* (New York: St. Martin's Press, 2011), 16, 83.

91. Jonathan Glover, *Humanity: A Moral History of the Twentieth Century*, 2nd ed. (New Haven, CT: Yale University Press, 2012), 339.

92. "Universal Declaration of Human Rights," preamble.

The second meaning of human dignity is respect for our reason and conscience. In the words of the Universal Declaration, "all human beings are born free and equal in dignity and rights. They are endowed with *reason* and *conscience* and should act towards one another in a spirit of brotherhood."[93] It is not enough for human dignity that we be treated like a valuable inert object, to be sheltered but never listened to or recognized as having our own lives to lead. This second meaning of human dignity is necessary to secure the full extent of human rights. Human rights guard against the threat of being infantilized as a silent and unreasoning subject of rule who cannot make moral claims or pursue lives of our own.[94]

I interpret our reason and conscience to refer to how we possess two capacities for freedom.[95] The first is our capacity for *moral agency*, or moral thought, action, and expression. We are respected as moral agents when we are regarded as human beings who can guide our actions by moral reason and advance moral claims about how we and others should be treated. We voice moral claims when we say, "We were treated unfairly," or, "We should end the unjust war." To be respected as a moral agent is to be free to participate in deliberation about how we and others should be treated. We express our moral agency in government through our democratic accountability rights. As moral agents with reason and conscience, we can be held responsible for how we use our reason to direct our actions toward other human beings.

Our second capacity, as persons with reason and conscience, is our freedom to *pursue our own lives*. In the Declaration of Independence's

93. "Universal Declaration of Human Rights," art. 1.

94. On dignity requiring non-infantilization, see the Ober's important essay "Democracy's Dignity."

95. These capacities bear an affinity with Rawls's moral powers of a sense of justice and capacity for a conception of the good. Rawls sees these two moral powers as the grounds of people being free and equal (*Theory of Justice*, 442), and of having human dignity (*Theory of Justice*, 289). There are two relevant differences with my conception. First, I am supporting human rights, which are entitlements of all human beings. Rawls is justifying the basic liberties, which are entitlements of citizens in a democratic society. Second, moral agency is broader than a sense of justice. We exercise our moral agency when deliberating about our own or other people's treatment. The sense of justice applies moral reasoning about our society's political and economic institutions.

felicitous phrase, this freedom is the right to the "pursuit of happiness."[96] Because we possess reason and conscience, we can make decisions regarding the relationships and purposes that define our happiness and endow our lives with meaning. We can chart our own course in the religion we believe, the family we cherish, the work we contribute, the associations we join, and the art we create. The pursuit of happiness contrasts with having our lives dictated by a master, whose happiness, and not our own, we are made to serve. Our freedom to pursue our lives is protected by many human rights, such as freedom of religion in article 18 and the human right to marry in article 23 of the ICCPR.[97] Our human rights to freedom of speech, the press, and association are indispensable to both our moral agency and to our freedom to pursue our lives. We partake of these human rights when we hold our government democratically accountable, and when we practice our familial, cultural, religious, associational, and other commitments that imbue our lives with meaning.

Suppose that an adult in possession of reason is prohibited from marrying unless approved by a master. She cannot go to the church of her choice, speak, or write without her master's permission. She has no say in the rules that regulate her conduct that the master sets and coercively enforces. She is not seen by the legal system as a morally responsible person who can file suit in a court, but as an article of property. She would be unfree and unequal. She would be disdained as a slave, made to serve other people's purposes as a tool. She is denied recognition of her human dignity as a human being with her own aspirations and life to pursue.

Frederick Douglass declared that human beings of all races possess dignity because of their capacity for reason and conscience. In his 1852 oration "What, to the Slave, Is the Fourth of July?" Douglass reminded his audience that the moral rights to freedom and equality from the

---

96. Declaration of Independence.

97. UN General Assembly, *International Covenant on Civil and Political Rights*, art. 18 and 23. On the importance of the right to marry, see Macedo, *Just Married*.

Declaration of Independence are fundamentally opposed to slavery.[98] The slave deserves freedom and equality, because he "is a moral, intellectual and responsible being."[99]

> Must I undertake to prove that the slave is a man? . . . The slaveholders themselves acknowledge it in the enactment of laws for their government. They acknowledge it when they punish disobedience on the part of the slave. . . . What is this but the acknowledgement that the slave is a *moral, intellectual and responsible being*? The manhood of the slave is conceded. It is admitted in the fact that Southern statute books are covered with enactments forbidding, under severe fines and penalties, the teaching of the slave to read or to write.[100]

Laws barring slaves from learning to read and write, said Douglass, make little sense, unless slaves are human beings with the capacity to think, reason, share their thoughts, and to take responsibility for their actions.

Responsibility is closely coupled with moral agency. Human beings are moral agents with the capacity to make *choices that are responsible*. They can regulate their actions through moral reason to respect other people's rights. For example, they can respect other people's right to personal integrity and choose to refrain from violence. That does not mean that they always act that way. But they have the capacity to do so. Since human beings are moral agents with the capacity for responsible choice, they can be *held morally and legally responsible for their choices* when they are of sound mind.[101] For instance, someone who commits a murder deserves moral blame and is held responsible by the law. A hero who braves danger to save a life merits moral praise for her heroism. She is held responsible when the government officially honors her.

98. Frederick Douglass, "What, to the Slave, Is the Fourth of July?" in *Autobiographies*, ed. Henry Louis Gates (New York: Library of America, 1994), 431.

99. Douglass, "What, to the Slave," 433.

100. Douglass, "What, to the Slave," 432–33.

101. Moral and legal responsibility may be mitigated when a person is not of sound mind or mentally competent. Justice Ward Hunt summarized the concept of "sound mind" from common law in Life Insurance Company v. Terry, 82 U.S. 580, 585 (1872): "Lord Mansfield holds the legal test of a sound mind to be the knowledge of right and wrong. . . . Lord Lyttleton held the test to be the state called *compos mentis* or sound mind."

Human beings are not inanimate objects, like a boulder rolling down a hill. It would be odd to resent and blame the boulder for the damage it leaves behind as it is pulled down by gravity.[102] The bounder should not be held responsible for its destructive path, because it is an unthinking object, not a moral agent capable of choices guided by reason. Douglass pointed out that slaveholders conceded that slaves are human beings "in the enactment of laws for their government."[103] The slaveholders implicitly granted that slaves are moral agents capable of responsible choice, who can be held morally and legally responsible for their choices: "What is this but the acknowledgement that the slave is a moral, intellectual and responsible being?"[104] This tacit admission should be transformed into the open acceptance that human beings of every race are entitled to human rights.

Our public servants are tasked with securing the equal human rights of citizens, while respecting the human rights of noncitizens. This is the substantive standard of justice in democracy as equal accountability.[105] Human rights safeguard our urgent interests in our human dignity. We possess dignity as members of the human family, who must never be dehumanized. We also deserve respect for our human dignity as free and equal moral agents capable of reason and conscience. We must not be despised as passive objects of rule without moral claims to voice or lives of our own to pursue. Human rights are the haven of our human dignity.

102. P. F. Strawson, "Freedom and Resentment," *Proceedings of the British Academy* 48 (1962): 1–25. A reactive attitude is a reaction we feel that morally evaluates how we or others are treated. For instance, resentment is the reactive attitude that we feel when others have treated us wrongly. Moral reactive attitudes are predicated on the other person being a moral agent, as opposed to an inanimate, unthinking object.

103. Douglass, "What, to the Slave," 433.

104. Douglass, "What, to the Slave," 433.

105. In chapter 6, I will show that democratic accountability rights qualify as human rights. Securing them for citizens is thus required by both the Equal Accountability Principle and by the Equal Human Rights Principle.

Democratic Accountability Includes Both Substantive and Procedural Standards

It might be claimed that citizens bear no duty to ensure that their public servants secure any human rights aside from rights to democratic accountability. While it might be thought that freedom as self-government only depends on procedural standards being met, would citizens really be self-governing if they were prey to torture, or lacked any substantive rights to life, liberty, and the pursuit of happiness?

The attempt to cast aside substantive requirements ignores three crucial considerations. First, many human rights are indispensable institutional conditions for democratic accountability. In the absence of substantive human rights, such as the right to personal integrity, officials would be able to injure or kill opposition candidates or citizens attempting to protest and vote. The proper direction of the citizen–public servant model would then be reversed. Citizens would no longer be self-governing, because their authority over their officials would be nullified.

Second, losing sight of the substantive standard of human rights would neglect the democratic duty of oversight. Citizens should exercise oversight and ensure that their public servants are using the coercive government power of government justly. This duty of oversight, which I introduced in chapter 2, is grounded in how citizens collectively own government power and employ public servants to use it as a democratically accountable trust. It would not be a just exercise of coercive power to debase the human rights and dignity of other human beings.

Third, citizens owe each other the democratic duty of solidarity to recognize one another's standing as equal authorities in the citizenry. This duty of solidarity creates a freely self-governing relationship where all citizens are included in democracy. One way that citizens can be excluded from democracy is if they are denied their democratic accountability rights. But citizens can also be marginalized through other forms of discrimination.

Suppose that a government secured the democratic accountability rights of marginalized citizens, but it scorned their substantive human rights by inflicting racial segregation.[106] Martin Luther King Jr. spoke of nondiscrimination as a substantive requirement of justice: "An unjust law is a code that a numerical or power majority group compels a minority group to obey but does not make binding on itself. This is difference made legal."[107] Racial discrimination excludes the marginalized from democracy by treating them as pariahs. Among a group of friends, a person would scarcely be regarded as having the standing of being an equal friend if she were violently bullied and belittled because of her race. It in no way excuses that derogatory treatment to say that she has an equal vote. She is marginalized and denigrated as an enemy because her substantive rights are assailed. The word "enemy" derives from the Latin combining "in" (meaning not) and "amicus" (meaning a friend).[108] An enemy is not a friend. Instead of being recognized as an equal friend, she is treated as an enemy by those who target her substantive human rights. It strips citizens of their equal standing when their substantive human rights are assaulted. The victims are turned into outcasts who are hounded in their own country. The antidote to this injustice is for citizens to meet their democratic duties of solidarity and oversight and hold their public servants democratically accountable for honoring human rights.

The Delegation Principle

Why is respect for the human rights of noncitizens part of the standards of democratic accountability, according to my Equal Human Rights Principle? Were the Manchester workers justified in protesting against their officials going to war on the side of the Confederacy and slavery? I set out the *Delegation Principle* that citizens can only delegate to their public servants rights that the citizens collectively possess. To delegate is to authorize a *trust,* or to give permission for another person to use one's right or property. Just as individuals cannot delegate to their real

---

106. "Universal Declaration of Human Rights," art. 2 and 7.
107. King, "Letter from Birmingham Jail."
108. *Oxford English Dictionary,* s.v. "enemy, noun and adjective," accessed March 15, 2025, https://doi.org/10.1093/OED/1767482398.

estate agent the right to sell a house they do not own, citizens cannot delegate to their public servants the right to wield the power of government unjustly. No one is entitled to the right to impose morally prohibited brute force in violation of human rights and dignity.

My Delegation Principle draws on John Locke. When citizens delegate the coercive power to enact and enforce laws to their officials, the citizens cannot entrust the use of any rights they lack. As Locke says in a pivotal passage, "no body can transfer to another more power than he has in himself."[109] We can view this argument through the lens of the principal-agent framework that we described in the previous chapter and recast as the citizen–public servant model. It is improper for principals to give permission for their agent to use something the principals do not own. For example, it is not within the power of a principal to delegate the right to sell a car she has stolen to her auto broker.

Locke's perceptive thought is that persons possess no right to coerce illegitimately, and so they cannot delegate the use of that right to their government: "Having in the state of nature no arbitrary power over the life, liberty, or possession of another, but only so much as the law of nature gave him for the preservation of himself, and the rest of mankind; this is all he doth, or can give up to the common-wealth."[110] Because persons have no right to coerce unjustly, they cannot delegate that right to their public servants. The upshot is that the government must respect the rights of both citizens and noncitizens for its coercive power to be morally legitimate.

For example, Locke speaks to the question of whether governments may wage unjust wars. He answers that citizens cannot delegate to their government a right to prosecute an unjust war, since they do not have that right in the first place to entrust to their officials: "The people [have] given to their governors no power to do an unjust thing, such as is to make an unjust war, (for they never had such a power in

---

109. John Locke, *Second Treatise of Government*, ed. C. B. Macpherson (Indianapolis, IN: Hackett, 1980), 70, §140.
110. Locke, *Second Treatise of Government*, 70, §135.

themselves)."[111] When our government unleashes an unjust war or inflicts atrocities on noncitizens, it breaches the *Delegation Principle* that citizens can entrust to their public servants only powers that the citizens legitimately own.

While my Delegation Principle is inspired by Locke, I differ from him in three aspects. First, the relevant rights that our public servants must respect are human rights that are morally justified by the actual deliberation test, and not Lockean natural rights that are self-evident to reason and derive from a particular religion. Second, I argue that since citizens employ public servants to wield the coercive powers of government, this vests citizens with the democratic duty of oversight. Citizens should hold their public servants democratically accountable for using government power justly.

A third difference with Locke is that I frame the coercive power of government as being *collectively* owned by citizens. Locke's approach bases government on individuals consenting, either tacitly or explicitly, to delegate their individual natural right to coerce to officials. But as the previous chapter showed, the coercive power of government is nonconsensual. Requiring the consent of all citizens for laws to be binding would prevent the government from securing our moral rights. A scofflaw could refuse to consent to laws that prohibit violence or discrimination. Equal accountability instead grounds legitimate government power on democratic accountability to the governed as equal citizens.

My Delegation Principle embodies how citizens collectively own government power and employ public servants to use it on their behalf as a democratically accountable trust. Citizens can only delegate to their public servants the use of power that they collectively own. No one owns the power to abuse the human rights of either citizens or noncitizens, in contempt of their human dignity. Respecting the human rights of noncitizens is a substantive standard of justice that citizens should hold their public servants democratically accountable for satisfying.

---

111. Locke, *Second Treatise of Government*, 93, §179 (parentheses in original).

Who Is Entitled to Citizenship:
The Inclusion Principle

The Equal Human Rights Principle obligates our public servants to secure the human rights of citizens, while respecting the human rights of
noncitizens. The Equal Accountability Principle directs our public servants to equally empower citizens with the capacity to use their democratic accountability rights to correct injustices. Since public servants
owe more demanding duties to the citizens they work for, this raises the
issue of how to determine who is entitled to citizenship. I propose the
Inclusion Principle to answer this question.[112]

> *The Inclusion Principle*: The fact that a person is governed under a
> state's jurisdiction is a strong reason to grant that person citizenship
> in that state.

While this is not the only reason to claim citizenship, the Inclusion
Principle is an important criterion rooted in the substantive and procedural standards of moral legitimacy.

My Inclusion Principle finds support from Robert Dahl and Michael
Walzer. Dahl maintains that "every adult subject to a government and its
laws . . . has an unqualified right to be a member of the demos" or citizenry.[113] Walzer agrees that we are owed citizenship when we are subject
to a state's authority to make and enforce laws: "Political power . . . can't
be exercised democratically without the ongoing consent of its subjects.
And its subjects include every man and woman who lives within the
territory over which those decisions are enforced."[114] Walzer's concern
is that if long-term immigrant workers are denied citizenship, they will
be exploited. The specter of deportation forces them to submit to dangerous and degrading work for paltry pay. Immigrant workers "are exploited or oppressed at least in part because they are disenfranchised,
incapable of organizing effectively for self-defense. Their material condition is unlikely to be improved except by altering their political status.

---

112. I am grateful to Philip Petrov for perspicacious remarks on my Inclusion Principle.
113. Dahl, *Democracy and Its Critics*, 127.
114. Walzer, *Spheres of Justice*, 58; see also 61.

Indeed, the purpose of their status is to prevent them from improving their condition."[115] In this view, immigrant workers should be granted a path to citizenship to safeguard them from exploitation. What I add is a democratic argument for the Inclusion Principle, grounded in human rights, democratic accountability, and self-government.

The Substantive Standard of Human Rights Supports the Inclusion Principle

On the two-level model of human rights duties, the governments of states assume the primary responsibility to secure—to respect, protect, and fulfill—human rights in their territory. The International Covenant on Civil and Political Rights lays down this duty: "Each State Party to the present Covenant undertakes to respect and to ensure to all individuals *within its territory* and *subject to its jurisdiction* the rights recognized in the present Covenant."[116] The ICCPR links the state's just power to coercively enact and enforce laws with the duty to secure human rights in its territory. As UN Secretary General Kofi Annan said, "When we read the [UN] Charter today, we are more than ever conscious that its aim is to protect individual human rights, not to protect those who abuse them."[117]

The state's power to coerce and its responsibility to secure human rights are closely connected, because the coercive power of government is necessary to protect human rights from domestic violence and external invasion. The state's government must secure human rights in its territorial jurisdiction, while respecting the human rights of noncitizens, for its coercive power to be just or morally legitimate.[118] The less morally

---

115. Walzer, *Spheres of Justice*, 59.

116. UN General Assembly, *International Covenant on Civil and Political Rights*, art. 2 (emphasis added).

117. Kofi Annan, "Two Concepts of Sovereignty," *Economist*, September 16, 1999, www.economist.com/node/324795.

118. It is commonly thought by political theorists that the requirements of moral legitimacy are weaker than those of justice. I challenge that premise. I regard justice as specifying the conditions of full moral legitimacy for the government's coercive power. The more unjust the exercise of that power, the less morally legitimate it is. When coercive power is less morally legitimate, it is more morally blameworthy. Citizens then have a more urgent duty of oversight to hold their

legitimate the coercive power, the greater moral blame it incurs, and the more urgent the duty of oversight for citizens to hold their public servants democratically accountable for correcting the injustice.

The government's coercive power must satisfy standards of moral legitimacy, as coercion confronts us with a disquieting moral problem. Coercive power imposes physical force that can injure and kill human beings. Coercion is the darkness of a prison cell, the impact from an officer's truncheon, the manacles that chain the detained, and the bullet fired from a soldier's gun. What could ever make that morally permissible and not prohibited? As we saw in the previous chapter, the justification cannot be that a government agent is acting on behalf of the preferences of a principal. That would wrongly excuse a mafioso who is the agent of his bosses or principals in the mob. The rationale cannot be that a group of people have taken a vote and that the majority has expressed the will to inflict force. That would exculpate in error the drug dealer who commits a murder after a vote of his cartel. Coercive force can only be morally legitimate if it secures our human rights, respects the human rights of noncitizens, and is democratically accountable to us, the governed, as equal citizens. Human rights provide the substantive standard of moral legitimacy, and equal democratic accountability comprises the procedural standard.

The Inclusion Principle aligns symmetrically the people who should be protected by the government, and the citizens who can hold it democratically accountable. This close congruence enables us as citizens to hold our government democratically accountable for securing our human rights.

The foremost defenders of democracy subscribed to this protective argument for democratic government. In his 1957 speech "Give Us the

---

officials democratically accountable for correcting the injustice. Moral legitimacy is a range property, which can vary in degree, and not a categorical property, or a matter of all or nothing. A categorical concept of moral legitimacy cannot explain why misuses of coercive power might vary in their degree of blameworthiness and differ in the intensity of the duty of oversight to correct those injustices. A categorical concept of moral legitimacy also finds it difficult to account for why increasing opposition, from civil disobedience to conscientious refusal, would be justified in response to escalating levels of moral illegitimacy. A theorist who shares my view that moral legitimacy is a matter of degree is Lucia Rafanelli (*Promoting Justice across Borders*, chap. 3).

Ballot," Martin Luther King Jr. proclaimed that "our most urgent request to the president of the United States and every member of Congress is to give us the right to vote. Give us the ballot, and we will no longer have to worry the federal government about our basic rights."[119] John Stuart Mill advanced the protective argument for democracy in his *Considerations on Representative Government*: "The rights and interests of every or any person are only secure from being disregarded, when the person interested is himself able, and habitually disposed, to stand up for them."[120] A person's rights are only secure when she participates democratically, because she is the person most motivated to defend her rights and most familiar with her interests: "The absence of its natural defenders, the interest of the excluded is always in danger of being overlooked; and when looked at, is seen with very different eyes from those whom it directly concerns."[121]

I argue that the *governed*, whose human rights must be secured by government, should be granted citizenship. Citizenship should extend where the state's writ of law runs. This renders the state's power to enact and enforce laws democratically accountable to those who are governed by those laws. The Inclusion Principle entitles the governed to citizenship so that they can secure their human rights, consistently with the Equal Human Rights Principle.

The Procedural Value of Self-Government Endorses the Inclusion Principle

In 1857 the Supreme Court handed down its most notorious ruling, asserting that African Americans could never be citizens under the Constitution, even if they resided for years in the United States and were governed

---

119. Martin Luther King Jr., "Give Us the Ballot," address delivered at the Prayer Pilgrimage for Freedom, Washington, DC, May 17, 1957, https://kinginstitute.stanford.edu/king-papers /documents/give-us-ballot-address-delivered-prayer-pilgrimage-freedom.

120. John Stuart Mill, "Considerations on Representative Government," in *Collected Works of John Stuart Mill*, vol. 19, 404. On Mill's protective and educative arguments for democracy, see Dennis F. Thompson, *John Stuart Mill and Representative Government* (Princeton, NJ: Princeton University Press, 1976), and Carole Pateman, *Participation and Democratic Theory* (Cambridge, UK: Cambridge University Press, 1970).

121. Mill, "Considerations on Representative Government," 405.

by it.[122] Chief Justice Roger Taney wrote that African Americans "were not intended to be included, under the word 'citizens' in the Constitution, and can therefore claim none of the rights and privileges which that instrument provides for and secures to citizens of the United States."[123] Justice Taney cited the fact that the Constitution allowed African Americans to be enslaved as evidence that they did not deserve citizenship. To take one example, the Constitution's Fugitive Slave Clause ordered that slaves who escaped to another state be "delivered up" to their human traffickers.[124]

Justice Taney's odious opinion was premised on the belief that legally recognized citizens have the right to impose their preference regarding who should become citizens. When the Constitution was being written, African Americans were not legally recognized as citizens in many states, and they could not vote on whether to ratify the Constitution with its pro-slavery articles. Taney brandished these provisions, passed without the votes of African Americans, to contend that the Constitution did not regard them as citizens.

The Inclusion Principle opposes the iniquity of the *Dred Scott* decision. The principle recognizes African Americans as equal citizens, since they are residents governed in the territorial jurisdiction of the United States. The match between being governed and granted citizenship is necessary to free the governed to be self-governing. For the governed to be the ones in charge of their government, they must be equal citizens who can hold their public servants democratically accountable. President Lincoln invoked the Declaration of Independence's principle that governments must derive their just power from the governed, in just this way:

> Our Declaration of Independence says . . . "That to secure these rights, governments are instituted among men, *deriving their just powers from the consent of the governed.*" . . . Now the relation of masters and slaves is, *pro tanto*, a total violation of this principle. The master not only governs the slave without his consent; but he governs him by a set of rules altogether different from those which he prescribes

122. Dred Scott v. Sandford, 60 U.S. 393, 405 (1857).
123. Dred Scott v. Sandford, 60 U.S. 393, 404–5 (1857).
124. U.S. Const. article IV, section 2, clause 3.

for himself. Allow ALL the governed an equal voice in the government, and that, and that only is self-government.[125]

When African Americans are governed but denied citizenship, they are not freely self-governing. As Lincoln said of African Americans, is it not "a total destruction of self-government, to say that he too shall not govern *himself*? When the white man governs himself, that is self-government; but when he governs himself and also governs *another* man, that is *more* than self-government—that is despotism."[126] Lincoln's argument that we must "allow ALL the governed an equal voice in the government" supports the Inclusion Principle.

Conclusion

When Thomas Jefferson reached the venerable age of eighty years, he wrote cordially to his close friend and fellow former president, James Madison. Looking back with fondness and reverence at the Declaration of Independence, Jefferson said, "The merit of the Draught therefore could only consist in a lucid enunciation of human rights, in a condensed enumeration of the reasons for such an exercise of them, and in a style and tone appropriate to the great occasion, and to the spirit of the American people."[127]

Taking inspiration from the Declaration of Independence, this chapter has explored the meaning of justice as a standard of democratic accountability. I have argued that justice requires that our public servants recognize all citizens as equal authorities and secure their human rights, while respecting the human rights of noncitizens. The primacy of human rights is grounded in how they protect our urgent human interests, especially our interest in our human dignity. We deserve human dignity as members of the human family, who must never

125. Lincoln, "Speech at Peoria, Illinois, October 16, 1854," 265–66 (emphasis in original).

126. Lincoln, "Speech at Peoria, Illinois, October 16, 1854," 266. The Declaration refers to "unalienable rights," which Lincoln calls "inalienable rights."

127. Thomas Jefferson, "To Thomas Jefferson from James Madison, 6 September 1823," Founders Online, National Archives, https://founders.archives.gov/documents/Jefferson/98 -01-02-3745.

be dehumanized. We also merit human dignity as moral agents with reason and conscience, who have moral claims to voice in deliberation, and lives to fulfill in our pursuit of happiness. We must never be degraded as mere instruments for others like slaves, or despised as the passive pawns of rule who deserve no say in our own government. To protect our human dignity, my Equal Human Rights Principle provides that our public servants must secure the human rights of citizens and respect the human rights of noncitizens. This is a substantive requirement of justice. We bear the duty of oversight as citizens to ensure that our public servants satisfy the Equal Human Rights Principle.

The procedural standard of justice is that our public servants must recognize the equal authority of all citizens to hold their public servants democratically accountable. We can evaluate whether our public servants satisfy that procedural standard by the Equal Accountability Principle: our public servants should guarantee the equal capability of all citizens to use their democratic accountability rights to correct injustices. The exercise of citizens' democratic accountability rights must not be hindered by their membership in a marginalized group. The marginalized are subject to the most abject human rights violations, yet the least able to correct them. To remedy this compound injustice, we should met our duty of oversight and hold our public servants democratically accountable for fulfilling the Equal Accountability Principle.

I offered the Delegation Principle to shed light on why our public servants should respect the rights of noncitizens. It is only morally legitimate for citizens to delegate to their public servants the use of rights that the citizens collectively own. Citizens cannot delegate to their public servants the right to abuse the human rights and dignity of either citizens or noncitizens.

I contributed the Inclusion Principle to determine who should be entitled to citizenship. According to the Inclusion Principle, the fact that a person is governed under a state's jurisdiction is a strong reason to grant that person citizenship in that state. This achieves two purposes. First, the Inclusion Principle aligns the people the state is responsible for protecting with the citizens who can hold the state democratically accountable. The governed can then hold their government democratically accountable for satisfying the state's responsibility to secure their human rights. Second, fulfilling the Inclusion Principle recognizes all of the governed as equal citizens who can hold their government democratically accountable. The Inclusion Principle is necessary to make the governed freely self-governing.

6

The Human Right to Democratic Accountability

DEMOCRATIC SELF-DETERMINATION

IN SOUTH AFRICA, a defendant stood to address the Pretoria Supreme Court, where he faced the death penalty. It was 1964, and the defendant was charged with acts of sabotage and conspiracy to overthrow the state.[1] The accused justified his actions as necessary to oppose apartheid. Citing the Universal Declaration of Human Rights, he said that apartheid denied the democratic right of all the governed to elect their government and shape their laws: "The African people were not part of the Government and did not make the laws by which they were governed."[2] The defendant protested the 1960 referendum that had created a white Republic. He urged that the state is owned by all its residents, who should be recognized as equal citizens: "We believe that South Africa belongs to all the people who live in it, and not one group, be it black or white."[3] The referendum was not an act of self-determination, but of despotism, as it excluded Black South Africans from casting a vote on the new Constitution: "Africans, who constituted approximately 70 per cent of the population of South Africa, were not

---

1. Kenneth S. Bruon, *Saving Nelson Mandela* (New York: Oxford University Press, 2012), 35.
2. Mandela, *In His Own Words*, 30.
3. Mandela, 31. This passage supports the Inclusion Principle for citizenship from chapter 5.

entitled to vote, and were not even consulted about the proposed constitutional change."[4] Closing his speech, the defendant looked the judge
defiantly in the eyes and resolved that South Africa would one day build
a multiracial democracy founded on freedom and equality for all:

> I have cherished the ideal of a democratic and free society in which
> all persons live together in harmony and with equal opportunities. It
> is an ideal which I hope to live for and to achieve. But if needs be, it
> is an ideal for which I am prepared to die.[5]

He was sentenced to life in prison. The prisoner spent his nights in the
dark confines of an eight-by-seven-foot cell and his days in forced labor
at a quarry, where the blinding glare of the sun against the bare, white
limestone permanently scarred his sight.[6] In 1990 an international campaign convinced the government to relent and release him after twenty-
six years of incarceration. In 1993 the former prisoner won the Nobel
Peace Prize for his "work for the peaceful termination of the apartheid
regime, and for laying the foundations for a new democratic South
Africa."[7] The following year, Nelson Mandela was elected president.

President Mandela inspires us to ask: Are we entitled to democracy
as a human right? If so, what form of democracy is required? These
questions are crucial from both an internal and external perspective.
Within the state, if democracy is a human right, then governments
should codify this right in their laws and constitution. Officials should
meet their duty of fidelity to respect, protect, and empower the human
right to democracy for their citizens. The significance of this right is
demonstrated by Mandela's anti-apartheid activism and the anti-
communist dissidents from Eastern Europe, including Václav Havel's
Charter 77 movement in Czechoslovakia and Lech Wałęsa's Solidarity
trade union in Poland. It sustained their efforts, in the face of laws that

4. Mandela, 31.
5. Mandela, 42.
6. Peter Limb, *Nelson Mandela: A Biography* (Westport, CT: Greenwood Press, 2008), 80.
7. Bill Keller, "Mandela Shares Nobel Accolade with De Klerk," *New York Times*, October 16,
1993.

punished their protests, to know that they were striving to secure a right that every human being deserves.

Respecting democracy as a human right means, from the external perspective, that governments must not deprive noncitizens of democracy, such as by supporting authoritarian rulers. Public servants must not depose democratic governments in other states, inflict colonialism on noncitizens, or arm authoritarians against their people. Citizens should fulfill their duty of oversight and hold their public servants democratically accountable for respecting the human right to democracy for noncitizens.

I argue in this chapter that human beings are owed a human right to democratic accountability as a moral right, which ought to be recognized as a legal right.[8] The first section presents evidence that the human right to democratic accountability has been accepted in inclusive deliberation across diverse states. This broad global support allays the concern that the right might be limited to the West. Against this Western-centric claim, I document how a multitude of states have drafted and ratified the international human rights treaties enshrining the human right to democratic accountability.

The human right to democracy should be interpreted as an entitlement to equal democratic accountability, and not to popular will accountability. The predicament of popular will accountability is that it permits groups to violate every other human right at the behest of plurality preferences. This runs counter to the internationally recognized tenets that human rights are *indivisible*, or inseparable from one another, and *interdependent*, or mutually supporting.[9] My *congruence argument* is that the human right to equal democratic accountability is compatible with other widely ratified human rights, such as freedom of speech,

---

8. Chapter 4 draws on Mill to distinguish moral rights from legal or positive rights. I thank Dan Edelstein, who thoughtfully asked whether the human right to democratic accountability is a moral or legal right, after my research presentation at the Princeton University Center for Human Values. When this chapter refers to the human right to democracy, it means the moral right to democratic accountability.

9. UN General Assembly, *Vienna Declaration and Programme of Action*, July 12, 1993, A/CONF.157/23, https://www.refworld.org/docid/3ae6b39ec.html.

press, protest, association, and the rule of law. These human rights are integral to holding the government democratically accountable.

To show that a good should be owed as a human right, we must identify how it secures an urgent human interest that is under threat. The second section of this chapter lays out how the human right to democratic accountability serves three urgent interests. The first is our interest in *freedom as self-government*, as declared in the Freedom Charter of the African National Congress. The second urgent interest is *respect for our human dignity* as free and equal persons capable of reason and conscience, a value that Frederick Douglass espouses. The third urgent interest is that democratic accountability *protects our other human rights* from abuse and neglect.

The moral lodestars of this chapter are the activists struggling for democracy. They are often omitted in philosophical considerations of whether democracy is a human right. We should listen to their voices, because human rights secure urgent interests from subjugation, disrespect, and oppression. The people with the closest contact with these dangers are the marginalized. They testify to the importance of democratic accountability.

The third section of the chapter answers three objections. First, I show that a peacefully promoted human right to democratic accountability coheres with the value of toleration. Critics cite toleration in an attempt to erase democracy from the list of human rights, depicting human rights as triggers for outside intervention. Against this criticism, I bring into greater prominence the *internal perspective* of human rights. The key claimants of human rights emerge from *within* a society. When Mandela was organizing against apartheid, he was falsely framed by the government as a foreign agitator and adversary. He replied in his Pretoria speech, "The suggestion made by the State in its opening that the struggle in South Africa is under the influence of foreigners or communists is wholly incorrect. I have done whatever I did, both as an individual and as a leader of my people, because of my experience in South Africa and my own proudly felt African background, and not because of what any outsider might have said."[10]

10. Mandela, *In His Own Words*, 27.

Second, I emphasize that the human right to democratic accountability should be promoted peacefully, through duties to avoid harm and provide aid, and not through military intervention. Military force can jeopardize the human right to personal integrity, violating the indivisibility requirement.

Third, I answer an objection based on self-determination. The right of self-determination is the freedom of a people to form a government and choose its political status, either as an independent state or a polity in a relationship with another state. It is commonly believed that self-determination entitles pluralities to choose any form of government they want, even an authoritarian regime. This theory of authoritarian self-determination licenses pluralities to select nondemocratic governments that discriminate against marginalized groups. The discriminatory government is then imposed by state coercion, as occurred in the 1960 South African referendum.

In place of authoritarian self-determination, I contribute a conception of *democratic self-determination*. It is innovative in combining democratic accountability with self-determination at two levels. First, there must be democratic accountability in the *input* of self-determination. Decisions regarding the constitution should be made by citizens who possess equal democratic accountability rights to openly deliberate the proposed constitution.[11] Second, I incorporate democratic accountability into the *output* of self-determination. All residents of the state should continue to enjoy the secure standing of being equal citizens after the referendum. This robust inclusion as equal authorities liberates citizens to be self-governing. Democratic self-determination respects citizens' human dignity as persons capable of reason and conscience and protects their other human rights from oppression and neglect. My theory of democratic self-determination places the values of equality and nondiscrimination at the core of democracy and human

11. Simone Chambers makes the persuasive point that constitutions should be established after free deliberation in the public sphere of civic society, in "Democracy and Constitutional Reform: Deliberative versus Populist Constitutionalism," *Philosophy and Social Criticism* 45, nos. 9–10 (2019): 1116–31.

rights. All citizens, including every race and sex, are owed the human right to what Mandela called "a democratic and free society."[12]

Intercultural Agreement on the Human Right to Democracy

The international community recognizes that democracy possesses greater moral legitimacy compared to other forms of government. Since World War II, popular movements have established democracy in over half of states globally. 106 states out of 195 are now democracies.[13] Even authoritarian governments concede the value of democracy by holding elections and calling themselves "democratic people's republics." Though the claims to be democratic may be hypocritical, they communicate the belief across cultures that democracy is a condition for the moral legitimacy of government. If this belief were not widespread, states would not wrap themselves in the mantle of democracy. Few governments base their legitimacy on the once-dominant alternatives to democracy, such as the divine right of kings or aristocracy.

An apparent exception to this democratic trend is the People's Republic of China. However, the PRC admits the principle of democracy and holds local elections. In a speech to the government's Chinese People's Political Consultative Conference (CPPCC), President Xi said, "The CPPCC needs to play the role of an organization specializing in deliberation and put deliberative democracy into practice throughout the whole process of its performance of duties. It needs to improve the system of political consultation, democratic oversight, and participation in the deliberation and administration of state

12. Mandela, *In His Own Words*, 42.

13. Freedom House, "Electoral Democracies in *Freedom in the World 2025*," *Freedom in the World 2025*, https://freedomhouse.org/sites/default/files/2025-02/List_of_Electoral_Democracies_FIW24.xlsx. However, there is little room for complacency. Freedom House observes, "Global freedom declined for the 19th consecutive year in 2024. Sixty countries experienced deterioration in their political rights and civil liberties, and only 34 secured improvements." Freedom House, "Uphill Battle to Safeguard Rights," *Freedom in the World 2025*, accessed June 28, 2025, https://freedomhouse.org/report/freedom-world/2025/uphill-battle-to-safeguard-rights.

affairs."[14] He based democracy on both the right to vote and broader rights to democratic participation: "Whether people enjoy democratic rights or not depends on whether they have the right to vote in elections, as well as whether they have the right to constantly participate in everyday political activities. Besides having the right to democratic elections, it also depends on whether they have the right to democratic decision-making, democratic management, and democratic oversight."[15] The PRC is currently not democratically accountable. But it is revealing that diverse states, including the PRC, admit the value of democracy.

174 state parties have recognized the human right to democracy in the ICCPR, which the PRC has signed.[16] The treaty guarantees in article 25 the democratic rights "to vote and to be elected at genuine periodic elections which shall be by universal and equal suffrage."[17] The ICCPR recognizes as human rights the democratic accountability rights to free expression, assembly, and the rule of law.[18] The international covenant pairs democracy with the human right to nondiscrimination in article 2. Democracy must not be denied based on race, sex, or religion.[19]

14. Xi Jinping, "Speech at the Meeting Marking the 65th Anniversary of the Founding of the Chinese People's Political Consultative Conference," *Guangming Daily*, September 22, 2014, http://en.theorychina.org/xsqy_2477/201411/t20141113_314382.shtml.

15. Xi Jinping, "Speech at the Meeting Marking the 65th Anniversary."

16. A state that *signs* a treaty is not yet legally bound by it, but it expresses the commitment to proceed with ratification. The signatory state is obligated not to commit acts that would defeat the treaty's purpose. *State parties* have ratified the treaty and are legally bound by it. See United Nations, Vienna Convention on the Law of Treaties, May 23, 1969, United Nations, Treaty Series, vol. 1155, p. 331, https://www.refworld.org/docid/3ae6b3a10.html. While the treaty is *legally* binding only for states that are parties to it, I argue that the human right to democratic accountability is a moral human right that is *morally* obligatory for all states.

17. UN General Assembly, *International Covenant on Civil and Political Rights*, art. 25. For current state parties to the ICCPR, see United Nations Treaty Collection, "International Covenant on Civil and Political Rights," accessed June 28, 2025, https://treaties.un.org/pages/viewdetails.aspx?chapter=4&clang=_en&mtdsg_no=iv-4&src=ind.

18. *International Covenant on Civil and Political Rights.* The ICCPR guarantees freedom of expression in art. 19, freedom of assembly in art. 21, free association in art. 22, equal protection of the law in art. 26, and legal due process in art. 9.

19. *International Covenant on Civil and Political Rights,* 173, art. 2. Peter Singer cites the ICCPR as upholding the human right to democracy in *One World Now: The Ethics of Globalization* (New Haven, CT: Yale University Press, 2016), 118–19.

A skeptic might say that some parties to the ICCPR are not demo-cratic. The worry is that their signing on to the international covenant might not reflect any real commitment to democracy. Does this mean that signing the treaty amounts to "cheap talk"? Against this view, re-search by Kathryn Sikkink and Thomas Risse has found that respect for human rights follows a three-stage sequence. In the first step, states openly oppose the very idea of human rights. In the second, "hypocriti-cal stage," states sign on to the principle of human rights, but their actions may be contrary to their avowed values. The third stage incor-porates the principle in practice. The state acts with integrity toward human rights.[20] The sequence is not inevitable, but we should not be discouraged too hastily by hypocrisy. It passes as an intermediate phase between opposition and open adherence to human rights. I add that when states sign human rights treaties, they join the international com-munity in affirming the validity of those rights. The excuse of authoritar-ians that human rights are culturally alien is untenable when their states have accepted the moral value of human rights, as reflected by their signing international human rights treaties.[21]

Why might the hypocritical stage lead later to integrity? One reason is that domestic movements can demand that their governments act in accordance with human rights. They can point to their government's agreement with international treaties to lend legitimacy to their de-mands. For example, the 1975 Helsinki Final Act resulted from a two-year international deliberation, negotiated over 761 sessions.[22] It com-mitted the thirty-five signatory states to "respect human rights and fundamental freedoms," including political and civil rights. These democratic rights "derive from the inherent dignity of the human per-son and are essential for his free and full development."[23] Skeptics

20. Thomas Risse and Kathryn Sikkink, "The Socialization of International Human Rights Norms into Domestic Practices: Introduction," in *The Power of Human Rights*, ed. Thomas Risse, Stephen C. Kopp, and Kathryn Sikkink (New York: Cambridge University Press, 1999), chap. 1.

21. I thank Theodora Welch, who contributed discussion of this idea.

22. Daniel C. Thomas, *The Helsinki Effect* (Princeton, NJ: Princeton University Press, 2001).

23. Organization for Security and Co-operation in Europe (OSCE), *Conference on Security and Co-operation in Europe (CSCE): Final Act of Helsinki*, August 1, 1975, point VII, https://www .refworld.org/docid/3dde4f9b4.html. Thomas, *Helsinki Effect*, 86.

scoffed at the human rights provisions as idle talk. Their expectations were belied when the act unleashed a torrent of social mobilization within the communist bloc "under the banner of human rights."[24] Václav Havel's Charter 77 movement in Czechoslovakia and Lech Wałęsa's Solidarity trade union in Poland shared the goal of spurring their governments to comply with the human rights ratified in the Helsinki Final Act.[25] The efforts of these activists contributed to restoring democracy in Eastern Europe. Their heroism is honored in a preserved portion of the Berlin Wall. Near the parliament of a united and democratic Germany, the fallen fragment is emblazoned with the words, "Trophy of Human Rights."[26]

A second impetus for integrity is what Jon Elster calls the "civilizing force" of hypocrisy.[27] Once officials in their public statements accept human rights, they face domestic and international audience costs if they act hypocritically. This brings public pressure to bear on officials to conform their conduct more closely to their professed principles. I suggest that this process took place when the Allies advocated self-determination in World War I. British Prime Minister David Lloyd George wrote that the motives for the Allies endorsing self-determination combined sincere belief with self-interest. The Allies anticipated that the multinational empires they were fighting could be fractured if the captive nationalities were encouraged to seek statehood: "It was discovered that the strength of the enemy might be undermined by taking advantage of disaffection amongst the subject races."[28] However, once the Allies admitted the value of national self-determination, the British had to grant its moral force within its own empire, a striking

24. Thomas, *Helsinki Effect*, 211.

25. On the pro-democracy dissidents in the Soviet Union who inspired the Helsinki Final Act and invoked it in their activism, see Benjamin Nathans, *To the Success of Our Hopeless Cause: The Many Lives of the Soviet Dissident Movement* (Princeton, NJ: Princeton University Press, 2024).

26. Morton Winston, "The Helsinki Effect," *Canadian Journal of Political Science* 35, no. 4 (2002): 982.

27. Jon Elster, "Deliberation and Constitution Making," in *Deliberative Democracy*, ed. Jon Elster (Cambridge, UK: Cambridge University Press, 1998), 97–122.

28. David Lloyd George, *The Truth about the Peace Treaties*, vol. 2 (London: Victor Gollancz, 1938), 755.

example of the civilizing force of hypocrisy. The prime minister wrote that the British were compelled to concede that "the principle of government with the consent of the governed should be extended to India."[29]

The influence of pro-democracy movements and the claims of governments to be democratic lead us to ask: What kind of democracy are the governed entitled to possess over their government? This chapter argues for a human right to democratic accountability. I understand democratic accountability to mean *equal accountability*, which is democratic accountability without discrimination against marginalized groups.

Answering the Diversity Objection to the Universality of Human Rights

Are human rights, which protect access to vital goods for human beings, compatible with cultural diversity? One reply is that rights can secure the freedom for the flourishing of a plethora of religions.[30] Freedom of conscience shields us from religious persecution. A critic might still worry that human rights are non-neutral in that they tend to make it more likely that certain faiths may gain disciples. People who live in a state that honors human rights might be more willing to join faiths that preach solidarity with all human beings. This concern about non-neutrality misses the fact that no moral framework is neutral in leaving cultures unaffected. A world where no human rights are recognized, as was the case before 1945, was not culturally neutral, but it permitted pervasive and vehement discrimination. A moral framework that protects human rights for all human beings evinces greater respect for cultural diversity. It was the ordeal of an intolerant world without human rights that rallied people from a global family of cultures to accept the Universal Declaration of Human Rights.

A second reply to the worry about diversity is to clarify what underpins the universality of human rights. These rights do not force people to adopt

---

29. Lloyd George, *Truth about the Peace Treaties*, vol. 2, 755.

30. Alexis de Tocqueville attributed the diversity and strength of religious belief in the United States to its religious freedom (*Democracy in America*).

the same culture.[31] The reason why human rights are universal is that human beings share similar vulnerabilities or threats to urgent interests.[32] Human rights protect our vital needs without dictating a particular way of life. A human right to subsistence does not mean that everyone must eat the identical food. A human right to freedom of conscience does not imply that everyone must worship the same God. Human rights shelter the diversity that can emerge once people's urgent interests are satisfied.

A third response to the cultural respect concern is that the human right to democracy has satisfied the *actual deliberation test*. Deliberation can scrutinize the validity of a moral requirement by examining it in public discussion. The actual deliberation test can offer evidence that a proposed human right is morally valid and defends genuine urgent interests that are broadly shared among human beings from many cultures. A salient site of deliberation is the drafting, ratification, and claiming of human rights declarations and treaties.

The Actual Deliberation Test and Ideal Deliberation Test

The human right to democratic accountability is a moral right, which gives states and the international community the urgent moral duty to protect it as a legal human right.[33] For instance, states codified the moral human right to democratic accountability as a legal human right when they ratified the International Covenant on Civil and Political Rights.[34]

The extensive deliberation that precedes the ratification of legal human rights expresses cultural respect and helps us to discern what moral human rights we are entitled to possess. This public discussion takes place at two levels. First, human rights declarations and treaties are drafted in deliberation over hundreds of sessions *between states*.

31. Gutmann, "Introduction."

32. Beitz, *Idea of Human Rights*, 109–10. Amartya Sen holds that human rights are universal in that people in different countries have strong reasons to value democracy ("Democracy as a Universal Value," *Journal of Democracy* 10 [1993]: 3–17).

33. A moral human right is a right that should be codified in national and international law (Christiano, "Instrumental Argument").

34. UN General Assembly, *International Covenant on Civil and Political Rights*.

Second, deliberation takes place *within states* when their governments and civil societies discuss whether to ratify the treaties.[35] A state that ratifies a treaty enters it as a party and agrees to be legally obligated by it.

A possible concern about the actual deliberation test is that it might be subject to a status quo bias. It seems to leave the content of moral human rights to be determined by the outcome of global agreement on international law. Actual deliberation needs a standpoint of scrutiny, since no discussion ever includes all the people who are subject to a proposed principle. One critical standpoint is supplied by the *ideal deliberation test*. It asks what people *would* agree to, consistent with their freedom and equality, if we held an ideal deliberation that is completely inclusive and free of duress or deception.[36] In the ideal deliberation test, we reflect on what would be acceptable to everyone bound by the decision. This reflection is needed, because procedures are imperfect, and it is impossible to include in actual deliberation everyone who is relevantly affected by a contemplated human right. We should treat the findings of actual deliberation as "provisional," as Amy Gutmann and Dennis Thompson write. The findings of public discussion are provisional in being "open to revision in an ongoing process of moral and political deliberation."[37]

I note that when we make actual deliberation more inclusive, its verdict becomes more conclusive and credible. As the conversation is freer and attends to more diverse voices, the actual deliberation test approaches more closely a completely inclusive, ideal deliberation.[38] Both

35. That internal deliberation is more open and free when the state is democratic.

36. Ideal deliberation tests include the ideal speech situation in Habermas, *Between Facts and Norms*, and the original position in Rawls, *Theory of Justice*.

37. Gutmann and Thompson, *Why Deliberative Democracy*, 97.

38. This thought aligns with Rawls's claim that principles are morally justified when they achieve "wide and general reflective equilibrium" (*Political Liberalism*, 384). In wide reflective equilibrium, an individual has settled on principles of justice after contemplating what people could accept in a hypothetical, ideal deliberation. Citizens then test their views of what ideal deliberation would require in actual deliberation with one another. The ideal deliberation and actual deliberation tests interact with one another. When their results concur, citizens reach *general reflective equilibrium* and principles of justice are fully morally justified. Citizens agree on principles of justice after having engaged internally in the ideal deliberation test, and externally in actual deliberation with each other.

actual and ideal deliberation are needed. Actual deliberation examines different people's interpretations of what ideal deliberation requires, while ideal deliberation provides a standpoint to reconsider the outcomes of actual deliberation. The highly inclusive deliberation both *between diverse states* in the drafting of human rights treaties and *within states* during the ratification of treaties weigh strongly in favor of the moral validity and cultural respect of human rights.

A second answer to the status quo concern is that making actual deliberation more inclusive can enrich our understanding of human rights. We benefit from moral learning when we listen to the experiences of marginalized people, who face threats to their urgent interests.[39] For instance, global deliberation with greater participation for women has deepened the appreciation of the moral human right to nondiscrimination. This more inclusive deliberation prompted the UN General Assembly to adopt the Convention on the Elimination of All Forms of Discrimination against Women (CEDAW) in 1979.[40]

To be clear, agreement does not imply that human rights are only morally binding for states that ratify them. Moral human rights are morally obligatory even for countries, such as apartheid South Africa, that repudiate them.[41] To recognize human rights violations, we must

39. Habermas, "Concept of Human Dignity," 467–68.

40. UN General Assembly, *Convention on the Elimination of All Forms of Discrimination against Women*, December 18, 1979, United Nations, Treaty Series, vol. 1249, 13–142, https:// treaties.un.org/doc/Publication/UNTS/Volume%201249/v1249.pdf. The treaty became legally obligatory after sufficient states ratified it in 1981.

41. Legal human rights are legally obligatory even for states that oppose them, once those human rights have been ratified by a "very large majority of States." Those rights then become jus cogens, or peremptory norms of customary international law. The International Law Commission, whose members are elected by the UN General Assembly, explains: "Acceptance and recognition by a very large majority of States is required for the identification of a norm as a peremptory norm of general international law (jus cogens); acceptance and recognition by all States is not required." See United Nations General Assembly, *Report of the International Law Commission, Seventy-First Session* (New York: United Nations, 2019), conclusion 7, p. 143. Ronald Dworkin holds that jus cogens is not based solely on consent ("A New Philosophy for International Law," *Philosophy and Public Affairs* 41, no. 1 [2013]: 8–10). Otherwise, a state could renounce the right against genocide, a core canon of customary international law, simply by not ratifying the Genocide Convention. I agree with Dworkin that human rights and other jus cogens norms are obligatory because respecting them is required for the coercive force of government and the international order of states to be morally legitimate. See Dworkin, "New Philosophy for International Law," 19–22.

understand human rights to be moral rights that remain morally binding when states transgress them. The relevance of agreement is that when people from many cultures ratify international statements of human rights, it shows that those rights respect plural cultures.

The third principle of cultural respect is to see whether citizens from diverse states claim human rights. One of the most pressing threats to human rights is the coercive force of states. The litmus test of whether human rights are culturally respectful cannot be if state officials who are among the most egregious rights violators adhere to the human rights treaties that their predecessors signed. When authoritarians disregard human rights, a sign that these rights are not culturally alien is that members of the culture seek to exercise them, as Mandela did.

Merging these three strands, statements of human rights exhibit cultural respect when we conduct actual deliberation in the drafting, ratification, and claiming of human rights. The freer and more inclusive the actual deliberation or public discussion, the closer it approaches a fully free and inclusive ideal deliberation, and the greater the validity of the requirements of human rights. The declarations and treaties that comprise the International Bill of Human Rights satisfy these principles of cultural respect. The Universal Declaration, which includes a human right to democracy in article 21 and other provisions, was written with all the original member states of the United Nations participating. The UN held over two hundred meetings to solicit comments from the widest possible set of state members, refining the Universal Declaration over 168 drafts.[42] Dr. Peng Chun Chang, a Confucian philosopher and statesman from China, presided as the vice-chair of the commission. Other influential members included Charles Malik, a Lebanese philosopher and diplomat, and the judge Hernán Santa Cruz from Chile.[43]

The work of these delegates in the UDHR drafting committee merits greater attention. An unwarranted source of skepticism about human

42. Sun Pinghua, "Pengchun Chang's Contributions to the Drafting of the UDHR," *Journal of Civil and Legal Studies* 5, no. 5 (2016): 1.

43. Mary Ann Glendon, "The Forgotten Crucible: The Latin American Influence on the Universal Human Rights Idea," *Harvard Human Rights Journal* 16 (2003): 27–39.

rights is the perception that they originated from the United States and Western Europe. This skeptical presumption neglects the signal efforts of other states as progenitors of human rights. Latin American states contributed the catalyst for the Universal Declaration. The Inter-American Conference, meeting in Peru, issued a "Declaration in Defense of Human Rights" as early as 1938.[44] In the 1945 sessions to found the United Nations, "delegates from Brazil, Canada, Chile, Cuba, the Dominican Republic, Egypt, France, Haiti, India, Mexico, New Zealand, Panama, and Uruguay" came together to champion a Universal Declaration of Human Rights.[45] The United States came around only after photographs of the Holocaust made evident the need for a declaration that would recognize human rights for all human beings.[46]

At the outset of the drafting process, the Chinese delegation presented a ten-article declaration of human rights.[47] The Chinese draft marked the genesis of article 21 and its human right to democracy. The Chinese draft affirmed, "Every person has the right to take part in the affairs of his government directly or through his representatives."[48] As the committee honed the language of article 21, it voted in favor of the Chinese delegation's version: "The will of the people is the source of the authority of government; this will shall be expressed in periodic elections, which shall be universal, genuine, equal, and held by secret ballot, or manifested in equivalent free voting procedures."[49]

Vice Chair Peng Chun Chang "introduced the concept of Chinese Confucian culture into the provisions of the Universal Declaration of Human Rights."[50] Chang brought attention to the Confucian concept of *ren* or the capacity for benevolence and co-humanity. The United Nations committee wove the Confucian notion of *Ren* into the first

44. Glendon, "Forgotten Crucible," 28.

45. Glendon, 17–18.

46. Glendon, 18.

47. Stephen C. Angle and Marina Svensson, eds., *The Chinese Human Rights Reader* (New York: Routledge, 2001), 208.

48. United Nations Economic and Social Council, document E/CN.4/AC.1/18, May 3, 1948, https://documents-dds-ny.un.org/doc/UNDOC/DER/NL4/818/25/PDF/NL481825.pdf ?OpenElement.

49. Morsink, *Universal Declaration of Human Rights*, 60.

50. Quoted in Pinghua, "Pengchun Chang's Contributions," 3.

article of the Universal Declaration. Article 1 grounds human rights in the dignity of human beings as persons with reason and conscience, who should act in solidarity and recognize each other's humanity.[51]

Some critics have charged that Confucian ideals are at odds with human rights. But the founder of modern China, Sun Yat-Sen, who is revered in both Taiwan and the People's Republic of China, proposed the Three Principles of the People. One of these principles is democracy or *mínquán*. Sun Yat-Sen held two elements to be foundational to democracy. The first is the Four Rights of the People, *zhèngquán*, including the rights of citizens to vote in elections, recalls, initiatives, and referenda. The second element of democracy is the separation of powers in the Five Power Constitution.[52] Alongside the legislative, judicial, and executive branches, Sun Yat-Sen drew on Chinese Confucianism to add the accountability branch and the civil service.[53] Taiwan has implemented the Five Power Constitution in its democracy. The accountability branch, whose members are nominated by the president and confirmed by the legislature, audits the government budget. It censures the corruption of officials, initiates impeachment, investigates human rights abuses, and proposes remedies. Kim Dae-jung, who served as president of South Korea, said, "There are no ideas more fundamental to democracy than the teachings of Confucianism, Buddhism, and Tonghak [South Korean neo-Confucianism]. Clearly, Asian has democratic philosophies as profound as those of the West."[54]

Following the drafting process, the ratification of human rights declarations and treaties has respected cultural diversity. The human rights

51. Pinghua, 3; "Universal Declaration of Human Rights," art. 1.

52. Audrey Wells, *The Political Thought of Sun Yat-Sen* (New York: Palgrave Macmillan, 2001). Macedo and Sen level strong criticisms against the Asian authoritarianism theory in Macedo, "Self-Sustaining Virtue of the Powerful," and Sen, "Democracy as a Universal Value."

53. To recall from previous discussion of this point, the accountability branch is the Control Yuan. The civil service is the Examination Yuan.

54. Kim Dae Jung, "Is Culture Destiny? The Myth of Asia's Anti-Democratic Values," *Foreign Affairs* 73, no. 6 (1994): 191. The PRC's economic success is cited by partisans of authoritarianism, but they ignore the fact that Taiwan, with its democratic government, has attained a higher per capita GDP of $34,430, compared to $13,690 in the PRC, measured by purchasing power parity. See "GDP per capita, current prices, 2025," International Monetary Fund, accessed June 28, 2025, https://www.imf.org/external/datamapper/NGDPDPC@WEO/ADVEC/WEOWORLD/TWN/CHN.

protected by the ICCPR and the Universal Declaration have garnered the free and reasoned assent of states from diverse cultures. The ICCPR, with its human right to democracy, has won the support of 174 state parties.[55] Though some states may violate rights in practice, their agreement with the principle of human rights in international treaties testifies to how those rights respect cultural pluralism.

A third sign of cultural respect is that diverse people have *claimed* human rights. Human rights can mobilize *domestic* opposition to abuses of power by governments.[56] As Rainer Forst notes, "the primary perspective of human rights is *from the inside*."[57] For example, human rights have legitimated the internal opposition of Black South Africans and Chinese dissidents to authoritarianism.[58] China's first winner of the Nobel Peace Prize, Liu Xiaobo, called on the PRC government to comply with the human rights that it accepted in its own constitution. He cited the PRC constitution's provision that "the state respects and guarantees human rights" and pointed out that "human rights have already become one of the fundamental principles of China's rule of law."[59] The PRC constitution explicitly endorses the human rights to "enjoy freedom of speech, of the press, of assembly, of association, of procession and of demonstration."[60] The advocates for human rights are not foreign interlopers but activists from within China appealing to their government's own constitution and treaty commitments.

In 2022 a wave of demonstrations swept across China after a fire killed ten residents of a barricaded building in Urumqi. Gathering around a candlelit memorial, a crowd held up white sheets of paper to

---

55. UN General Assembly, *International Covenant on Civil and Political Rights*.

56. Sen criticizes the "external imposition" view for ignoring the diversity of Western and non-Western peoples. Westerners can be human rights violators, and non-Westerners can be human rights advocates ("Democracy as a Universal Value").

57. Rainer Forst, "The Justification of Human Rights and the Basic Right to Justification: A Reflexive Approach," *Ethics* 120 (2010): 727.

58. Risse and Sikkink, "Socialization," 5. I thank Jamie Mayerfeld, who helpfully suggested that I discuss Charter 08.

59. Liu Xiaobo, "Nobel Lecture in Absentia," December 10, 2010, available at https://www.nobelprize.org/prizes/peace/2010/xiaobo/lecture/; *Constitution of the People's Republic of China* (rev. 2004), art. 33, available at https://www.refworld.org/pdfid/4c31ea082.pdf.

60. *Constitution of the People's Republic of China*, art. 35.

protest censorship, chanting, "Need human rights, need freedom." Other protestors exhorted that the communist party should step down: "Don't want dictatorship, want democracy!"[61] The protesters waved the Chinese flag and sang the national anthem to pledge that they are Chinese citizens seeking the human right to democracy.[62]

Governments may violate human rights, but it is specious for them to assert that these rights are culturally alien to their citizens. Liu gave voice to the human right to democratic accountability when he said, "Freedom of expression is the foundation of human rights, the source of humanity, and the mother of truth."[63] Liu's message reverberated with his fellow Chinese citizens, which is why the regime saw it as a challenge to their single-party rule. If the message had been culturally incomprehensible, as the regime claimed, there would have been no risk that it would find a receptive audience. It was because Liu's advocacy of human rights struck a chord with the Chinese people that the security forces cracked down on him.

The government detained Liu in solitary confinement as one of the authors of the Charter 08 manifesto. Signed by over ten thousand people before censors hastily suppressed it, Charter 08 commemorates the sixtieth anniversary of the Universal Declaration of Human Rights.[64] Charter 08 invokes Sun Yat-Sen's principles of representative democracy. In language that resonates with democracy as equal accountability, it seeks the "public control of public servants," a "democratically regulated and accountable system of public finance," the separation of powers, and competitive multiparty elections.[65] Charter 08 declares that "the government exists for the protection of the human

61. CNN's Beijing's Bureau and Nectar Gan, "Protests Erupt across China in Unprecedented Challenge to Xi Jinping's Zero-Covid Policy," CNN, November 28, 2022, https://www.cnn.com/2022/11/26/china/china-protests-xinjiang-fire-shanghai-intl-hnk/index.html.

62. Tessa Wong and Nathan Williams, "China Covid: Protests Continue in Major Cities across the country," BBC News, November 27, 2022, https://www.bbc.com/news/world-asia-63771109.

63. Liu Xiaobo, "Nobel Lecture in Absentia."

64. Editorial Board, "The Spirit of Liu Xiaobo," New York Times, June 14, 2017.

65. "Charter 08," trans. Perry Link in The Journey of Liu Xiaobo, ed. Joanne Leedom-Ackerman et al., trans. Stacy Mosher and Andréa Worden (Lincoln, NE: Potomac Books, 2020), 491–92.

rights of its citizens," a principle that the Equal Human Rights Principle embodies in chapter 5 of this book.[66] Human rights attract the allegiance of people from plural cultures.

Activists within states are often overlooked in debates about the human right to democracy. However, the function of human rights is to protect urgent human interests from threats. Few people are as qualified to speak about those threats as the marginalized who are stricken by the state's repressive powers. They have endured prison and persecution for the sake of democracy. Their voices deserve to be heard on human rights, instead of being shunted aside in undue deference to the autocrats who are incarcerating them.

The leading proponents of human rights and democracy have welcomed each other as allies across cultures. Liu was nominated for the Peace Prize by Václav Havel and the South African Nobel laureate Bishop Desmund Tutu.[67] Havel was one of the founders of Charter 77.[68] The secret police hounded and detained Havel, but he later led the Velvet Revolution restoring democracy as the president of Czechoslovakia and later the Czech Republic. Liu and his coauthors christened their petition Charter 08 in homage to Havel's Charter 77. Before the prison sentence that would end his life, Liu said, "I, filled with optimism, look forward to the advent of a future free China. For there is no force that can put an end to the human quest for freedom, and China will in the end become a nation ruled by law, where human rights reign supreme."[69]

66. Quoted in Michael Wines, "A Manifesto on Freedom Sets China's Persecution Machinery in Motion," *New York Times*, April 30, 2009, https://www.nytimes.com/2009/05/01/world/asia/01beijing.html.

67. Václav Havel, Dana Němcová, and Václav Malý, "A Nobel Prize for a Chinese Dissident," *International Herald Tribune*, September 20, 2010, https://www.nytimes.com/2010/09/21/opinion/21iht-edhavel.html.

68. "Czech Republic/Slovakia: Text of Charter 77," *Radio Free Europe*, January 9, 1997, https://www.rferl.org/a/1083022.html.

69. Liu Xiaobo, "Nobel Lecture in Absentia."

The Human Right to Democratic Accountability Is Consistent with Other Human Rights

My *congruence argument* explains why we should construe the right to democracy as a human right to democratic accountability, which interprets democracy consistently with our other human rights in two ways. First, equal accountability secures the equal standing of all citizens, so that all citizens are freely self-governing. To have equal standing, citizens must possess equal human rights. Second, equal accountability integrates several human rights, such as free speech and the rule of law, into democratic accountability itself.

All five core elements of equal accountability are guaranteed by the ICCPR as human rights. The core elements of equal accountability are the rights to *authorize* our public servants to hold office, to *evaluate* and *sanction* their conduct during office, to *remove* them from office, and to *run for office and campaign for candidates*. We evaluate and sanction our public servants with our human rights to free speech and the press in article 19, the freedom to protest in article 21, free association in article 22, and the rule of law in at least eight provisions of the ICCPR.[70] We authorize and remove our officials through our democratic accountability rights to vote and run for office in article 25.[71]

A central canon of human rights interpretation is that they are indivisible and interdependent. The Vienna Declaration, which was adopted by 171 states, stands for the principle that "all human rights are universal, indivisible and interdependent and interrelated."[72] Human rights are interdependent, because they rely on each other to be secured: "One set of rights cannot be enjoyed fully without the other."[73] To exercise

---

70. The ICCPR upholds the human right to the rule of law in art. 6 (right to life protected by law), art. 7 (right against cruel, inhuman, or degrading punishment), art. 9 (rights to liberty and security of the person and habeas corpus), art. 10 (rights of the accused and prisoners), art. 14 (right to equality before the law and due process), art. 15 (right against punishment by ex post facto laws), art. 16 (right to legal recognition as a person before the law), and art. 17 (right to protection of law against arbitrary search and seizure). UN General Assembly, *International Covenant on Civil and Political Rights*.

71. *International Covenant on Civil and Political Rights*, articles 2 and 25.

72. UN General Assembly, *Vienna Declaration*.

73. Office of the High Commissioner for Human Rights, accessed March 15, 2025, https://www.ohchr.org/en/what-are-human-rights.

the human rights to vote and run for office, members of opposition parties must be protected by the human right to the rule of law against the arbitrary power of the state to arrest and prosecute them.

By contrast, the popular will theory severs democracy from other human rights. It would transform democracy into an aberrant human right that can negate every other human right based on plurality preferences. This anomaly follows from the neutrality of the popular will theory, which imposes plurality preferences as coercive law, even if those preferences hollow out the rights of other citizens. To avert this problem, we should interpret the right to democracy as a human right to democratic accountability. Equal accountability combines democracy with the human right to nondiscrimination, making democratic accountability equal and honoring Mandela's call for a multiracial democracy.

The Human Right to Democratic Accountability Protects Urgent Interests

I put forward three urgent interests advanced by the human right to democratic accountability. First, democratic accountability grants us the freedom to govern ourselves as the ones in charge of our government. Undemocratic regimes exclude us from government and subordinate us to unaccountable rule. The second urgent interest is respect for our human dignity as free and equal persons capable of reason and moral conscience.[74] Authoritarianism and colonialism demean our human dignity, condemn us to political passivity, and disparage us as deficient in reason and conscience. Third, democracy empowers us to demand that our public servants secure our other human rights. Authoritarianism and colonialism leave us chronically vulnerable to unaccountable power that can strike down our human rights with impunity. Activists from the ranks of marginalized people, like Nelson Mandela

---

74. Chapter 5 explicates how we deserve human dignity, both as members of the human family, and as persons with reason and moral conscience.

and Frederick Douglass, have invoked all three of these urgent interests to support democracy.

Our Urgent Interest in Freedom as Self-Government

South African apartheid, meaning "separateness," segregated society based on race, and cast out nonwhites from self-government. The Group Areas Act of 1950 confined nonwhite South Africans to ghettos, which they could not leave without a pass.[75] The deceptively termed Promotion of Bantu Self-Government Act of 1959 evicted 3.5 million Black South Africans from lands where they had lived for generations. They were deprived of their citizenship and condemned to the impoverished Bantustans, which were restricted to only 14 percent of South Africa's territory.[76] Abandoned by their government, Black South Africans "were forced to survive on meagre rations of corn meal and to drink contaminated water."[77] Malnutrition, tuberculosis, and cholera ran rampant. An escalating series of repressive laws clamped down with brutal force on dissent. The Suppression of Communism Act of 1960 ordered the police to arrest protestors as foreign agents. The Indemnity Act of 1961 unleashed the police to torture and kill outside of the rule of law.

As the South African government sank into an abyss of injustice, the leading pro-democracy organizations assembled at the Congress of the People in June 1955 near Johannesburg. The 2,888 delegates drew up a statement of their principles of democracy and human rights.[78] The Freedom Charter declares the value of democratic self-government as being grounded in the inclusion of all the governed in government: "The People Shall Govern! Every man and woman shall have the right to vote for and to stand as a candidate for all bodies which make laws; All people shall be entitled to take part in the administration of the

75. Adrian Guelke, *Rethinking the Rise and Fall of Apartheid* (New York: Palgrave Macmillan, 2005).

76. Laura Evans, *Survival in the "Dumping Grounds": A Social History of Apartheid Relocation* (Boston: Brill, 2019), 2; Uriel Abulof, *The Mortality and Morality of Nations* (Cambridge, UK: Cambridge University Press, 2015), 241. On rights to territory, see Stilz, *Territorial Sovereignty*.

77. Evans, *Survival in the "Dumping Grounds,"* 3.

78. United Nations Centre against Apartheid, *Freedom Charter of South Africa*, 2.

country; The rights of the people shall be the same, regardless of race, colour or sex."[79]

Against the injustice of racial segregation, I combine self-government with the *Inclusion Principle*. All the governed who reside within the territorial jurisdiction of a state should be recognized as equal citizens, as I wrote in chapter 5. The Inclusion Principle finds expression in the Freedom Charter: "South Africa belongs to all who live in it, black and white," and "no government can justly claim authority unless it is based on the will of *all* the people."[80]

In equal accountability, we are freely self-governing when we can hold our public servants democratically accountable and our equal human rights are secured. This accords with the Freedom Charter, which entitles citizens to equal democratic accountability rights: "The law shall guarantee to all their rights to speak, to organize, to meet together, to publish."[81] The Freedom Charter stresses the democratic accountability right to the rule of law. Without this human right, citizens can be driven out of democracy by the lawless power of the government to imprison and injure citizens: "All shall be equal before the law! No one shall be imprisoned, deported or restricted without a fair trial; No one shall be condemned by the order of any government official; The courts shall be representative of all the people."[82] The authors of the Freedom Charter knew the need for the rule of law against the compulsory power of the state. 156 of the delegates who founded the Freedom Charter were arrested and tried for treason.[83]

The human right to democratic accountability serves our urgent interest in freely governing ourselves. As the African National Congress and its allies sought to shake off the shackles of apartheid, they worked in solidarity to attain the standing of freely self-governing, equal citizens: "We the people of South Africa, black and white together—equals, countrymen and brothers . . . pledge ourselves to *strive together*, sparing

79. *Freedom Charter of South Africa*, 3.
80. *Freedom Charter of South Africa* (emphasis added).
81. *Freedom Charter of South Africa*, 5.
82. *Freedom Charter of South Africa*, 4.
83. *Freedom Charter of South Africa*, 2.

neither strength nor courage, until the democratic changes set out here have been won."[84]

Our Urgent Interest in Respect for Our Reason and Conscience

The second urgent interest that the human right to democratic accountability promotes is respect for our reason and moral conscience. Article 1 of the Universal Declaration grounds human rights in our dignity as human beings. Human dignity expresses our profound value as members of the human family, and as moral agents capable of reason and moral conscience, which I described in chapter 5. Dignity is the high moral standing that requires that our rights be secured.

I interpret our reason and moral conscience as the possession of two capacities for freedom. The first is our capacity for *moral agency*, or moral thought, action, and speech. To be respected as a moral agent is to be free to participate in deliberation about how you and others should be treated, including by the government. We exercise our moral agency in government through our democratic accountability rights. With these rights, we morally evaluate the conduct of our public servants, sanction their injustices during office, and deliberate together about whether our public servants deserve to be authorized or removed from office in elections. We use our moral agency when we fulfill our democratic duties of oversight and solidarity.

Our second capacity is our freedom to *pursue our own lives*. Because we possess reason and conscience, we can make decisions regarding the relationships and purposes that endow our lives with meaning and happiness. This element of our human dignity is protected by several human rights, such as freedom of religion in article 18 and our human right to marry in article 23 of the ICCPR.[85] Our human rights to freedom of speech, the press, and association are indispensable to both our moral agency and our freedom to pursue our lives.

84. *Freedom Charter of South Africa*, 3 (emphasis added).
85. UN General Assembly, *International Covenant on Civil and Political Rights*, articles 18 and 23.

Authoritarian and colonial regimes disrespect our human dignity as
moral agents. This disrespect is especially corrosive because it manifests
inequality in such a visible, public forum. The ruling race in the authoritarian or colonial power is exalted as possessing moral agency, with the
full capacity for moral speech, thought, and action as adults in government. But the subject races are denigrated as inferior in their moral
agency. They are treated as unreasoning and deserving of servitude. This
inequality despises the subjects of unaccountable rule as hapless
children or "barbarians," in the derisive epithet of colonial powers.

Arthur James Balfour, who later served as the British prime minister,
struck this infantilizing tone toward the colonized Irish in a speech
when he was chief secretary for Ireland:

> But in one respect they are our inferiors. . . . They are politically in-
> capable of self-government. . . . The Irish are no more fit to be trusted
> with the control of their destinies than your little children are fitted
> to be left in charge of your house, to pay rates and taxes, to direct the
> servants, to manage the household. . . . There is my policy in Ireland
> in a nutshell. I am in charge of the mutinous nursery.[86]

At the root of authoritarianism and colonialism is the condescending
prejudice that entire groups of adult human beings are so lacking in
moral agency that they are condemned to be permanent wards of the
state. This disrespects their human dignity as moral agents.

After the Civil War, Frederick Douglass held that it was not enough
to end slavery. He was not content with so-called benign authoritarianism. Instead, he held firm to the principle that the government must
respect the reason and conscience of African Americans by recognizing
their democratic right to vote.[87] Excluding someone from democracy
sends an unequivocal message of inequality that is publicly pronounced:
"To rule us out is to make an exception, to brand us with the stigma of

---

86. Quoted in "Character Sketch: November. The Right Hon. Arthur J. Balfour, M.P.," *The Review of Reviews*, vol. 4, *July—December 1891*, ed. W. T. Stead (London: Review of Reviews, 1891), 575–76.

87. Frederick Douglass, "What the Black Man Wants," speech delivered in Boston, Janu-ary 26, 1865, in *The Essential Douglass: Selected Writings and Speeches*, ed. Nicholas Buccola (In-dianapolis, IN: Hackett, 2016), 192.

inferiority," said Douglass. "It declares before the world that we are unfit to exercise the elective franchise."[88] Furthermore, he wrote, the denial of democratic rights will "lead us to undervalue ourselves, to put a low estimate upon ourselves, and to feel that we have no possibilities like other men."[89]

Douglass's moral integrity led him, ahead of his time, to envision that the right to vote must be extended to women to respect their reason and moral conscience. Douglass declared, "I hold that women, as well as men, have the right to vote."[90] Proudly calling himself a "woman's-right-man," Douglass said that "moral intelligence and the ability to discern right from wrong, good from evil, and the power to choose between them" were "the true basis of Republican government."[91] Possessing the capacity for moral agency, women should have "the right of choice in the selection of the persons who should frame the laws, and thus shape the destiny of all the people, irrespective of sex."[92] When Douglass referred to "moral intelligence" and the "ability to discern right from wrong," he meant that women and African Americans should be respected as having moral agency.

Like Douglass, John Stuart Mill supported the right to vote for women. Mill spoke in favor of the franchise for women in a pioneering 1867 address before Parliament:

Meanwhile an unworthy stigma would be removed from the whole sex. The law would cease to declare them incapable of serious things; would cease to proclaim that their opinions and wishes are unworthy of regard, on things which concern them equally with men, and on many things which concern them much more than men. They would no longer be classed with children, idiots, and lunatics, as incapable of taking care of either themselves or others, and needing that everything should be done for them, without asking their consent.[93]

88. Douglass, "What the Black Man Wants," 192.
89. "What the Black Man Wants," 192.
90. "What the Black Man Wants," 192.
91. Frederick Douglass, *Life and Times of Frederick Douglass* (Hartford, CT: Park, 1881), 423.
92. Douglass, *Life and Times*, 423.
93. Mill, "Admission of Women," 157.

To deprive women of democracy is to deprecate their status as moral agents. It would class them not as adults who can make moral claims, but as infants, except in the case of women, their tutelage would be lifelong. In language that echoes Douglass on the exclusion of African Americans, Mill proclaimed that the denial of democratic rights stains women with "an unworthy stigma."[94]

The wound that political segregation inflicts on the self-respect of the marginalized cuts as deeply as the damage wrought by segregation in education. The Supreme Court ruled in *Brown v. Board of Education* that racial segregation in public schools was an affront to the equal protection of the law in the Constitution's Fourteenth Amendment. In a unanimous decision, Chief Justice Warren wrote that the stigmatizing message of segregation is internalized by minorities: "To separate them from others of similar age and qualifications solely because of their race generates a feeling of inferiority as to their status in the community that may affect their hearts and minds in a way unlikely ever to be undone."[95]

Soon after the *Brown v. Board of Education* decision was issued, Dr. Martin Luther King, Jr. condemned segregation for debasing the self-respect of racial minorities: "As you seek to explain to your six-year-old daughter why she cannot go to the public amusement park," you can "see the depressing clouds of inferiority begin to form in her little mental sky."[96] King lamented that being shut out from public spaces leaves you "forever fighting a degenerating sense of 'nobodiness.'"[97] Political segregation, like segregation in education and public accommodations, ostracizes the people it oppresses. It publicly pronounces the excluded to be unworthy of participating in democracy, and it demeans their human dignity as persons with reason and moral conscience. The children who are raised under this regime of inequality are left to ask why they, unlike their peers, will grow up without attaining democratic rights and full citizenship.

94. Mill, "Admission of Women," 157.
95. Brown v. Board of Education, 347 U.S. 483 (1954).
96. King, "Letter from Birmingham Jail."
97. King, "Letter from Birmingham Jail."

The work of John Rawls helps to illuminate why inclusion in democracy is requisite for the self-respect of citizens. In his *Theory of Justice*, Rawls refers to "self-respect and a sure confidence in the sense of one's own worth" as "perhaps the most important primary good."[98] A primary good is a resource that can be used to pursue a meaningful life of our own.[99] To possess self-respect is to value our lives and to have confidence that our plan of life is worth fulfilling. What makes self-respect so indispensable is that "without it nothing may seem worth doing, or if some things have value for us, we lack the will to strive for them. All desire and activity becomes empty and vain, and we sink into apathy and cynicism."[100] Because self-respect is such a crucial condition to pursue our life plans, we "would wish to avoid at almost any cost the social conditions that undermine self-respect."[101]

Our self-respect is shaped by our public standing in the eyes of our government and fellow citizens. As social creatures, our self-respect withers when other people despise us, and thrives when our peers esteem us. As Rawls says, "For our sense of our own value, as well as our self-confidence, depends on the respect and mutuality shown us by others."[102] Frederick Douglass prefigured this thought when he wrote, "Men are so constituted that they derive their conviction of their own possibilities largely by the estimate formed of them by others."[103] Like Douglass, Rawls links our self-respect to our democratic standing as equal citizens: "Self-respect is secured by the public affirmation of the status of equal citizenship for all."[104] If the government spurned the rights of equal citizenships for a group of the governed, it would "have

98. Rawls, *Theory of Justice*, 349. I thank Steve Macedo and Michael Blake for an enlightening conversation on Rawls and the social bases of self-respect in a 2021 American Political Science Association panel on the fiftieth anniversary of Rawls's *Theory of Justice*, where we were joined by David Estlund, Katrina Forrester, and Samuel Freeman.

99. Rawls, *Theory of Justice*, 54.

100. Rawls, *Theory of Justice*, 386.

101. Rawls, *Theory of Justice*, 386.

102. Rawls, *Political Liberalism*, 319.

103. Douglass, "What the Black Man Wants," 192.

104. Rawls, *Theory of Justice*, 478. Shklar regards the vote as a crucial marker of inclusion and equal standing for citizens in *American Citizenship: The Quest for Inclusion* (Cambridge, MA: Harvard University Press, 1991).

the effect of publicly establishing their inferiority as defined by the basic structure of society." The resulting "subordinate ranking in public life would indeed be humiliating and destructive of self-esteem."[105] Discrimination in our democratic rights is palpably humiliating because it announces our inherent inferiority on a public stage before the entire citizenry.

Douglass, Rawls, Mill, and King impart the lesson that discrimination in democratic rights delivers a degrading message of inferiority to the discriminated. I argue that the human right to democratic accountability acknowledges our human dignity as moral agents capable of reason and conscience, who can advance moral claims in deliberation and participate in democratic accountability.

Our Urgent Interest in Protecting Our Human Rights

The human right to democratic accountability affords security for our other human rights, such as our rights to personal integrity.[106] Inequality in democratic rights not only excludes the governed from freedom as self-government and detracts from the self-respect of the citizens. It leaves the politically excluded more exposed to injustice.

Unequal political rights pose a grave risk, because of the coercive power of governments. Coercion employs armed force to detain, imprison, and punish human beings. The people at greatest risk of wanton violence by the state are political dissidents and marginalized groups. To find refuge from oppression, we must possess the human right to democratic accountability. This right empowers us to protest the misdeeds of our officials, criticize them in speech and the press, and petition the courts to remedy their injustices and punish their crimes through the rule of law. Under the aegis of democratic accountability,

---

105. Rawls, *Theory of Justice*, 477.

106. The human right to democratic accountability can protect not only substantive but also procedural human rights. For instance, the participants in the Civil Rights Movement exercised their democratic accountability right to protest in order to secure their democratic accountability right to vote.

we can march in free association, organize opposition parties, run against our officials, and vote them out of office.

Frederick Douglass valued the right to vote because it protects us from abuse, in addition to respecting our moral agency and freeing us to be self-governing. Douglass asked President Andrew Johnson, who opposed democratic rights for the newly liberated slaves, "how can you, in view of your professed desire to promote the welfare of the black man, deprive him of all means of defense . . . ? Can it be that you would recommend a policy which would arm the strong and cast down the defenseless?" Without being able to participate in democracy, African Americans would be "abused with the greatest impunity," warned Douglass.[107] In a speech at the Massachusetts Anti-Slavery Society, Douglass defended the right to vote for African Americans: "Without this, his liberty is a mockery; without this, you might as well almost retain the old name of slavery for his condition. . . . He is at the mercy of the mob, and has no means of protecting himself."[108] Democratic accountability guards us from arbitrary power.

The architect of the US Constitution, James Madison, regarded elections as necessary to secure citizens against misgovernment. In an essay published in 1800, Madison lauded elections as "intended by the Constitution to preserve the purity, or to purge the faults of the Administration." By voting, "the great remedial rights of the people were to be exercised, and the responsibility of their public agents to be screened."[109] For citizens to protect themselves, they must have both elections and the democratic rights to freedom of speech and the press. Introducing the Bill of Rights in 1789, Madison said of the First Amendment, "The people shall not be deprived or abridged of their right to speak, to write, or to publish their sentiments; and the freedom of the press, as one of the great bulwarks of liberty, shall be inviolable."[110]

107. Frederick Douglass, "Reply of the Colored Delegation to the President," February 7, 1866, in Scott Yenor, *Reconstruction: Core Documents* (Ashland, OH: Ashbrook Press, 2018), 48.

108. Douglass, "What the Black Man Wants," 191.

109. James Madison, "Report on the Resolutions," in *Writings of James Madison*, vol. 6, 395.

110. James Madison, "Adding a Bill of Rights to the Constitution," speech delivered to Congress, Washington, DC, June 8, 1789, in *Selected Writings of James Madison*, ed. Ralph Ketcham (Indianapolis: Hackett, 2006), 167.

Amartya Sen ascribes democracy's protective effect to the power of freedom of speech and the press when combined with the vote. Sen explains that democracies prevent famines through the rights of citizens to speak freely against government misconduct, and to vote oppressive or negligent officials out of power.[111] These barriers are absent in authoritarian and colonial regimes. For example, British colonial rule neglected to protect Indians from the 1943 Bengal Famine, which killed two to three million people.[112] In China under Mao, Cambodia under Pol Pot, the Soviet Union under Stalin, and Latin American dictatorships, authoritarians have afflicted their subjects with mass hunger and political persecution. From 1937 to 1938, Stalin's secret police, the dreaded NKVD, imprisoned 1.5 million people and shot 750,000 victims, who were lined in execution pits outside of cities.[113] Chile's authoritarian regime, ruled by Augusto Pinochet, drugged political dissidents and threw them from helicopters and planes to drown at sea.[114] The UN Working Group on Enforced or Involuntary Disappearances has counted 57,149 enforced disappearances from 1980 to 2018 perpetrated by authoritarian governments globally.[115]

During the "Great Leap Forward," Chinese communists coerced farmers into laboring on communes and diverted legions of farmers to iron production. Sen estimates that the ensuing 1958–1961 famine was the largest in history, ending the lives of thirty million people.[116] The eradication of the democratic rights of free speech, the press, and multiparty competition impeded the free flow of information and stymied accountability for officials. As mass famine engulfed the country, "the Chinese authorities mistakenly believed that they had 100 million more metric tons of grain than they actually did."[117] People who can hold

---

111. Sen, *Development as Freedom*, chaps. 6–7, and idem, *Idea of Justice*, chaps. 15–16.

112. Sen, *Development as Freedom*, 180.

113. Robert Service, *Stalin: A Biography* (Cambridge, MA: Harvard University Press, 2005), 356.

114. Ilas Bantekas and Lutz Oette, *International Human Rights: Law and Practice* (Cambridge, UK: Cambridge University Press, 2020), 396.

115. Bantekas and Oette, *International Human Rights*, 396.

116. Sen, *Development as Freedom*, 181.

117. Sen, *Development as Freedom*, 181.

their government democratically accountable are less likely to starve or be killed.

Thomas Christiano and the political scientists Christian Davenport and David Armstrong have examined the relation between the Political Terror Scale and the Polity IV dataset measuring whether countries are authoritarian or democratic. When the quality of democratic institutions reaches the threshold of 8 (on a 0 to 10 scale with 10 being the most democratic), state-sponsored political terror, such as torture and enforced disappearances, sharply decline. At the same time, respect for human rights to personal integrity consolidates. The key features of democratic institutions that register at least an 8 are constitutional checks on the executive, free and fair multiparty elections, and electoral accountability for the executive and legislature.[118] Christiano sums up these findings: "In multivariate analysis, minimally egalitarian democracy turns out to be a very strong independent variable for explaining the protection of human rights to personal integrity."[119] This remains the case even after controlling for "population size, per capita GDP, civil war, interstate war, and the presence of international nongovernmental organizations (NGOs)."[120]

The marginalized are the people who most urgently seek the shield of democracy. Liu Xiaobo and his fellow authors of Charter 08 strove for democratic accountability to prevent authoritarian catastrophes, like the Great Leap Forward and the Cultural Revolution, from befalling the people of China in the future: "The Chinese people, who have endured human rights disasters and uncountable struggles across these same years, now include many who see clearly that freedom, equality, and human rights are universal values of humankind and that democracy and constitutional government are the fundamental framework for

118. Christiano, "Instrumental Argument," 151–52.

119. Christiano, 152, citing Christian Davenport and David Armstrong, "Democracy and the Violation of Human Rights: A Statistical Analysis from 1976 to 1996," *American Journal of Political Science* 48 (2004): 538–54; Christian Davenport, *State Repression and the Domestic Democratic Peace* (Cambridge, UK: Cambridge Press 2007); and Emilie Hafner-Burton and Kiyoteru Tsutsui, "Human Rights in a Globalizing World: The Paradox of Empty Promises," *American Journal of Sociology* 110, no. 5 (2005): 1373–411.

120. Christiano, "Instrumental Argument," 152.

protecting these values."[121] An official Communist Party report admitted that Mao's regime was responsible for the deaths of eighty million people from famine, state-sponsored violence, and political purges.[122] This toll is greater than the entire present-day population of either France (67.5 million) or the United Kingdom (67.3 million).[123]

The greatest testament to the universality of the human right to democratic accountability is how ruthlessly authoritarians suppress it.[124] Officials in apartheid South Africa realized that the democratic accountability right to protest could shake their regime to its foundations. On March 21, 1960, officials ordered police to open fire on peaceful marchers in Sharpeville, killing sixty-nine people, including twenty-nine children.[125] The marchers had gathered to demonstrate against the internal passport laws that had prohibited them from leaving Black neighborhoods without a government issued pass.

The Sharpeville massacre set off a wave of global protests, leading the UN General Assembly to adopt the International Convention on the Elimination of All Forms of Racial Discrimination (ICERD) in 1965.[126] Since then, 182 states have joined the international convention as legally obligated parties to the treaty.[127] Article 5 guarantees democratic rights for people of all races. ICERD protects, as democratic accountability rights, the freedom to "vote and to stand for election," the "freedom of opinion and expression," the "freedom of peaceful assembly and association," and the "equal protection of the law."[128] To honor the protestors,

121. Perry Link, trans., "Charter 08," *New York Review of Books*, January 15, 2009.

122. Valerie Strauss and Daniel Southerl, "How Many Died? New Evidence Suggests Far Higher Numbers for the Victims of Mao Zedong's Era," *Washington Post*, July 17, 1994, https://www.washingtonpost.com/archive/politics/1994/07/17/how-many-died-new-evidence-suggests-far-higher-numbers-for-the-victims-of-mao-zedongs-era.

123. World Bank, "Population 2021," https://databankfiles.worldbank.org/data/download/POP.pdf.

124. See my revealed preferences argument in chapter 4.

125. Tom Lodge, *Sharpeville: An Apartheid Massacre and Its Consequences* (New York: Oxford University Press, 2011).

126. UN General Assembly, *International Convention on the Elimination of All Forms of Racial Discrimination*, December 21, 1965, United Nations, Treaty Series, vol. 660, p. 195 (emphasis added), available at: https://www.refworld.org/docid/3ae6b3940.html.

127. UN General Assembly, *International Convention on the Elimination of All Forms of Racial Discrimination*.

128. *International Convention on the Elimination of All Forms of Racial Discrimination*, art. 5.

President Mandela signed the new constitution of South Africa's multiracial democracy in Sharpeville.

The universality of the human right to democratic accountability tracks the ubiquity of the threat to freedom. Authoritarian regimes tread a common path to servitude. Just as the apartheid government of South Africa banned the African National Congress and the Congress of Democrats, the Third Reich persecuted Jews and outlawed opposition parties. In the lead-up to the war, the Nazis amassed power by banning all opposition parties before the November 12, 1933, Reichstag election.[129] With a manufactured vote in a sham election at his back, Hitler cynically descanted in August 1934, "Every year I take the opportunity to submit my authority to the approval of the German people. . . . We barbaric Germans are better democrats than other nations."[130] If elections are not to devolve into a crude implement of propaganda, they must be competitive, in accordance with the democratic accountability rights of citizens to associate in opposition parties, speak freely, and run for office under the auspices of the rule of law. The gravity of the threat must be matched by the universality of the right. We are owed democratic accountability as a human right to safeguard us all from oppression.

Defending the Human Right
to Democratic Accountability

The human right to democratic accountability is affirmed in an impressive array of international human rights treaties and declarations. Despite this, the prevailing view in academic political theory, at least in the United States, opposes a human right to democracy.[131] The main worry

129. Evans, *Third Reich in Power*.

130. Hedwig Richter and Ralph Jessen, "Elections, Plebiscites, and Festivals," in *The Oxford Illustrated History of the Third Reich*, ed. Robert Gellately (New York: Oxford University Press, 2018), 90.

131. Rawls, *Law of Peoples*, 59–77; Beitz, *Idea of Human Rights*, 174–85; Joshua Cohen, "Is There a Human Right to Democracy?" in *The Egalitarian Conscience: Essays in Honour of G. A. Cohen* (New York: Oxford University Press, 2006), chap. 11; Miller, "Is There a Human Right to Democracy?"; Ignatieff, *Human Rights as Politics and Idolatry*. The exceptions who support a human right to democracy, as I do, include Allen Buchanan, *The Heart of Human Rights* (New York: Oxford University Press, 2013); Christiano, "Instrumental Argument"; Sen, "Democracy

is that a right to democracy would be intolerant of nondemocratic societies and deprive people of the right to self-determination to choose their government, including an authoritarian regime if they wish.[132]

The skeptical position stumbles over two hurdles. First, it deviates from the terms of the Vienna Declaration that human rights are *indivisible*. The United Nations convened the largest meeting on human rights in history during the 1993 World Conference on Human Rights. The conference spanned 171 states, eight hundred nongovernmental organizations, and seven thousand official participants.[133] It forged a consensus to embrace the human right to democracy in the Vienna Declaration and Programme of Action, which laid out the guiding principles for the international community and the United Nations that "all human rights are universal, indivisible and interdependent and interrelated."[134]

Human rights are *universal*, because they are entitlements of every human being, without racial or gender discrimination. They are *indivisible*, in that human rights should not be divided from one another. It would violate the indivisibility requirement to designate a constricted set of human rights as "basic rights," while denigrating other human rights as so-called non-basic rights. Many skeptics of a human right to democracy admit that democracy is the most just form of government, because it respects the freedom and equality of citizens.[135] However, the skeptics attempt to estrange democracy from its companion human rights by lowering its status to a "non-basic right," which does not deserve to be treated as a real human right.[136] However, this attempt to demote democracy runs counter to the indivisibility requirement. As

as a Universal Value" and *Idea of Justice*; and Carol C. Gould, *Globalizing Democracy and Human Rights* (Cambridge, UK: Cambridge University Press, 2004). I am grateful to Carol for her comments at our APSA panel.

132. I thank Jack Pitblado for helpful discussion of this point.

133. Office of the United Nations High Commissioner for Human Rights (OHCHR), "World Conference of Human Rights, Vienna, 1993," https://at20.ohchr.org/conference.html.

134. "World Conference of Human Rights, Vienna," art. 5.

135. Rawls, *Law of Peoples*, 62. Rawls writes that a "constitutional democracy is, in fact, superior to other forms of society," but he claims that there is no human right to democracy, because he does not count it as a basic right.

136. Ignatieff, *Human Rights as Politics and Idolatry*, contends that the only human rights are basic rights to personal integrity against violence.

the Vienna Declaration puts it, states and the international community should regard all human rights "in a fair and equal manner, on the same footing, and with the same emphasis."[137]

The second obstacle confounding the skeptical view is that it does not meet the actual deliberation test. The test seeks to verify whether proposed conceptions of human rights are culturally respectful and morally valid. The human right to democratic accountability has been confirmed in deliberation encompassing people from diverse cultures. The human right to democracy is to be secured for women and men of all races, as declared in the ICERD and the CEDAW. These human rights treaties have been ratified by 182 states and 189 states respectively.[138] The human right to democratic accountability cannot be overturned without upending the core treaties that protect the human right to nondiscrimination.

Building on the Vienna Declaration, the United Nations Commission of Human Rights explicitly endorsed the human right to democracy in 1999. The fifty-one diverse states serving on the commission voted to accept the "Promotion of the Right to Democracy" resolution, and none opposed it.[139] The resolution defines democracy as including not only elections but the full set of our democratic accountability rights.[140] It integrates into democracy the right to "transparent and *accountable* government institutions."[141] In line with equal accountability, the resolution includes in democracy our human rights to freedom of speech, the press, association, assembly, the rule of law, transparency, and the rights to vote and run for office.

A striking development confirming the human right to democratic accountability is that 192 states have ratified the United Nations Convention against Corruption, which entered into force in 2005. States must implement policies that "reflect the principles of the rule of law,

137. Ignatieff.

138. United Nations Office of the High Commissioner for Human Rights, "Status of Ratification Interactive Dashboard," June 28, 2025, https://indicators.ohchr.org/.

139. UN Commission on Human Rights, *Promotion of the Right to Democracy*, April 27, 1999, E/CN.4/RES/1999/57, https://www.refworld.org/docid/3b00f02e8.htm.

140. UN Commission on Human Rights, *Promotion of the Right to Democracy*.

141. *Promotion of the Right to Democracy* (emphasis added).

proper management of public affairs and public property, integrity, transparency and *accountability*."[142] The treaty proclaims that corruption endangers "the institutions and values of democracy," especially "the rule of law."[143] The UN Convention on Corruption is the latest in a prolific line of treaties and resolutions recognizing our human right to democratic accountability.

The human right to democratic accountability has been ratified by an overwhelming host of the world's states. It is a key element of jus cogens, or the peremptory norms of international law binding for the whole international community.[144] Actual deliberation over decades bridging many of the world's cultures in multiple venues has substantiated the human right to democratic accountability and its indivisibility from other human rights.

The Human Right to Democratic Accountability Should Be Promoted Peacefully

Some authors believe that a human right to democracy would lead to military interventions to install democratic governments.[145] I oppose the forcible imposition of democracy by one state on another. The violence of invasion is destructive of the human rights to life and personal integrity. The proper means of promoting democracy are not violent, but rather the *peaceful* means of giving constructive support to democratic governments and not interfering with democracy.[146] The peaceful support of democracy makes the human right to democratic accountability indivisible with the human rights to life and personal integrity, which protect against killing and injury. Giving aid in establishing

---

142. UN General Assembly, *United Nations Convention against Corruption*, October 31, 2003, A/58/422, art. 5 https://www.refworld.org/docid/4374b9524.html (emphasis added).

143. UN General Assembly, *United Nations Convention against Corruption*, preamble.

144. UN General Assembly, *Report of the International Law Commission*, 143.

145. Miller, "Is There a Human Right to Democracy?" and Rawls, *Law of Peoples*, 62.

146. Rafanelli, *Promoting Justice across Borders*; Brettschneider, *When the State Speaks*, conclusion. I suggest that at minimum, the government bears the duty to respect the human rights of noncitizens. But citizens and their public servants may choose to go further and provide aid to help fulfill the human right to democratic accountability. International organizations like the UN may have, as part of their purpose, the duty to fulfill human rights.

democratic government would satisfy the *duty to fulfill* the human right to democracy. Not interfering with the human right to democracy would meet the *duty to respect* that right.

One way that states should respect democracy is by not overthrowing democratic governments. This might seem like a minor duty, as it only requires states to refrain from acting, but it would have far-reaching repercussions. The United States overthrew the democratically elected government of Iran in 1953, supported a coup in 1954 against President Jacobo Árbenz, the elected leader of Guatemala, and funded armed opposition to President Allende of Chile.[147] In 1973, Allende was overthrown by Augusto Pinochet, who unleashed a reign of terror executing or forcibly disappearing "more than 3,200 people, and scores of thousands more were detained and tortured or exiled."[148] Our public servants should respect the human right to democratic accountability and not overthrow democracies in other states.

The duty to respect also requires curbing *indirect* interference with human rights, such as military aid for dictatorships. The human right to democratic accountability gives citizens and corporations the duty not to arm authoritarians with the means of repression, such as censored Internet search engines, surveillance technology, and weaponry.[149] The human right to democratic accountability prohibits banks from lending to corrupt governments. This rule is codified in the Federal Corrupt Practices Act.[150]

To fulfill the human right to democratic accountability peacefully, states and international organizations can donate expertise and assistance in setting up courts, electoral systems, and the rule of law in democratizing countries.[151] The United Nations "supports the civil society to

147. Tirman, *Deaths of Others*.

148. Jonathan Kandell, "Augusto Pinochet, Dictator Who Ruled by Terror in Chile, Dies at 91," *New York Times*, December 11, 2006.

149. Li Yuan and Daisuke Wakabayashi, "Google, Seeking a Return to China, Is Said to Be Building a Censored Search Engine," *New York Times*, August 1, 2018. This is one of the areas where the ethics of technology is relevant to the human right to democratic accountability. I thank Rob Reich for insightful conversations on this topic.

150. Foreign Corrupt Practices Act of 1977, 15 U.S.C. § 78dd-1; Diamond, *Ill Winds*, chap. 10.

151. Larry Diamond, *The Spirit of Democracy: The Struggle to Build Free Societies Throughout the World* (New York: Times Books, 2008).

strengthen democratic institutions and accountability, ensures self-determination in decolonized countries, and assists in the drafting of new constitutions in post-conflict nations."[152] The UN contributes to fulfilling the human right to democracy through its UN Democracy Fund (UNDEF), the UN Development Programme (UNDP), and other agencies.

Answering the Toleration Objection

Rawls worries that the human right to democratic accountability would not tolerate undemocratic but decent hierarchical societies. I offer two responses. First, I focus on the *internal perspective* of human rights. Rawls views human rights as *external triggers* for foreign intervention when they are violated.[153] He says that where human rights are respected, it serves "to exclude justified and forceful intervention by other peoples."[154] I join with Rawls in opposing military force to promote democracy. Military coercion in these cases would contravene the human right to personal integrity and contradict the indivisibility of human rights. But I want to foreground how human rights mobilize *domestic* opposition to abuses by governments. This assuages the concern that the human right to democratic accountability does not tolerate nondemocratic states.

It is the state's own citizens who are rallying in support of democracy. We saw this in the pro-democracy associations led by Nelson Mandela and Bishop Desmund Tutu from South Africa, Liu Xiaobo of the People's Republic of China, Kim Dae-jung in South Korea, Václav Havel

---

152. "Democracy," United Nations, accessed March 16, 2025, https://www.un.org/en/global-issues/democracy.

153. I include an external perspective on human rights, but I focus this external standpoint on our duty to respect the human rights of noncitizens and avoid complicity with the violation of those rights.

154. Rawls, *Law of Peoples*, 80. Jeremy Waldron compellingly criticizes the idea that human rights serve only as triggers for external intervention in "Human Rights: A Critique of the Raz/Rawls Approach," in *Human Rights: Moral or Political?* (New York: Oxford University Press, 2018), chapter 3, 117–38. Waldron holds that the external intervention approach to human rights shortchanges the individualism of human rights and how those rights should be integrated into national law.

in the Czech Republic, and Lech Wałęsa in Poland. The human right to democratic accountability protects the internal advocates of democracy both from oppression by their own government and from complicity by foreign governments. Political scientist Beth Simmons attributes the impact of human rights to their incorporation into *domestic* law and institutions.[155] The human right to democratic accountability amplifies the domestic voice and influence of citizens.

My second response to Rawls is that his own principles entail that nondemocratic, hierarchical societies are unlikely to be decent. Rawls portrays a hierarchical society as united by a single comprehensive conception of the good. It is governed by a "state religion," which is "the ultimate authority within society and may control government policy on certain important matters."[156] The society grants unequal political rights on the basis of religion: "One religion may legally predominate in the state government, while other religions, though tolerated, may be denied the right to hold certain positions."[157] The religious discrimination imposed by a hierarchical society violates the human right to nondiscrimination in the Universal Declaration and article 2 of the ICCPR. Yet Rawls predicts that a hierarchical society would be decent in his work criticizing a human right to democracy.[158]

However, in his writings focused on religious toleration, Rawls admits the "fact of oppression." It holds that uniting a society under a single religion will tend to incite the state persecution of minorities.[159] I maintain that the fact of oppression means that an undemocratic, hierarchical society is unlikely to be decent. There may be exceptions to

155. Beth Simmons, *Mobilizing for Human Rights: International Law in Domestic Politics* (New York: Cambridge University Press, 2009).

156. Rawls, *Law of Peoples*, 74.

157. Rawls, *Law of Peoples*, 65n2.

158. Rawls, *Justice as Fairness*, 74. Rawls acknowledges that if empirical research showed that democracy is needed to respect human rights, then there would be a strong case for a human right to democracy (*Law of Peoples*, 75n16).

159. On the fact of oppression, see Rawls, *Political Liberalism*, 37 and idem, *Justice as Fairness*, 34, 84.

this rule.[160] Rawls cites the Ottoman Empire as a possible case.[161] But the authors of the Universal Declaration and ICCPR recognized that religious regimentation is often imposed by oppressive state power. They learned that lesson from the resurgence of discrimination that preceded and marked the world wars.[162] Historian Taner Akçam records how the Ottoman Empire inflicted crimes against humanity on the Armenian Christians in the Hamidian massacres of 1894–1897, the Adana massacre of 1909, and the Armenian genocide of 1915. Akçam writes that in Anatolia, "the prewar population (estimated at approximately 17.5 million in 1914) was so completely disrupted over the next six years that almost a third of the inhabitants were internally displaced, expelled, or annihilated."[163] The pattern of religious persecution is sufficiently common to justify both the human right to freedom of religion and the human right to democracy without religious, racial, gender, or other discrimination.[164]

Rawls tries to avoid the implication that pluralism can be eliminated only by oppression. He adds a proviso that pluralism only "characterizes a society with free institutions."[165] It might be thought that a hierarchical society's lack of free institutions precludes diverse religions and other comprehensive doctrines from arising. Since hierarchical societies ostensibly lack diversity, there is no need to use oppression for the society's official religion to prevail.

160. Beitz notes that the justification of a human right does not depend on a danger to urgent human interests always arising without exception. Rather, the human right is justified if it protects against a "standard threat," or a predictable pattern of danger to urgent human interests. See *Idea of Human Rights*, 58, 111.

161. Rawls, *Law of Peoples*, 76n17.

162. Morsink, *Universal Declaration of Human Rights*, 329.

163. Taner Akçam, *The Young Turks' Crime against Humanity: The Armenian Genocide and Ethnic Cleansing in the Ottoman Empire* (Princeton, NJ: Princeton University Press, 2012), xvi.

164. ICCPR art. 2 prohibits discrimination based on religion, race, sex, political opinion, and other status. ICCPR art. 25 sets out the human right to democracy, which explicitly refers to article 2 on non-discrimination. The human right to democracy is also embodied in article 19 on freedom of expression and the press, article 21 on free assembly, article 22 on free association, and a multitude of provisions on the rule of law. See UN General Assembly, *International Covenant on Civil and Political Rights*.

165. Rawls, *Justice as Fairness*, 3.

However, the proviso's premise that pluralism emerges only under free institutions does not bear scrutiny. Rawls's examples of the fact of oppression are drawn from societies *without* free institutions, such as the Spanish monarchy during the Inquisition and the Wars of Religion in sixteenth- to seventeenth-century Europe.[166] Earlier in history, the Roman Empire, which lacked free institutions, persecuted Christians. The Byzantine Empire and medieval Spain murdered Jews and Muslims for their religion. It took a two-decade military campaign to suppress the Cathars, a Christian sect, in the thirteenth-century Albigensian Crusade. The lawyer Raphael Lemkin, who coined the term genocide, said that the Albigensian Crusade was "one of the most conclusive cases of genocide in religious history."[167]

These examples reveal that societies without free institutions can still contain pluralism. But if pluralism can emerge in societies that are not free, then uniting those societies under a single orthodoxy with unequal political rights would rely on oppressive state power. A hierarchical society cannot be decent because of the fact of oppression.

Although Rawls is not a proponent of a human right to democracy, there are reasons that we can discover from his work to endorse this right. Equal political rights recognize the dignity and self-respect of citizens: "The hardships arising from political and civil inequality, and from cultural and ethnic discrimination, cannot be easily accepted," Rawls writes. "When it is the position of equal citizenship that answers the need for status, the precedence of the equal liberties becomes all the more necessary."[168]

Democratic Self-Determination

The third objection to the human right to democratic accountability claims that the right to self-determination allegedly entitles pluralities to choose any form of government. This view generalizes the popular

166. Rawls, *Law of Peoples*, 21–22.
167. Raphael Lemkin, *Lemkin on Genocide*, ed. Steven Leonard Jacobs (New York: Lexington Books, 2012), 71.
168. Rawls, *Theory of Justice*, 478.

will theory to claim that a plurality of citizens should select not only legislators but the type of government. Since the approach allows a plurality to choose the output of an authoritarian government and does not guarantee respect for democratic rights in the input of choosing the government, it should be called "authoritarian self-determination."[169] The theory licenses pluralities to select nondemocratic governments that discriminate against citizens based on their race, gender, or religion. The type of government is then coercively imposed by the state on the rest of the citizenry, even if they disagree with it. Just as the members of a club can decide on their rules, citizens can determine whether to adopt an authoritarian or democratic constitution.

I challenge authoritarian self-determination, because it draws a false analogy between citizenship in a state and consensual membership in a club. States, however, fall in a different category due to their coercive power, their urgent duties, and their nonconsensual force. First, the state wields the coercion of imprisonment, the police, and the military. A chess club or baseball league cannot send armed police to apprehend their members and arraign them before a court. State coercion is the darkness of the prison cell, the chains binding a detainee, and the bullet fired from a soldier's gun. This coercion confronts us with such a dire threat to our lives and liberty that it raises the question of whether it can ever be morally legitimate. It is only because anarchy and foreign invasion endanger our lives and liberty to an even greater extent that it is morally legitimate to form a government with the coercive power to enact and enforce laws. But to be morally legitimate, the government must be democratically accountable to the governed as equal citizens, secure their equal human rights, and respect the human rights of noncitizens, as I argued in chapter 5. These requirements of justice are expressed by my Equal Accountability Principle, the Equal Human Rights Principle, and the Delegation Principle.

A second distinguishing aspect of states is that they shoulder the primary responsibility for securing human rights in their territorial

---

169. I am grateful to Jack Pitblado, who asked why the theory should be called authoritarian self-determination.

jurisdiction. The 1933 Montevideo Convention on the Rights and Duties of States defines a state as an entity with a permanent population, a territory, a government to enact and enforce laws in its territorial jurisdiction, and the ability to enter into relations with other states.[170] I wrote in chapter 5 that states need these features to secure the human rights of the people governed in their territory, who are entitled to equal citizenship according to the Inclusion Principle. The ICCPR in article 2 specifies the duty of states to secure human rights in their territory.[171] States are the only institutions equipped to protect and fulfill human rights in their territory, because they wield the necessary resources, monopoly on coercion, and ability to enact and enforce laws. Officials must secure the human rights of their citizens, and respect the human rights of noncitizens, for the coercive power of government to be morally legitimate.

Third, states belong to a separate category than clubs in that states exercise power that is nonconsensual and unavoidable. The power is nonconsensual, because we are obligated to obey morally legitimate laws even if we disagree with them, voted against the representatives who passed them, and never signed the state's constitution, as chapter 4 pointed out. The coercive power of government is unavoidable, given that the costs of citizens to exit from their state are highly onerous.[172] Stateless persons who leave the protection of their state are woefully vulnerable to violence and neglect. "To be a stateless individual," says Judith Shklar, "is one of the most dreadful political fates that can befall anyone in the modern world."[173] Authoritarian decision-procedures might be tolerable in a club that lacks the capacity for coercive, physical violence. We can leave the club and find safe haven in the law. But a government differs in being armed with coercive force that cannot be

170. Convention on Rights and Duties of States adopted by the Seventh International Conference of American States (signed December 26, 1933, entered into force January 8, 1936), in *League of Nations Treaty Series*, vol. 165 (1936), art. 1, 21.

171. UN General Assembly, *International Covenant on Civil and Political Rights*, art. 2.

172. Rawls lays out how the authority of the state is not consensual, because the costs of leaving it are so high (Rawls, *Justice as Fairness*, 93–94). These considerations support my point in chapter 4 that democracy should be based not on the consent of the governed but on democratic accountability to the governed.

173. Shklar, *American Citizenship*, 4.

escaped. Thus the analogy between a state and a voluntary club is untenable.

Due to the coercive power they indirectly wield in the office of the citizen, citizens bear democratic duties of solidarity to recognize each other's equal authority. I add in this chapter that citizens should recognize one another's equal authority when they exercise self-determination in choosing their constitution. Consider South Africa's 1960 constitutional referendum. South African officials contended that it was an act of self-determination to decide on the form of government. The referendum ratified a new constitution and founded an apartheid regime. Nelson Mandela contested the referendum because it did not recognize the democratic right of Black South Africans to participate in the act of self-determination: "Africans, who constituted approximately 70 per cent of the population of South Africa, were not entitled to vote, and were not even consulted about the proposed constitutional change."[174]

I argue that acts of self-determination, to be morally legitimate, must satisfy both *procedural* standards of justice in the *input* of how the government is chosen, and *substantive* standards in the *output* of the type of government that is created. South Africa's 1960 referendum violated these standards, as it was decided without the input of black South Africans and produced the output of a viciously discriminatory apartheid state.

In contrast to authoritarian self-determination, my conception of *democratic self-determination* requires that self-determination be democratic in both its input and output.[175] On the input side, all the residents governed in a state's territorial jurisdiction must be able to speak freely and cast an equal vote as citizens, in line with the Inclusion Principle. Black South Africans, as residents of South Africa, should have been entitled to vote and freely debate the constitutional referendum.

Democratic inclusion in the input of self-determination conforms with the 1952 United Nations General Assembly resolution, "The Right of Peoples and Nations to Self-Determination." The resolution sets forth

---

174. Mandela, *In His Own Words*, 31.
175. I discuss democratic self-determination in my article "Democratic Self-Determination."

that the right of self-determination shall be exercised "according to the principles and spirit of the Charter of the United Nations in regard to each Territory and to the freely expressed wishes of the peoples concerned, the wishes of the people being ascertained through plebiscites or other recognized *democratic means*."[176] Self-determination should be democratic in its procedural input. I hold that this requires democratic accountability rights to vote on the referendum, as well as free speech, the press, association, protest, petition, and the rule of law to deliberate freely on the terms of the constitution, without fear of reprisal or persecution.

Authoritarian self-determination goes awry in permitting undemocratic inputs into self-determination. This confronts us with the *problem of the false mandate*. Authoritarians can claim a false mandate to rule by asserting that their power resulted from the self-determination of their subjects. Their mandate is false because the authoritarians hold the referendum in undemocratic conditions. They censor and imprison the critics of the referendum, like the members of the African National Congress. To avert the problem of the false mandate, we should require that self-determination be exercised through the democratic input of all the governed with equal democratic accountability rights to deliberate about and vote on the constitution.

The substantive requirement of democratic self-determination is that the *output* of the referendum should be a constitution that secures the equal democratic accountability rights of all the governed as equal citizens. The 1960 referendum betrayed this requirement by coercively imposing on Black South Africans an authoritarian regime that denied their equal citizenship and was unaccountable to them.

Three important reasons favor democratic self-determination over authoritarian self-determination. First, democratic self-determination respects the core canon of human rights interpretation that they should be treated as indivisible, as set out in the Vienna Declaration signed by 171 states.[177] Human rights should be treated as indivisible in not being

176. UN General Assembly, *The Right of Peoples and Nations to Self-Determination*, December 16, 1952, A/RES/637, available at: https://www.refworld.org/docid/3b00f0791c.html.
177. UN General Assembly, *Vienna Declaration*.

separated from each other. For this reason, the right to self-determination should be embedded within the larger structure of human rights. For example, the International Covenant on Civil and Political Rights declares the right to self-determination.[178] But for self-determination to be indivisible with other human rights, including the human right to democracy in article 25 of the ICCPR, it must respect those human rights in the input and the output of self-determination. By allowing prejudice to warp the constitution, authoritarian self-determination imposes an intolerable burden on the human right to nondiscrimination.

Discrimination must not be entrenched into the constitution. While ordinary laws can be overturned by a simple act of legislation, self-determination makes a coercively enforced choice of constitution that distributes the fundamental political rights of citizens. The political disadvantage of marginalized citizens would be cemented into the basic rules and institutions of government. Discrimination that is hardened into the structure of government is resistant to reform, since it distorts the political process and can only be altered by an extraordinary process of amendment or by replacing the entire constitution.

The second reason for democratic self-determination is that states are diverse. Authoritarian self-determination assumes that the territory of a state corresponds with a single nation. Unequal political rights may seem less objectionable when states contain just one cultural unit, with no minorities to be marginalized. But this picture of a state with a single unitary nation is a myth. We can glean from history how states contain internal diversity.

At the drafting of the Treaty of Versailles, the leaders of the Allies redrew the map of the world in the wake of World War I, which shattered the multinational German, Russian, Ottoman, and Austro-Hungarian Empires. The statesmen tried to apply self-determination based on nationality in piecing together the fragments. The Versailles peacemakers, however, did not view self-determination as overriding democracy, with peoples being able to choose any form of government, no matter how authoritarian. Self-determination was coupled with

---

178. UN General Assembly, *International Covenant on Civil and Political Rights*, art. 1.

democracy and equal rights. Prime Minister Lloyd George enunciated this view: "It is undoubtedly desirable that there should also be such a geographical adjustment of the map of Europe, on the basis of recognising national rights, as will prevent trouble in future, secure a more permanent peace, and also make firmer and more solid the foundations of *democratic freedom* in Europe."[179] But the principle of self-determination proved more vexing to implement than anticipated, because multiple nationalities coexist in the same territory. Lloyd George put this point memorably: "No human ingenuity could avoid incorporating . . . a numerous population alien in language, origin and religion to the predominant race. In the Central European States one could find areas, not only on the frontiers but far into the interior, where there existed an inextricable mixture of races."[180]

To protect diverse citizens who live in the same territory, the Versailles peacemakers signed the Minority Treaties with the newly created states mandating that minorities receive equal treatment and protection. The Minority Treaty with Poland provided the template. It stipulated that all inhabitants "in territory which is or may be recognized as forming part of Poland" shall have a right to Polish citizenship.[181] This provision, which recognized all residents of a state's territory as equal citizens, respected the Inclusion Principle. The Minority Treaty sought to guarantee equal legal and political rights to all citizens, of every ethnicity and religion. It proclaimed that all "shall be equal before the law and shall enjoy the same civil and political rights without distinction as to race, language or religion."[182] This requirement accorded with my Equal Human Rights Principle. The treaty also honored the output requirement of democratic self-determination that the constitution should secure the equal rights of all citizens. The subsequent disavowal of the Minority Treaties in several states fanned the flames of genocide

179. David Lloyd George, *The Truth about the Peace Treaties*, vol. 1 (London: Victor Gollancz, 1938), 63 (emphasis added).

180. Lloyd George, *Truth about the Peace Treaties*, vol. 2, 1363–64.

181. Lloyd George, *Truth about the Peace Treaties*, vol. 2, 1384.

182. Quoted in Lloyd George, *Truth about the Peace Treaties*, vol. 2, 1385.

in the years leading to World War II, with minorities losing their equal political rights.

In Africa and Asia, numerous ethnicities intermingle in the same state. This is in many ways the result of how European empires drew borders to separate ethnic groups in a tactic of divide and rule, to make it harder for them to resist colonialism. For instance, Tanzania is home to "120 nationalities, each with its own territory, language, culture, and traditions."[183] It is not viable to assign every nationality its own state. African governments have instead prioritized the territorial integrity of existing states to prevent the outbreak of nationalist or irredentist wars seeking to alter borders.[184]

Since states contain myriad religious and ethnic groups, I argue self-determination should be democratic in both its input and output. This secures for all citizens their human rights and inclusion in democracy without discrimination. W. Arthur Lewis, the first Black Nobel Laureate in Economics, emphasized that self-determination should result in democracies that respect the equal rights of citizens. Equal democratic rights are crucial to preventing ethnic conflict.[185] "The democratic problem in a plural society," said Lewis, "is to create political institutions which give all the various groups the opportunity to participate in decision-making, since only thus can they feel that they are full members of a nation, respected by their more numerous brethren, and owing equal respect to the national bond which holds them together."[186]

A third reason for democratic self-determination is that it avoids the three objections that I raised in chapter 5 against popular will

183. John Quigley, "Prospects for the International Rule of Law," *Emory International Law Review* 5, no. 2 (1991): 316.

184. Organization for African Unity Assembly of Heads of States and Government, "Border Disputes among African States," AGH/Res. 16(1) (1964), https://au.int/sites/default/files/decisions/9514-1964_ahg_res_1-24_i_e.pdf.

185. Authoritarian self-determination neglects how respect for the rights of minorities can alleviate the risks of civil war by reducing the intensity and stakes of political conflict. Barry R. Weingast elucidates this role of rights in mitigating conflict in "The Political Foundations of Democracy and the Rule of Law," *American Political Science Review* 91 (1997): 245–63. I am grateful to Weingast for discussion of these ideas.

186. W. Arthur Lewis, *Politics in West Africa* (New York: Oxford University Press, 1965), 66–67.

accountability. Authoritarian self-determination, like popular will accountability, might assert that the fair way to settle disagreements among citizens is to allot them an equal vote and to allow the plurality to prevail. Popular will accountability selects representatives in elections, while authoritarian self-determination chooses the constitution in a referendum. However, both procedures run into three similar problems. First, our considered convictions about fairness require fair substantive outputs, not merely equal procedural inputs. It was unfair for a brutal apartheid government to be imposed as the output of the 1960 South African referendum. Second, authoritarian self-determination, like popular will accountability, is unfair in failing to protect citizens' continuing input into procedures. Both views permit citizens to be disenfranchised, preventing them from participating politically. Black South Africans were excluded from both the 1960 constitutional referendum and the system of government it created. Third, authoritarian self-determination and popular will accountability unfairly prioritize preferences at the expense of citizens' equal standing. But securing our standing is more fundamental, according to my Bounded Grounds argument, because the standing of being citizens is the reason for listening to preferences in the first place.

After years of persecution, South Africans ended apartheid and founded a constitution enshrining an inclusive and multiracial democracy. The 1996 constitution proclaimed that "South Africa belongs to all who live in it, united in our diversity."[187] To include all citizens in democracy, it states that their equal human rights must be secure: "This Bill of Rights is a cornerstone of democracy in South Africa. It enshrines the rights of all people in our country and affirms the democratic values of human dignity, equality, and freedom."[188] The purpose of the constitution is to "heal the divisions of the past and establish a society based on democratic values, social justice and fundamental human rights."[189] The 1996 constitution shines as a beacon of democratic

187. South Africa, Constitution of the Republic of South Africa, preamble.
188. Constitution of the Republic of South Africa, chap. 7.
189. Constitution of the Republic of South Africa, preamble.

self-determination, because it included South Africans of all races in democracy as equal citizens.

Conclusion

In August 1973 agents from the South Korean dictatorship abducted a man from his hotel in Tokyo.[190] They blindfolded him and forced him to board a boat. He was about to be hurled into the darkness of the sea when a light from the sky pierced the gloom. A Japanese plane had tracked the kidnappers. The abductee was Kim Dae-jung, a dissident who was later elected president of South Korea after it had adopted democracy. Kim received the Nobel Peace Prize to honor "his work for democracy and human rights in South Korea and in East Asia."[191]

This chapter ranges us on the side of pro-democracy activists and stands for a human right to democratic accountability. The South Korean authoritarian regime followed the pattern of countless autocrats. But their fear of democratic accountability rights is the greatest evidence of the power of these rights. The peacefully promoted human right to democratic accountability protects us from abuse. Democratic accountability frees us to be self-governing as equal authorities, and it expresses respect for our human dignity as moral agents capable of reason and moral conscience.

190. South Korea was ruled by authoritarians until the June 29 Declaration in 1987.
191. "Kim Dae-jung—Biographical," The Nobel Prize, accessed August 3, 2025, https://www.nobelprize.org/prizes/peace/2000/dae-jung/biographical/.

Conclusion

THE EQUAL ACCOUNTABILITY THEORY
OF DEMOCRACY

YEARS AFTER LEAVING THE OFFICE of president, Theodore Roosevelt
protested the Sedition Act of 1918. The law, passed by Congress and
signed by President Woodrow Wilson, criminalized speech and print
that was critical of the government.[1] Defying President Wilson's Sedition
Act, Roosevelt defended the right of citizens to speak out against the
misdeeds of their officials. Roosevelt wrote the following in the *Kansas
City Star* during World War I:

> The President is merely the most important among a large number
> of public servants. He should be supported or opposed exactly to the
> degree which is warranted by his good conduct or bad conduct. . . .
> Therefore it is absolutely necessary that there should be full liberty
> to tell the truth about his acts, and this means that it is exactly neces-
> sary to blame him when he does wrong as to praise him when he does
> right. . . . To announce that there must be no criticism of the

1. Pub.L. 65–150, 40 Stat. 553, May 16, 1918; Stone, *Perilous Times*, chap. 3. The Sedition Act
of 1918 followed the pattern, from 120 years earlier, of President John Adams' Sedition Act of
1798 (1 Stat. 596). James Madison and Thomas Jefferson founded an opposition party, the
Democratic-Republicans, to defend the right to criticize the government against the Sedition
Act of 1798. The passage of the two acts demonstrates that the dangers to democracy from
elected authoritarians are not new trends, but are recurrent threats. See Corey Brettschneider,
*The Presidents and the People: Five Leaders Who Threatened Democracy and the Citizens Who
Fought to Defend It* (New York: W. W. Norton, 2024).

President, or that we are to stand by the President, right or wrong, is not only unpatriotic and servile, but is morally treasonable to the American public.[2]

Roosevelt believed that the "full liberty" to discuss whether the president "does wrong" is crucial to democracy. The precepts that we are free when our officials work as our public servants, and we have the duty to criticize them, offer a promising start. However, Roosevelt wrote on these points only briefly. He left for us the vital task to develop a new theory of democracy that can answer the challenges from elected authoritarians and discrimination against marginalized citizens.

This book offers a new vision of democracy centered on *equal accountability*. It explains how we can govern ourselves freely as citizens in a representative democracy. How can we be self-governing, or the ones in charge of our government, when officials have the power to enact and enforce the laws? How can we overcome the danger of being excluded from democratic self-government by officials or groups that violate our rights? James Madison drew our attention to this problem in Federalist 51: "It is of great importance in a republic not only to guard against the oppression of its rulers, but to guard one part of the society against the injustice of the other part."[3] The "oppression of its rulers" is the threat to self-government from elected authoritarians. The need to "guard one part of the society against the injustice of the other part" arises because of factions hostile to the rights of marginalized citizens. In today's crisis of democracy, the perils of elected authoritarians and factions loom larger than ever.

My book pursues a three-part strategy to secure our freedom as self-government against these threats. First, equal accountability strengthens our *democratic accountability rights* and institutions. We are freely self-governing, or the ones in charge of our government, when we can hold our public servants democratically accountable both during their terms in office and in elections. Democratic accountability depends on

2. Theodore Roosevelt, "Sedition, a Free Press, and Personal Rule," May 7, 1918, in *Roosevelt in the Kansas City Star: War-Time Editorials by Theodore Roosevelt* (New York: Houghton Mifflin, 1921), 147–48.

3. Madison, "Federalist No. 51," 254.

an array of rights and institutions that include but go beyond elections. Second, equal accountability protects our democratic accountability rights through the *democratic duties* of citizens and public servants. Citizens have duties of oversight and solidarity, and public servants bear duties of fidelity. Third, equal accountability safeguards democratic rights from foreign interference through the *human right to democratic accountability*. This right entitles human beings to democratic accountability without racial or gender discrimination.

To outline briefly each of these three parts of my strategy to secure self-government, the first broadens our democratic accountability rights to encompass rights and institutions in addition to elections. Although officials enact and enforce laws, we can still be the ones in charge if we hold them accountable as our public servants. We are free when our public servants answer to us. Democratic accountability consists of the authority, or set of rights, to impose enforceable duties on our public servants. What makes the duties enforceable is that our public servants must work in *offices* that are subject to the rule of law and limits on their power. To rein in elected authoritarians, we must possess rights to hold our public servants democratically accountable *during office*. We exercise democratic accountability during office with our rights to free speech, the press, protest, petition, association, transparency, and the rule of law. Our authority over our public servants, who work for us, must be ensured by institutions that are independent of the officials being scrutinized. These institutions range from courts to audit agencies, impeachment, law enforcement, inspectors general, and congressional or parliamentary oversight. These independent institutions serve as the *eyes* of citizens, informing us of the actions of our public servants. They are the *shield* of citizens, protecting our rights to participate in democracy. And they are the *sword* of citizens, allowing us to sanction or correct the misconduct of our officials.

The second part of my strategy guarantees our democratic accountability rights using the *democratic duties* of citizens and public servants. Supreme Court Justice Louis Brandeis said, "The most important office, and the one which all of us can and should fill, is that of private citizen. The duties of the office of private citizen cannot under a republican form of government be neglected without serious injury to the public."[4] Justice Brandeis leads us to ask: What are the duties of the office of the citizen? Why would neglecting those duties seriously injure the public?

I explain that the duties of citizens and public servants are necessary to secure our democratic accountability rights. I identify three sets of democratic duties in this book: the duty of oversight, the duty of solidarity, and the duty of fidelity. Citizens should fulfill their *duty of oversight* to hold their public servants democratically accountable for using the coercive power of government justly. I ground the duty of oversight in how citizens collectively own the power of government, and employ public servants to use that power on their behalf.[5] John Rawls describes how citizens collectively own government power: "In a democracy, political power, which is always coercive power, is the power of the public, that is, of free and equal citizens as a collective body."[6] James Madison similarly traces the "fountain of authority" to "the people."[7]

I argue that since citizens own government power, they bear the democratic duty of oversight to hold their public servants democratically accountable for using that power justly. The duty of oversight applies to the *vertical relation* between citizens and their public servants. Oversight flows downward from citizens as the equal authorities to the public servants they employ. The democratic duty of oversight follows from the concept of freedom as self-government. Citizens freely govern themselves when they are in charge of their government. But since citizens possess authority over their public servants, citizens should ensure their public servants are using the coercive power of government justly. Citizens are like townspeople who have lent a gun they own to a sheriff. They should hold their sheriff democratically accountable for using that power to secure rights, and not to terrorize anyone, either citizens or noncitizens. For example, citizens fulfilled the duty of oversight when

4. Mason, *Brandeis*, 122.
5. The best work on citizens' complicity in the injustices of their government is Beerbohm, *In Our Name*.
6. Rawls, *Political Liberalism*, 216.
7. Madison, "Federalist No. 51," 252.

they marched in mass demonstrations against President Lyndon Johnson. The democratic accountability right of protest sanctioned President Johnson for the grave injustice of the Vietnam War, which killed 58,220 Americans and 3.6 million Vietnamese, including 2.4 million Vietnamese civilians.[8] The weight of protest forced Johnson to drop out of running for reelection in 1968.

The duty of *solidarity* calls on citizens to respect, protect, and empower each other's equal authority or standing as the ones in charge of their government. Solidarity applies to the *horizontal relation* among citizens. The democratic duty of solidarity, like the duty of oversight, is founded on the value of freedom as self-government. The horizontal relation of solidarity protects the vertical relation of democratic accountability. When our standing is attacked by elected authoritarians or factions, other citizens should come to our aid and defend our equal authority.

If there were no democratic duty of solidarity, we would be forsaken by our fellow citizens and left defenseless when preyed upon by factions and elected authoritarians. The Anglo-Irish statesman Edmund Burke wrote, after the attempts of King George III to corrupt and subvert Parliament: "When bad men combine, the good must associate, else they will fall one by one, an unpitied sacrifice in a contemptible struggle."[9] Citizens who stand alone against authoritarianism will be defeated individually, but they can prevail when they act united in solidarity.

Citizens should associate together and act on the duty of solidarity by *respecting* our equal authority in their own actions, *protecting* our equal authority from threats, and *empowering* us with material resources and civic education to exercise our democratic accountability rights. To see the significance of democratic duties, consider what our

8. National Archives, "Vietnam War U.S. Military Fatal Casualty Statistics: Electronic Records Reference Report," 2018, https://www.archives.gov/research/military/vietnam-war/casualty-statistics; Tirman, *Deaths of Others*, 167. These casualty statistics are confirmed by President Kennedy's and Johnson's defense secretary, Robert McNamara. See Robert S. McNamara et al., *Argument without End: In Search of Answers to the Vietnam Tragedy* (New York: PublicAffairs 1999). The death toll inflicted in Vietnam covers both the Johnson and Nixon administrations.

9. Edmund Burke, "Thoughts on the Present Discontents," in *The Works of the Right Hon. Edmund Burke*, vol. 1 (London: Holdsworth and Ball, 1834), 150.

government would look like without them. Suppose that citizens had no duty to *respect* each other's equal authority. They would then be allowed to attack one another's democratic accountability rights with impunity. For example, during the near century of Jim Crow from 1877 to 1965, African Americans were subject to a relentless reign of racial segregation and ruthless terror, both by factions of other citizens and elected authoritarian officials. More than four thousand African Americans were lynched.[10] If citizens were exempt from any democratic duty to *protect* each other's equal authority, then citizens could look away while elected authoritarians and factions blotted out the equal authority of the marginalized. This callous indifference allowed, in the absence of public protest, the mass internment in concentration camps of 120,000 innocent Japanese American citizens during World War II.[11] If citizens had no democratic duty to *empower* one another's equal authority, marginalized citizens would be too impoverished to participate in democratic accountability. The right to vote is futile when a person cannot afford transportation to the voting booth.[12] The marginalized are further disempowered when they are bereft of a civic education. Citizens must have a robust civic education to understand their democratic accountability rights and to know how to use these rights in order to safeguard themselves and each other.

When we act on our democratic duty of solidarity to protect other citizens from factions, we strengthen our security against elected authoritarians. A time-tested stratagem of elected authoritarians is to stoke factions and hostility among citizens, so that they are too consumed by conflict to coordinate against the autocrats. The ancient Romans referred to this insidious tactic as *divide et impera*, divide and conquer.

10. Gates, *Stony the Road.*

11. Richard Reeves, *Infamy: The Shocking Story of the Japanese-American Internment in World War II* (New York: Henry Holt, 2015), xiii. The Japanese American internment was upheld by the Supreme Court in Korematsu v. United States, 323 U.S. 214 (1944), a decision overturned in Trump v. Hawaii, No. 17-965, 585 U.S. 667 (2018).

12. Alex Karner and Dana Rowangould found that when Texas restricted secure ballot drop-off locations to only one per county, it disproportionately burdened Asian, African American, and Latino voters. See Karner and Rowangould, "Access to Secure Ballot Drop-off Locations in Texas," *Findings*, May 25, 2021, https://findingspress.org/article/24080-access-to-secure-ballot-drop-off-locations-in-texas.

The ancient Greek philosopher Aristotle set out with singular clarity how tyrannies embroil citizens into factions. To entrench tyranny, "another way is to stir up strife and set friends against friends, people against notables and the rich against each other."[13] Tyrants aim to keep citizens uneducated and riled against one another: "Do not allow schools or other gatherings where men pursue learning together, and do everything to ensure that people do not get to know each other well, for such knowledge increases mutual confidence."[14] Aristotle's warning reverberates to this day, as Prime Minister Viktor Orbán is waging a campaign against Central European University in Hungary, and universities are under increasing pressure in the United States.[15] Tyrants *disempower* citizens by depriving them of the civic education and material resources to exercise their democratic rights.

How can we unravel the vicious cycle of elected authoritarians, factions, and powerlessness? My answer is that citizens should work together in solidarity and participate in democratic accountability. Citizens should meet their democratic duty of solidarity and *protect* each other's equal authority. Coming to one another's defense, citizens stave off the elected authoritarians who incite factions. When citizens act in solidarity to *empower* each other's equal authority, they urge their public servants to provide the material resources and civic education needed to exercise democratic accountability rights.[16] Civic education nurtures trust and civic skills among citizens, teaching them how to cooperate in

13. Aristotle, *The Politics*, trans. T. A. Sinclair and Trevor J. Saunders (New York: Penguin, 1992), 345 [1313b16].

14. Aristotle, *Politics*, 344–45.

15. Scheppele, "Autocratic Legalism."

16. On the importance of empowering citizens through civic education, see Ben-Porath, Gutmann, and Thompson, "Teaching Competition and Cooperation"; Macedo, "Against Majoritarianism"; Allen and Reich, *Education, Justice and Democracy*; Manville and Ober, *Civic Bargain*; Gutmann, *Democratic Education*; Taylor, *Horace Mann's Troubling Legacy*; Satz, "Equality, Adequacy, and Education"; and Ober, *Demopolis*, 71–76. Among the conditions needed to exercise democratic accountability rights is sufficient free time to participate democratically. See Rose, *Free Time*. Freedom as capabilities require the resources to exercise rights, according to Sen, *Development as Freedom*, and Anderson, "What Is the Point of Equality?" 287–337. A capability is a substantive freedom to act or to achieve a valuable condition. See Martha Nussbaum, *Women and Human Development: The Capabilities Approach*, rev. ed. (Cambridge, UK: Cambridge University Press, 2001).

holding their public servants democratically accountable. This alleviates the threat of elected authoritarians practicing the tyrant's techniques of disempowering citizens and pitting them against each other.

Citizens who work as public servants should abide by their *democratic duty of fidelity*. This duty is vertical and flows upward from public servants to the citizens they work for. Our public servants should cooperate with democratic accountability, enact and enforce laws that respect, protect, and empower all citizens, and aid us in countering elected authoritarians and factions. Representatives Liz Cheney and Adam Kinzinger admirably met their duties of fidelity when they took leading roles in the January 6th investigative committee in the House of Representatives. They faithfully strove to protect the democratic accountability rights of the citizens they serve.

The third prong of my book's response to the democratic crisis is to defend the *human right to democratic accountability*. This right requires our public servants to secure our democratic accountability rights, while respecting or not violating those rights for noncitizens. Our public servants must not overthrow foreign democracies, arm authoritarians against their own people, or supply the technology of repression. The peacefully promoted human right to democratic accountability respects democracy not only as an entitlement for ourselves, but for all human beings, without racial or gender discrimination.

In brief, my argument in this book shows how we can surmount the deepening crisis in democracy. We should strengthen our democratic accountability rights, secure those rights through our democratic duties, and recognize democratic accountability as a human right.

Protecting Each Other's Inclusion in Democracy

To prevail in the global crisis of democracy, we must meet the threat from every quarter: elected authoritarian officials, factions of rights-violating citizens, and the powerlessness of the marginalized. These perils spiral into a vicious cycle. Elected authoritarians divide citizens into factions to prevent them from coordinating to oppose tyranny. Elected authoritarians rob citizens of their education and resources, rendering them defenseless. Factions in turn instigate elected authoritarians into imposing laws that discriminate against and exclude the marginalized.

But if we work together as citizens and act on our democratic duties, we can create a virtuous circle. When we fulfill our duty of oversight, we work together to curb the injustices committed by our officials. As we empower one another, we gain the civic education and resources to exercise our democratic accountability rights, so we can coordinate even more effectively against elected authoritarians. When we fulfill our duty of solidarity and participate in democratic accountability to protect each other, we replace the malice of faction with the spirit of civic friendship. We join in a united front against our common dangers, and we cooperate to include all citizens equally in self-government.

The bond between citizens is rooted in how we can find refuge and strength in one another. Devoted to each other's freedom and equality, do we not express love in our actions, protecting one another as friends? "Love does not delight in evil but rejoices with the truth. It always protects, always trusts, always hopes, always perseveres."[17] Love is indeed the "more excellent way."[18] To complete the passage beginning this book, we remember the words of John Lewis, invoking Martin Luther King Jr.: "Democracy is not a state. It is an act, and each generation must do its part to help build what we called the Beloved Community, a nation and world society at peace with itself."[19]

17. 1 Cor 13 (New International Version). In civic friendship, the relevant form of love is not *erōs*, or romantic love, but *philia*, or the good will and love among friends, described by Aristotle in the *Rhetoric*: "Let loving, then, be defined as wishing for anyone the things which we believe to be good, for his sake but not our own, and procuring them for him as far as lies in our power. A friend is one who loves and is loved in return, and those who think their relationship is of this character consider themselves friends." Aristotle, *The Art of Rhetoric*, ed. John Henry Freese (New York: G. P. Putnam's Sons, 1926), 193 [1380b37–1381a2]. The ancient Greek word *philia* is the root of the city name Philadelphia, translated as "the city of brotherly love." Since the Beloved Community is a nation and world society at peace with itself, it also manifests *agápē*, or love of humanity, which is central to King's thought and Christianity. *Agápē* is the form of love in the passage from Corinthians. As King writes, "*agape* means understanding, redeeming good will for all men" (Martin Luther King, Jr., *A Testament of Hope: The Essential Writings and Speeches*, ed. James Washington (New York: HarperCollins, 1986), 19.

18. *Agápē* or love of humanity is the "more excellent way" that St. Paul invites us to follow in 1 Cor 12.

19. Lewis, "Together, You Can Redeem"; 1 Cor 12.

INDEX

accessibility, 74

Achen, Chris, 48n26, 131, 142–46

activism, 147–48, 215, 228–30, 232–33.
See also protest

activist networks, 150

actual deliberation test, 186–87, 203, 222–25,
247–48. See also deliberation; ideal
deliberation test

Adams, John, 38–39

agent-principal duties, 94

Agnew, Spiro, 72

Akçam, Taner, 252

Allen, Danielle, 103n50, 124

Allende, Salvador, 249

Alliance for Civics in the Academy,
124–25

American Revolution, 38

anarchy, 4n14, 133, 254

Annan, Kofi, 205

Anthony, Susan B., 149, 152

apartheid, 8, 37, 45, 47–48, 83, 144, 212–13,
215, 233–35, 244–45, 256, 261. See also
segregation; slavery

Árbenz, Jacobo, 249

Aristotle, 119, 184n44, 269, 271n17

Armstrong, David, 243

Athenians, 4n14, 16–17

authoritarianism, 8–11, 48–49, 217, 228, 232,
236, 242–45, 253, 257–61. See also elected
authoritarians

authorization, 41–42, 46, 51–54, 57–60, 64,
67, 85, 231. See also elections

Balfour, Arthur James, 236

Barr, William, 12–13, 30

Bartels, Larry, 48n26, 131, 142–46

Basic Law of Germany, 52

Bedi, Sonu, 6n20

Beerbohm, Eric, 49n29, 74n103, 266n5

Beitz, Charles, 188, 190, 252n160

Ben-Porath, Sigal, 120

Bett, Mum, 87–89

Biden, Joseph, 107

Bipartisan Campaign Reform Act
(BCRA), 118

Black, Hugo, 3n10

Borough of Duryea v. Guarnieri, 76

Bostock v. Clayton County, 72

bounded ground, 28–29, 37, 179–80, 261

Brandeis, Louis, 87, 92, 100–101, 265–66

Brennan, Jason, 18, 48

Brennan, William, 100–101

Brettschneider, Corey, 20n65

Brom and Bett v. Ashley, 88–89

Brown v. Board of Education, 68, 106, 238

Buchanan, Allen, 73n98, 74n103, 190n70,
245n131

Buckley v. Valeo, 118

Burke, Edmund, 267

campaign finance, 117–19, 126

capability theory of freedom, 108–9, 184.
See also freedom (discussion of)

Caplan, Bryan, 18

Carpenter, Daniel, 4n14, 76

Carrese, Paul, 124
Chambers, Simone, 216n11
Charter 08, 229–30, 243
Charter 77, 213, 220, 230
checks and balances, 17–19, 25. *See also*
  separation of powers
Cheney, Liz, 270
Chinese Exclusion Act, 36
Chinese People's Political Consultative
  Conference (CPPCC), 217–18
Christiano, Thomas, 243
circumstances of justice, 161n120
citizen–public servant model, 32–33, 93n20,
  158, 164–68, 200
citizenship, 35–36, 175–76, 204–9, 254,
  265–66
Citizenship National Curriculum, 122–23, 151
Citizens United v. FEC, 118
civic education, 47, 119–25, 146, 151, 173,
  269, 271. *See also* empowerment
civic empowerment gap, 120
civic friendship, 103n50, 271n17
Civil Liberties Act, 2
Civil Rights Act of 1964, 7, 43, 72, 99
Civil Rights Movement, 5, 8, 43, 84–85,
  93, 125, 153, 240n106. *See also* racial
  injustice; segregation; *specific activists*
Clark, Mary, 124–25
Code of Federal Regulations, 59
coercion (government), 33–34, 60, 71,
  95–97, 138, 141, 154, 163–67, 172–73, 190,
  192, 203–6, 240–42, 254–56
Cohen, Joshua, 156n105
colonialism, 232, 236, 260
Commonwealth v. Jennison, 127n1
concentration camps, 1, 5, 18, 47, 195, 268
Confucianism, 226–27
Congress of the People, 233
congruence argument, 214–15, 231
consent theory, 130–35, 167, 203. *See also*
  individually decisive
Considerations on Representative Government
  (Mill), 68n86, 207

Constitution of the United States. *See* US
  Constitution
Convention on the Elimination of All
  Forms of Discrimination against Women
  (CEDAW), 224, 247
correlative duties, 94–95
COVID-19 Hate Crimes Act of 2021, 8
cultural diversity, 221–22, 225–28
Cultural Revolution, 243
Cushing, William, 127n1

Dahl, Robert, 156n105, 204
Davenport, Christian, 243
"Declaration in Defense of Human
  Rights," 226
Declaration of Independence, 36, 52–53, 88,
  132, 149, 171, 173–76, 181–82, 186, 196–98,
  208–9. *See also* Federalist Papers; pursuit
  of happiness; US Constitution
deep state, 22
Delegation Principle (discussion of),
  35, 175, 201–3, 210, 254. *See also* Equal
  Accountability Principle (discussion of);
  Equal Human Rights Principle
  (discussion of); Inclusion Principle
  (discussion of)
deliberation, 34, 46–47, 66–70, 77, 101, 112,
  147–52, 181, 183n42. *See also* actual
  deliberation test; ideal deliberation test
deliberative justification, 69–72, 75, 77
democracy (discussion of), 213–19,
  246–49, 264
Democracy in America (Tocqueville), 149–50
Democracy and Its Critics (Dahl), 156n105
Democracy for Realists (Achen and Bartels),
  142–43
democratic duties (discussion of).
  See citizen–public servant model;
  correlative duties; duty to empower
  democratic accountability rights; duty
  of fidelity; duty of oversight; duty of
  solidarity; norm diffusion; oversight;
  solidarity

democratic norms, 14n50, 26, 150n84.
See also norm diffusion
democratic relationship, 49–51, 85, 90, 103–5,
126
democratic self-determination, 37–38,
216–17, 220–21, 254, 256–62, 264.
See also self-determination
democratic standing, 29
Demopolis (Ober), 158–59
Department of Justice. See US Department of Justice
Dewey, John, 184n44
direct democracy, 44n17
direct injustice, 106
discursive politics, 147
disinformation, 123
dissent, 10–12, 233, 240
Douglas, Stephen, 128–30, 132, 162, 167
Douglass, Frederick, 36, 43, 144, 197–99, 215,
233, 236–41
Dred Scott v. Sandford, 36, 127–28, 175, 207–8
Du Bois, W.E.B., 89, 97, 172
Duda, Andrzej, 77
duty of care. See fiduciary duties
duty to empower democratic accountability
rights, 3–4, 6n22, 9, 15, 17, 19, 31–33, 47,
50–51, 90–91, 94–95, 102, 105, 108–26, 137,
141, 146, 153, 155, 167–68, 174, 176, 184–85,
204, 213, 267–71; with access to vote,
114–17; with civic education, 119–25; with
equitable campaign finance, 117–19; with
legal counsel, 110–11; with the resources
to participate in deliberative democracy,
111–14
duty of fidelity, 6–10, 26, 32–33, 42, 60–61,
74, 85, 91–94, 106–9, 121, 125–26, 138–39,
167, 213, 265–66, 270. See also fiduciary
duties; public office
duty to fulfill human rights, 188, 191–192, 249
duty of good faith. See fiduciary duties
duty of loyalty. See fiduciary duties
duty of oversight, 6–8, 9–10, 26, 30–31, 33, 82,
90–94, 97, 98–101, 106, 108, 109–10, 125, 131,

137, 138, 152–55, 166–68, 175, 193, 200, 203,
205–6, 210, 214, 266–67, 271: and campaign-
ing/voting, 98; and citizenship, 33, 125, 166;
and civic education, 121; and complicity,
152–53; and empowerment, 109–10, 126;
failures, 8; and freedom of speech, 138–39;
and government power, 6–7, 41, 90, 93,
95–98, 106, 108, 138, 153, 167–68, 265–67; and
human rights, 9–10, 200–201, 206; and
justice, 26, 82, 91, 99, 101, 132, 137; and
morality, 74; principal-agent, 94; and
transparency, 15, 70, 75. See also oversight
duty to protect human rights, 95, 103, 106–8,
191, 268
duty to respect human rights, 95, 105–6, 191,
249
duty of solidarity, 6–8, 19, 26–27, 32, 90–94,
99, 102–9, 125, 130–31, 132–42, 147–50,
153–54, 161, 164–66, 200–201, 265–70; and
citizenship, 50, 93, 137, 165–66, 267; and
civic associations, 149–50; and civic
education, 121; and deliberative
justification, 72; and the democratic
relationship, 51; and injustice, 7–8, 26–27,
161, 234–35; and the law, 106–8; and
marginalization, 29, 32, 94, 99, 102–4,
109–10, 125–26, 131–32, 138, 153, 200–201;
as a message, 105, 154; opposition to, 130;
and self-governance, 10, 90–91, 104; and
senseless voting, 143. See also solidarity
Dworkin, Ronald, 17–18, 132, 224n41

economic opportunity, 14
Educating for American Democracy
(EAD), 124
Eisenhower, Dwight, 143
elected authoritarians: and accountability
rights, 5–6, 14–16, 25, 38, 41–42, 44, 50, 58,
144–45, 264, 267, 269–70; and checks and
balances, 17–18; and democratic duties, 27,
131, 268; discussion of, 270–71; and
impeachment, 30; and independent
institutions, 15–17, 22, 55–56; and the law, 7;

elected authoritarians (*continued*)
and the popular will, 12–13, 19–21, 64, 160;
and public servants, 60–61; and voting,
114–16. *See also* authoritarianism;
presidential power

elections, 19–25, 31–32, 40–41, 44, 67n81,
81–82, 85, 245. *See also* authorization;
removal from office

elective despotism, 42, 63

Ellison, Ralph, 105

empowerment, 109–20, 126, 146, 155, 184–85,
268–69. *See also* civic education

emulation, 151–52

epistocrats, 48, 145n62

Equal Accountability Principle (discussion
of), 32, 34–36, 38, 174–75, 183–86, 210, 254.
See also congruence argument; Delegation
Principle (discussion of); elected
authoritarians; empowerment; Equal
Human Rights Principle (discussion of);
evaluation; fidelity; freedom (discussion
of); Inclusion Principle (discussion of);
independent institutions; justice
(discussion of); marginalization; oversight;
social minimum; solidarity

equal authority (discussion of), 4, 83, 91,
94–95, 102, 105, 117, 256, 267–69

Equal Human Rights Principle (discussion
of), 35, 175, 186, 188, 193–94, 201, 207, 210,
230, 254, 259. *See also* Delegation
Principle (discussion of); Equal
Accountability Principle (discussion of);
Inclusion Principle (discussion of)

Erdoğan, Recep Tayyip, 10–11

Estlund, David, 132

evaluation, 41, 66–69, 72, 80–82, 85–86

Executive Order 9066, 2

external rule, 48

factions, 5–7, 27, 60, 106–7, 160–61, 165, 268–71

false mandates, 257

Family Assistance Plan of 1969, 111

famine, 109, 113, 242–44

Federal Corrupt Practices Act, 249

Federalist Papers, 18, 52–53, 58, 62, 64, 67,
70–71, 78n120, 80–82, 92, 165, 264.
See also Declaration of Independence;
US Constitution

Feldman, Jan, 6n20

Ferejohn, John, 25, 156–57

fidelity. *See* duty of fidelity

fiduciary duties, 58–61, 79, 85, 126; duty of
care, 59; duty of good faith, 59; and duty
of loyalty, 59. *See also* duty of fidelity

fiduciary trust, 57–61, 79, 126

Fifteenth Amendment, 108

filibustering, 115

First Amendment, 3n10, 76–77, 101, 122, 241.
See also freedom of speech/press

Five Power Constitution, 227

For the People Act, 114–15

Forst, Rainer, 228

Four Rights of the People, 227

Fourteenth Amendment, 40, 108, 238

Fowler, Anthony, 143

freedom (discussion of): of association,
68–69; and civic education, 121, 123; and
correlative duties, 140; and equal
democratic accountability, 89, 134; and
external rule, 48; and self-governance,
46, 54, 85, 128–30; and solidarity, 50,
104–5; substantive, 108–9, 112–13.
See also capability theory of freedom

Freedom Charter of the African National
Congress, 36, 104, 215, 233–34

Freedom House, 217n13

freedom of speech/press: and deliberation, 66–67, 138–39; and democratic
accountability rights, 3–4, 15, 25, 32, 37,
40–42, 144, 242, 257; and equal
authority, 47; and the Founders, 18; and
moral criticism, 137–38, 142; and norm
diffusion, 150–51; and the PRC
constitution, 228; and privacy, 140; and
resources, 109; and sanctioning, 76–77,
98–99, 101; and the Sedition Act, 13, 92;

and the Supreme Court, 100–101, 118.
See also First Amendment
Freeman, Elizabeth, 87–89, 91, 110
French Declaration of the Rights of Man
and the Citizen of 1789, 16
French Revolution, 50
Friedman, Milton, 111–12
Fugitive Slave Act of 1850, 182
Fukuyama, Francis, 61
Fuller, Lon, 74n104

Gandhi, Rahul, 11–12, 22
Garland, Merrick, 7, 60, 98
gatekeeping, 18n59
general reflective equilibrium, 183n42
genocide, 195, 253, 259–60
Gerber, Alan S., 83n131
Gilens, Martin, 117
"Give Us the Ballot" (King Jr.), 206–7
Gladstone, William, 171
Goodin, Robert, 148n78
governance dilemma, 96
Government Accountability Office
(GAO), 75
government maintenance, 141
Grant, Ulysses, 43, 60, 108, 138
Great Leap Forward, 242–43
Green, Donald P., 83n131
Group Areas Act of 1950, 233
Gutmann, Amy, 120, 157n107, 187, 223

Habermas, Jürgen, 183n42
Hall, Andrew, 143
Hamilton, Alexander, 43, 53n39, 62, 67, 71,
80, 82, 115. *See also* Federalist Papers
Hammond, James Henry, 170–71
Hammond, William Gardiner, 63n71
Hampton, Jean, 43–44
Harsayni, John, 177n24
Hart, H.L.A., 96
hate incidents, 5, 107
Havel, Václav, 213, 220, 230, 250
Helsinki Final Act of 1975, 219–20

Herodotus, 16–17
Hersh, Eitan, 155
hierarchical societies, 250–53
Histories (Herodotus), 16–17
Hitler, Adolf, 245
Hobbes, Thomas, 57, 135–36
homelessness, 112–13
Hoover, Herbert, 143
How Democracies Die (Levitsky and
Ziblatt), 17–18
human dignity, 36, 40, 126, 139, 174–75, 189,
194–99, 209–10, 215, 227, 232, 235–40
human rights: Abraham Lincoln on, 172;
definition of, 174; and Delegation
Principle, 201–3; distinction with natural
rights, 186; and Equal Human Rights
Principle, 186–88; George Washington
on, 174; and human dignity, 194–99;
human rights duties, 191–94; and
Inclusion Principle, 204–9; James
Madison on, 35; meaning and importance of, 189–90; and standards of
democratic accountability, 200–201;
Thomas Jefferson on, 209. *See also* actual
deliberation test; citizenship; cultural
diversity; Declaration of Independence;
democracy (discussion of); duty to
fulfill; duty to protect; duty to respect;
Equal Human Rights Principle
(discussion of); hypocrisy; Inclusion
Principle (discussion of); internal
perspective; justice (discussion of);
toleration; treaties; Universal Declaration of Human Rights
Hume, David, 161n120
Hunt, Ward, 198n101
hypocrisy, 219–21

iCivics, 124
ideal deliberation test, 223–24. *See also*
actual deliberation test
ideal theory, 161, 169
"I Have a Dream" (King Jr.), 99, 103

illiberal democracy, 13–14

impeachment, 23–24, 30–31, 65–66, 79–80. *See also* sanctioning

incarceration, 97. *See also* policing

Inclusion Principle (discussion of), 36, 46, 175, 204–8, 210–11, 234, 256, 259. *See also* Delegation Principle (discussion of); Equal Accountability Principle (discussion of); Equal Human Rights Principle (discussion of)

Indemnity Act of 1961, 233

independent institutions, 13, 15–17, 22–24, 41, 74, 77–79, 265

individually decisive, 133. *See also* consent theory

Inouye, Daniel, 56

Inspector General Act of 1978, 74–75

Inter-American Conference, 226

internal perspective, 215, 250

International Bill of Human Rights, 194, 225

International Convention on the Elimination of All Forms of Racial Discrimination (ICERD), 244, 247

International Covenant on Civil and Political Rights (ICCPR), 191–92, 194, 197, 205, 218–19, 222, 228, 231, 235, 252, 258

Invisible Man (Ellison), 105

Iran-Contra, 56, 70

Island Vote case, 177–78

Jackson, Ketanji Brown, 64–65

Jay, John, 43

Jefferson, Thomas, 38, 42, 92, 209, 263n1

Jim Crow. *See* segregation

Johnson, Andrew, 241

Johnson, Christopher, 116

Johnson, Lyndon, 267

judicial review, 5, 18, 54n47, 126. *See also* rule of law

justice (discussion of), 33–34, 172–73, 181–83, 201, 209–10

justice cascade, 151

Kant, Immanuel, 77, 96

Kateb, George, 195n89

Keck, Margaret, 150

Kennedy, Anthony, 76, 78

Keohane, Robert, 74n103, 96

Kim Dae-jung, 227, 250, 262

King, Martin Luther Jr.: background on, 39–40; and deliberative justification, 72; and democratic accountability, 42–43, 84–85, 271; and injustice, 1, 125, 201; and the *New York Times*, 100; and self-respect, 238, 240; and a social minimum, 111; speeches/writings of, 68, 96, 99, 102–3, 206–7

King George III, 267

Kinzinger, Adam, 270

Kolodny, Niko, 49

Korematsu v. United States, 5

Ku Klux Klan, 108, 138

Kymlicka, Will, 157n108, 178n27

Lane, Melissa, 4n14, 16n54, 17n57, 73n101

Laws (Plato), 73n101

legal human rights, 224n41

Lemkin, Raphael, 253

Lessig, Lawrence, 20n66

"Letter from a Birmingham Jail" (King Jr.), 96

Levi, John, 110–11

Levine, Peter, 124

Levitsky, Steven, 17–18, 145

Lewis, John, 1, 8, 271

Lewis, W. Arthur, 260

LGBT citizens, 72, 103, 107, 148, 152

Life Insurance Company v. Terry, 198n101

Lijphart, Arendt, 160n119

Lincoln, Abraham, 2, 54, 81n128, 128–30, 132, 166–67, 170–72, 186, 208–9

Liu Xiaobo, 228–29, 243–44, 250

Lloyd George, David, 220, 259

Locke, John, 29n85, 58n54, 202–3

Lovett, Frank, 18n62

Macedo, Stephen, 5n16, 11n35, 48n27, 103n49, 119n117, 120n118, 159n113, 197n97, 227n52, 239n98, 269n16

Madison, James: and authorization, 52–54; and consent theory, 133–34; and constitutional democracy, 69; and democratic duties, 92–93; and elections, 241; and elective despotism, 18, 38, 42; and equal accountability theory, 19, 264, 266; and factions, 5, 165; and fiduciary trust, 58; and freedom of speech, 18, 66–67, 263n1; and human rights, 35; and impeachment, 79–80; and independent institutions, 70; and justice, 64, 170; and presidential power, 61–62; and regular elections, 81; and the right to run for office, 83–84; and self-government, 43; and the separation of powers, 77–78. See also Federalist Papers

majoritarianism, 17, 19, 158–60, 173, 180–81, 187

Malik, Charles, 225

Mandela, Nelson, 36, 45–47, 83, 104, 212–13, 215, 232–33, 245, 250, 256

Manin, Bernard, 21

Manville, Brook, 2n6

Mao Zedong, 244

March on Washington for Jobs and Freedom of 1963, 98–99

marginalization: and civic education, 120; definition of, 94n23; and democratic duties, 99–100, 106, 131, 268; and discrimination, 45, 96; and empowerment, 35, 109–10, 174, 268; and equal authority, 34, 47; and human rights, 6, 200–201, 230, 243; and responsibility, 152–53; and solidarity, 31–32, 102–5, 126; and stigmatization, 10–12; and violence, 107, 240, 243–44. See also activism

Marshall, Thurgood, 68–69

Mason, George, 80

Massachusetts Constitution, 39, 88, 93, 127

mass internment. See concentration camps

Matthew Shepard and James Byrd, Jr. Hate Crimes Prevention Act of 2009, 107

May, Kenneth, 157n108, 158

McConnell, Mitch, 115

McGahn, Don, 64–65

media literacy, 123

mediated accountability, 23–25, 30, 72, 77–80, 85

mediated injustice, 106

military intervention, 216, 248, 250

Mill, John Stuart, 33n94, 44–47, 68, 130, 138–42, 151, 172–73, 181, 207, 237–38

Milley, Mark, 55

minority, 6n20

Minority Treaties, 259

Modi, Narendra, 11–12, 22

Montesquieu, 77

Montevideo Convention on the Rights and Duties of States of 1933, 255

Montgomery Bus Boycott, 40, 43, 72, 84

moral agency, 196, 198–99, 236–41, 262

moral criticism, 138–42

moral legitimacy, 205–6, 217, 254–56

moral rights, 173–77, 180–81, 186, 189, 192, 197–99, 214, 222, 224–25

mortality rates, 113–14

Mounk, Yascha, 13–15

Müller, Jan-Werner, 11n36

mutual aid, 105n56

national security, 73n98

National Strategy to Counter Antisemitism, 107

natural rights, 186–87

Navalny, Alexei, 84

negative income tax, 112

neopatrimonial rule, 61

New York Times v. Sullivan, 100–101

Nicholas II (Czar), 61

Nineteenth Amendment, 152

Nixon, Richard, 8, 23–24, 31, 65, 79–80, 111

nonideal theory, 160, 169, 180

normative innovation, 148–49, 151–52, 168

normative reframing, 147, 149, 151–52, 168

norm diffusion, 146–51, 168. *See also* democratic norms

Nozick, Robert, 51n34

Nuremberg trials, 56n52

Nussbaum, Martha, 108, 112, 156n106

Obama, Barack, 98

Ober, Josiah, 2n6, 11n35, 16n54, 103n51, 119n117, 120n118, 124–25, 158–59, 196n94, 296n16

O'Connor, Sandra Day, 124

office (discussion of), 4, 6n21, 16–19, 22–23, 24–25, 32–33, 39, 41–42, 52–56, 84–86; authorization is to hold office as an accountable trust, 57–61; in contrast to a king, 64–65; with fiduciary duties, 58–61; with limited powers and duration, 61–65, 85; subject to democratic accountability right to authorize to hold office, 51–56; subject to democratic accountability right to remove from office, 81–82; subject to democratic accountability right to run for office, 82–84; subject to democratic accountability rights to evaluate and sanction during office, 65–80; subject to impeachment, 79–80; subject to oath of office, 55–56; subject to separation of powers, 77–79. *See also* Carpenter, Daniel; deliberative justification; duty of fidelity; fiduciary duties; Lane, Melissa; self-governmentofficials (definition of), 6n21, 17

"On Liberty" (Mill), 139

Orbán, Viktor, 269

Ostrom, Elinor, 26

oversight. *See* duty of oversight

Page, Benjamin, 117

Painter, Richard W., 22n71

Parks, Rosa, 39–40, 43, 72

patrimonial rule, 61

Patten, Alan, 160n119

Peirce, Charles Sanders, 183n42

Peng Chun Chang, 225–26

The People vs. Democracy (Mounk), 13

Perry, D. LaRouth, 106n59

Perry, Ravi K., 106n59

petitions, 31, 76–77, 101, 110–11

Petrov, Peter, 14n50

Pettit, Philip, 18n62, 112

Pinochet, Augusto, 242, 249

Plato, 73n101

Plessy v. Ferguson, 5

policing, 22, 31–32, 96–97, 233. *See also* incarceration

Political Terror Scale, 243

Politics (Aristotle), 184n44

Pol Pot, 242

Polybius, 77

popular will theory: and accountability, 16–17, 20–21, 23–24; compared to equal accountability theory, 41, 157; and democratic duties, 25, 131–32, 155–57; discussion of, 10–11; and elected authoritarians, 14, 19–20; and fairness, 176–80, 261; and independent institutions, 22–23; and the marginalized, 45; and moral rights, 173; and plurality voting, 159–60, 162; and preference neutrality, 157–59, 177n25, 178–79, 232; and racial justice, 31–32; and responsiveness, 27–29; and the role of president, 12–13; and self-determination, 37–38, 158; and subjectivity, 156–57, 162–63. *See also* elections; ideal theory; nonideal theory

populism, 13–14, 19–20

poverty, 113

presidential power, 61–65, 79–80. *See also* elected authoritarians

principal-agent duties, 93–95, 158, 162–65, 167, 202

principal-principal duties, 93–94, 102, 164–65, 167

prison. *See* incarceration

privatization, 93n22

Promotion of Bantu Self-Government Act of 1959, 233

property rights, 29n85, 52n35

protest, 38–40, 43, 67–68, 98–99, 244, 267. *See also* activism

Proust, Marcel, 97

Przeworski, Adam, 21, 24n78

public office. *See* office

pursuit of happiness, 175, 186, 196–97, 210, 235. *See also* Declaration of Independence

Putin, Vladimir, 84

Putnam, Robert, 150n84

racial inequality, 31–32, 113–14

racial injustice, 25, 68, 85, 91, 96–97. *See also* apartheid; Civil Rights Movement; mortality rates; segregation; slavery

racism. *See* apartheid; Civil Rights Movement; segregation; slavery

Rawls, John, 50n31, 96n29, 103n50, 105n56, 112, 117–18, 136n27, 139n33, 140n42, 148, 156n106, 160–61, 177n24–25, 183, 185n49, 186n53–54, 192n81, 193n82, 196n95, 223n38, 239–40, 246n135, 250–53, 255n172, 266

Raymond, Leigh, 147, 149, 151

reactive attitude, 199n102

Reagan, Ronald, 2, 56

Reconstruction, 131, 145

Reeve, Tapping, 88

Regional Greenhouse Gas Initiative (RGGI), 147

Reichstag Fire Decree of 1933, 144

religion, 251–53

Remembrance of Things Past (Proust), 97

removal from office, 41, 46, 66–67, 81–86, 231

republicanism, 18n62

responsiveness, 27–29

retrospective accountability, 143, 156

revealed preferences argument, 131, 144–46

Rhetoric (Aristotle), 271n17

Richardson, Elliot, 8

"The Right of Peoples and Nations to Self-Determination," 256–57

Risse, Thomas, 219

Roberts, John, 24

Rodden, Jonathan, 116

Roman Republic, 124

Roosevelt, Franklin, 2

Roosevelt, Theodore, 185, 263–64

Rose, Julie, 6n20

Rousseau, Jean-Jacques, 20n65, 44

Rubenstein, David, 110–11

rule of law: under attack, 10; and citizen empowerment, 15, 22, 43; and democratic accountability, 110–11, 232, 257, 265; and elections, 245; and enforceable duties, 4–6; and government power, 71; and public office, 63–65. *See also* judicial review

running for office and campaigning for candidates, 41, 46–47, 82–83, 85–86, 231

sanctioning: and deliberative justification, 46, 72; and equal accountability, 231; and injustice, 70, 85–86, 99; and mediated accountability, 79–80; and moral criticism, 67, 101, 139; during office, 23, 32, 41, 65–66, 155, 265; and petitioning, 76, 110; and protest, 67–68; social, 151. *See also* impeachment

Santa Cruz, Hernán, 225

Satz, Debra, 112

Scanlon, Tim, 50–51, 156n106

Schumpeter, Joseph, 21, 23–24, 44

Sedgwick, Theodore, 88

Sedition Act of 1798, 53, 92, 263n1

Sedition Act of 1918, 13, 263

segregation, 5, 8, 18, 39–40, 68, 99, 106, 116, 125, 131, 141, 146, 201, 238, 268. *See also* apartheid; Civil Rights Movement; racial injustice; slavery

Seila Law v. Consumer Financial Protection Bureau, 24n77

self-determination, 233–34, 245, 253, 256–62. *See also* democratic self-determination

self-governance. *See* authorization; evaluation; freedom (discussion of); removal from office; running for office and campaigning for candidates; sanctioning

self-respect, 105, 238–39

Sen, Amartya, 108–9, 112, 156n106, 228n56, 242

separation of powers, 24n77, 66, 77–79, 85, 227. *See also* checks and balances

sexism, 19

Sharpeville massacre, 244–45

Sheffield Resolves, 87–88

Shiffrin, Seana, 105n57

Shklar, Judith, 34, 190, 255

Sidgwick, Henry, 133

Sikkink, Kathryn, 150–51, 219

Simmons, Beth, 251

Simpson, Thomas, 18n62

Skinner, Quentin, 18n62

slavery, 19n63, 26, 87–89, 127–30, 145, 170–72, 182, 197–99, 207–8, 241. *See also* apartheid; Civil Rights Movement; racial injustice; segregation

Smith, Adam, 111

social capital, 150n84

social choice theory, 21n67

social egalitarianism, 49–50

social minimum, 111–14, 126, 184

social welfare. *See* welfare

solidarity. *See* duty of solidarity

Solidarity trade union, 213, 220

Sotomayor, Sonia, 42n8

Souter, David, 123–24

Stalin, Joseph, 242

states (discussion of), 255–56

St. Clair, James, 65

Stilz, Anna, 132, 160n119

Stokes, Susan, 21

Sullivan, E. Thomas, xii, 22n71, 67n83

Sun Yat-Sen, 77, 227, 229

Suppression of Communism Act of 1960, 233

Swaine, Lucas, 6n20

Taney, Roger, 127, 208

taxes, 27–28

Theory of Justice (Rawls), 239

Third Enforcement Act of 1871, 108

Thirteenth Amendment, 89, 182

Thompson, Dennis F., 120, 157n107, 187, 223

Three Principles of the People, 227

Till, Emmett, 40, 91

Tocqueville, Alexis de, 69, 149–50, 221n30

toleration, 215

transparency, 70, 72–75, 125

treaties, 218n16, 219–20, 222–25, 228. *See also* *specific treaties*

Treaty of Versailles, 258–59

Trump v. United States, 22n71, 42n8

Tutu, Desmund, 230, 250

Twenty-Fourth Amendment, 90, 99

UN Democracy Fund (UNDEF), 250

UN Development Programme (UNDP), 250

United Nations Commission of Human Rights, 247

United Nations Convention against Corruption, 247–48

United Nations Declaration on the Elimination of Violence against Women of 1993 (DEVAW), 148

Universal Declaration of Human Rights, 188–90, 194, 196, 212, 221, 225–28, 235, 252

US Constitution, 54–56, 59, 61, 65, 79–80, 90, 207–8. *See also* Declaration of Independence; Federalist Papers; *specific amendments*

US Department of Justice, 60–61, 108, 138

US Freedom of Information Act (FOIA), 73

US National Strategy to Counter Islamophobia and Related Forms of Bias and Discrimination, 107–8

US Uniform Code of Military Justice, 56

usurpation, 52–53, 57, 78

utilitarianism, 157n108, 176–78
Utilitarianism (Mill), 140

value theory of democracy, 20n65
Veal, Christopher Thomas, 96n30
Vienna Declaration, 231, 246–47, 257
voting, 179
voting rights, 60–61, 82, 90–91, 98–99,
    114–17, 126, 145–46, 149–52, 178,
    236–38
Voting Rights Act of 1965, 99

Waldron, Jeremy, 74n105, 155–58, 160,
    162–63, 178, 180, 187, 250n154
Wałęsa, Lech, 213, 220, 251
Walzer, Michael, 184, 204
Warren, Earl, 238
Washington, George, 120–21, 174
Wasow, Omar, 98n38
Watergate, 8, 23, 74, 80
Wealth of Nations (Smith), 111
Weber, Max, 61

Weingast, Barry R., 260n185
Welch, Theodora, 93n22, 164n130
Weldon, S. Laurel, 147–49, 151
welfare, 117
"What, to the Slave, Is the Fourth of July?"
    (Douglass), 197–98
White, Byron, 118
White Citizens' Councils, 106, 141
Whitney v. California, 100–101
Wilson, Woodrow, 12–13, 143, 150, 263
Woman Suffrage Procession, 150
women, 45–47, 116, 148–52, 224, 237–38
Women's Political Council, 43
World Conference on Human Rights of
    1993, 246

Xi Jinping, 217–18

Young, Iris Marion, 94n23

Zakaria, Fareed, 13, 15
Ziblatt, Daniel, 5–6n19, 17–18, 27n84, 145

A NOTE ON THE TYPE

This book has been composed in Arno, an Old-style serif typeface in the classic Venetian tradition, designed by Robert Slimbach at Adobe.